Port-Royal

AND OTHER PLAYS

Port-Royal

AND OTHER PLAYS

Edited, with an Introduction

by

RICHARD HAYES

A MERMAID DRAMABOOK

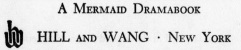

HILL AND WANG · NEW YORK

BIOGRAPHICAL NOTES

François Mauriac, the novelist and playwright, was born in 1885 in the country about Bordeaux. He is a classic instance of the French *homme de lettres*: distinguishing himself variously in the novel and the theatre; as biographer, critic, and polemicist. The profundity and paradox of his Catholic spirit are reflected in works so disparate as his life of Christ, *The Son of Man*, and *God and Mammon*, the latter his analysis of the special situation of the Christian artist. He was awarded the Nobel Prize for Literature in 1952. Among his novels in English are *The Desert of Love*, *Viper's Tangle*, *Thérèse*, and *Woman of the Pharisees*. Though *Asmodée* is his most notable work for the stage, he has written three other plays as yet untranslated: *Les Mal-Aimés*, *Passage du Malin*, and *Le Feu sur la Terre*.

Henry de Montherlant, ever since his birth in 1896 to an old French family of Catalonian origin, has enjoyed articulately the privileged pleasures of social deference, of physical excellence, and of talent. He was a bullfighter at fifteen, served with valor in World War I, and later withdrew into a life of quasi-monastic seclusion in North Africa. His plays, to which he turned after great success as a novelist, were events of provocation and celebrity in the postwar Parisian theatre. Of the translation of his major works now in progress, two recent instances are *The Bachelors*, a novel, and *Selected Essays*.

Paul Claudel spent most of his adult life in the French diplomatic service—at Washington, Tokyo, and Brussels—after the mystical revelation of faith he experienced in his eighteenth year (1886) at Nôtre Dame, on Christmas Day. He is the poet of the *Cinq Grandes Odes*, the contemplative visionary of *A Poet Before the Cross*, the dramatist of *Break of Noon*, *The Tidings Brought to Mary*. and the untranslated cosmic and terrestrial masterpiece, *Le Soulier de Satin*. His correspondence with André Gide is one of the remarkable documents of French spiritual and literary life. He died in 1955, on Ash Wednesday, the grandeur and audacity of his theater triumphantly confirmed by the brilliant productions of Jean-Louis Barrault and Louis Jouvet.

Jacques Copeau, who died in 1949 at the age of seventy-one, is remembered as the founder and director of the Vieux Colombier, whose "activities, theories and ideals form the most significant single contribution to the modern French theater" (Wallace

v

Fowlie). His influence and his work drew tribute from the actress Duse, from Stanislavsky and Appia and Gordon Craig. The interest in possibilities of a religious theatre, which is most beautifully reflected in *Le Petit Pauvre*, dominated his later years, and led him finally to abandon the practical stage, though the moral heritage of his example is incalculable.

ACKNOWLEDGMENTS

Mr. Georges Borchardt first proposed the idea of this collection, and to him, as equally to Mr. Arthur Wang who has been a publisher of unremitting patience and generosity, go my first and deepest thanks.

I much appreciate the kindness of Mr. Eric Bentley, who brought to my attention the existence of Copeau's *Le Petit Pauvre*, and of Mother Adele Fiske, R.S.C.J., of Manhattanville College, who suggested Claudel's *L'histoire de Tobie et de Sara*.

I am especially grateful to Mr. Beverly Thurman, who so very graciously undertook, on short notice, to translate *Le Petit Pauvre*, and to his wife, the actress Elizabeth Farrar—who created the role of Marcelle in the American premiere of *Asmodée*—for the uncommon theatrical sensibility and tact she contributed to these stage renderings.

It will be evident to the most casual observer how crucially my knowledge of French drama, and of so much beyond that, draws on the distinguished works of Mr. Wallace Fowlie. For those illuminations, and for his personal example, I hope to record here, however inadequately, something of my debt.

Finally, I wish to thank my friend, Mr. James Kane Brinker of New York, for much personal kindness to me during the preparation of this manuscript.

CONTENTS

CONTENTS

INTRODUCTION

In *A Guide to Contemporary French Literature*, that illuminating passage he conducts through the bewildering signs and symbols of a complex imagination, Mr. Wallace Fowlie throws into relief as its most salient marking the French writer's acknowledged awareness that his art is "knowingly the renewal of tradition and not the discovery of the new." It is an arresting observation: to an English or American contemporary, busy with his categories, his advances and retreats, his anxious interment or resuscitation of old and new "forms," it seems to announce a commitment which may seem defeating or perverse, scandalous even. How, he might ask, shall art be served? A little reflection would carry him beyond shock to irony, to the paradox that French art is also, and knowingly, the *violation* of tradition: Rimbaud, *Waiting for Godot*, the anti-novel. For as Mr. Fowlie continues:

The French genius, however, cannot be defined solely by this habit of integration with the past. . . . After establishing a relationship with the past, it then establishes another kind of relationship with the present. . . . No major view on man, and no particular kind of sensitivity is allowed to exist alone in France for very long. The French genius asserts itself by creating some miracle of equilibrium. It discovers in its own age an opposing voice, usually of power equal to its own, and therefore is able to grow more vibrantly according to its own distinctive qualities. . . .

Dialogue, then, even when no hope of reconciliation may be entertained—Descartes/Pascal, Corneille/Racine, Gide and Claudel—is the condition of French genius. Yet it is the dialogue characteristic of a race for whom eloquence is a rite and a ceremony: one—again and finally to draw on Mr. Fowlie—in which each of the opposing voices, gifted with that "exceptional power of spiritual discernment" which is the ground of French singularity, join their twin solitudes ("arias sung in the midst of great silence") to mount a psychological inquest of man, to avow and unmask his spiritual torment and aspiration.

It should be apparent immediately, to anyone either tutored in or accessible to religious experience, what congruence will exist between the habit of such an imagination and the texture of Christian sensibility. For the Christian, the French writer's "knowing renewal of tradition" will be analogous to his own relation to the scheme of time and eternity, his place within the metaphysical reality of the Communion of Saints. He will see in the dialectic of opposing voices an anguished reflection of his own intimate disorder, warring dualities of nature and grace: the principle of contradiction which underlies his thirst for transcendence and his limited possibility. And that "spiritual discernment" in the service of a psychological inquest must become, for the Christian, the energy of all his days, laborious: "scouring our skin of its daily deposit of dirt," as Claudel puts it: "keeping mind, will, and feeling permanently mobilized against passion and against any cheap skepticism."

It is one of the moral and social grandeurs of French spirit to have given articulate and mastering voice to this principle of contradiction in that art which is the very forum of its consciousness: the theatre. To the French audience, religious substance is not, as almost invariably it *is* to one of Anglo-Saxon heritage, a *frisson*, a pietism, a social embarrassment, an ethical utility or an aggression. The writer who elects it as his primary motif is not compelled to elaborate strategies of accommodation, as is Mr. T. S. Eliot, or to the intermittent subterfuges and brutalities of direct assault. (M. Mauriac, confronted with the novels of Mr. Graham Greene, professed his admiration, yet recorded his sensation that he was entering upon Christianity through some back door.) To the French mind—literary as well as social, and whatever its personal commitment or didacticism—the omission of such a burden of experience, range of spirit, so much achieved and defensible insight, would seem a mutilation of consciousness, witless if not intolerable, and hostile ultimately to those very springs of self-inquisition which are the fountainhead of the French image of man.

When he turned to writing for the stage in those years of uneasy calm before World War II, François Mauriac resumed the experience of several novelists previous and subsequent to himself—one thinks of Henry James and Mr. Graham Greene—who have also sought the more immediate impact of the theatre. He brought, that is, an established personality to his new venture: a constancy of theme and uniqueness of vision so dominating as ultimately to command for him the Nobel Prize in Literature.

The constancy of theme is, of course, that deepest preoccupation of all great literature, the tragic margin between illusion and reality. The uniqueness of vision is rooted in the echoing harmony of Mauriac's landscapes of the soul with that other first world, fierce in its wild solitude, of the sandy forests about Bordeaux, of *les Landes*: the province translated into poetry. One knew this acrid, piney scent from the novels, incendiary heat and resin smoking the air: afternoons without end, terrible in their connivance—that chance encounter by the path—and terrible in their self-knowing. In *Asmodée*, the most celebrated and tenacious of his plays, M. Mauriac ventilated that pungent scene, dilated it with remembrance and with love. He sought to evoke, with some of Chekhov's taut languor—that dramatic form, he has confessed, to which he most aspires—the spacious days of the heart's rise and fall, evenings heavy with moonlight and the drone of cicadas. Nothing is gentler here than the recurrent image of the broken little mill, at which these lovers—the tormented as well as the voluntary—make their trysts: it is the place of nostalgia, of sweetness, and of loveliest communion.

Within the great house, muffled, all is as one had known: draperies drawn against the heat and, by symbolic inference, against the invading clamor of passion. The *Asmodée* of the title is a legendary demon who lifted the roofs of houses to glimpse the roiling life within; it is one of Mauriac's ironies that he should take the form here of an English student, trembling on the threshold of manhood, and full of the large, free English innocence and grace. In this waiting household, his presence is like one of the winds which stir the pine trees, or like those sudden fires which devastate the forests at high noon. To the women of the house, both of whom vie subtly for his attention, he brings an irrevocable release from illu-

sion. The daughter comes out of her exquisite piety of
devotion into a headiness of love, the very intensity of
which foreshadows the shape of "all her future suffering."
The mother, a young widow and a figure in the Racinian
line drawn here with that infallible French austerity
which runs so passionately cross-grained to a rich sensuous
solicitation—she sees in the boy a last ardor and grace,
but renounces finally the possibility he suggests with
that conscious splendor of the heart at its deepest pitch of
grieving knowledge.

One member only of the household resists the young
man's appeal, wars actively, indeed, against it: that is
the tutor Blaise Couture, the quintessential Mauriac
"case of conscience" and an obsessive moral "type"
Molière would dimly have recognized. In a provincial
society, Couture exercises the magnetism of the pure
moralist: the world is but a field for his sowing of guilt.
He must panic at the entrance of its impulses and distractions, because they challenge his power; he *must* seek
to close the house against time and change because,
within its heavy stillness, he is desperately counterfeiting
an identity. Mauriac sees Couture as a more significant
figure than Molière's Tartuffe because he is not a *conscious* hypocrite, because he acts always, and destructively,
in good faith. And indeed, as a study in a certain kind
of moral pathology—of the man who does not live up
to his own best being—Couture is a most telling creation.

It is instructive, since Mauriac has invoked Tartuffe,
to consider how Molière might have regarded Blaise
Couture, whose relation is less to that pawing hypocrite
than it is to Alceste in *Le Misanthrope*, another impure
critic of an impure society and a more ambitious figure,
devious and blighted—an instance of *waste*—yet one
whom all the will and energy in the world cannot provoke
into tragic consequence. Mauriac has himself a passage
elsewhere on Alceste which is to the point:

The whole misfortune of Alceste, of that Alceste who is in all
of us, lies in a psychological need of the absolute that we bring
to love which is the most relative of human feelings.

He could not have underlined more suggestively the character of Blaise Couture, yet the irony of Alceste as well

as Couture is that both are involved not in love, but in
an intimidating enterprise of vanity; to it they bring every
rhetoric, force, cruel indifference and stratagem of those
trapped by their own nothingness. And what indeed can
be one more miscalculation of reality—even religious—
amid such swamps of self-delusion as these two personages
inhabit?

Mauriac's audacity in *Asmodée* has been to introduce
a figure—monster, moral type, humor, what one will—
drawn from the Molière daylight world of solidity and
generous reason, into the passionate upheaval and chi-
aroscuro, the terrible reason, of the Racinian abyss. If
the supreme enterprise of the French literary mind is to
record the colloquy of the lucidity which is Molière's
heritage, with the secret knowledge which is Racine's
torment, then Mauriac's translation of that dialogue to
the sphere of sanctity and grace and evil has deepened
and enriched it. His subdued rendering of states of innocence and illusion shows a great Christian imagination
at the tide of fullest passionate encounter and recognition: in language luminous yet exact, François Mauriac
does grave justice at once to the world and to the absolute demands of that spirit which, knowing, must suffer
and transcend the world.

* * *

Port-Royal—"that ample and thickly wooded play,"
Henry de Montherlant has called it: curious image for
a work of such linear austerity, so fluent and implacable
an itinerary of spiritual collision—was written by the
dramatist in 1953, and received its first performance at
the Comédie Française in December, 1954. Yet by the
subtler chronology of involvement one might make claim
for it as the first of his dramas: engaged—as possible
substance—so early as 1940, then abandoned; resumed
again, with wholly other an emphasis, in 1948; brought
at last to a clarified finality five years later. The interval
had seen seven plays, all of a militant personal audacity,
not least the celebrated *Le Maître de Santiago*, that work
the ambiguities of which *Port-Royal* at once qualifies and
sustains.

The provocation, allure even, for Montherlant of so
divisive and harassing a crisis of French spirit was not
wholly fortuitous. In that episode—convulsion, rather—
which had exercised Pascal and Racine, the history of
which Sainte-Beuve chronicled with laborious majesty,
and upon which, indeed (to the degree that a Frenchman
elects *for* or *against* Port-Royal) it would be possible still
to distinguish the lineaments of his sensibility, Montherlant found an echoing chamber in which to dramatize the
principle of "alternation" he takes as his singularity, the
fountainhead of his temperament: his sovereignty and
heraldic pride and contemptuous Catalonian maleness;
his taste for the intoxications at once of asceticism and
excess, and that hero's element Malraux has remarked
elsewhere of expecting forgiveness from nobody but himself. All of this Montherlant has contemplated in his
journals and his novels—less perhaps in his plays—with
an acquiescent exaltation and something of the unconscious fanaticism of the narcissist.

"There is in my work," Montherlant writes, "a Christian vein and a 'profane' (or worse than profane) vein,
and I nourish them alternately—I was going to say simul-
taneously. This is quite right, since everything in this
world deserves both attack and defense, and since we are
bound, concerning whatever truth we live in, to say to
ourselves what every married man has said to himself at
least once about his wife: 'Why that one?' " *Port-Royal*
is the issue of that first vein: dark and ceremonious a
ritual of sacrifice* as those other *auto-sacramentales*—
Le Maître de Santiago and the unproduced *La Ville dont
le prince est un enfant*—with which its creator sees it
forming a triptych: *l'ordre de chevalerie, le collège, le
couvent*. Remote though its impulse and passion and
quarrel must seem to Anglo-Saxon preoccupation, *Port-
Royal*'s subtlest strangeness may flow ironically less from
what is complex in it than from what is simple. The
study Montherlant proposes in lucidities of spiritual power
is without baroque elaboration or dissemblance. Lines of
force are marshaled and drawn with a kind of vehement

---

* "The sacrifice of Abraham is decidedly an obsession in my
work for the stage!" (Note to *Le Maître de Santiago*.)

precision. The destinies of Sœur Angélique and Sœur
Françoise approach, intersect, and diverge in a rigorous
geometry of the soul. Implicit everywhere, and only,
is that passionate quest Montherlant (with Wagner)
announces as his own: ". . . the eternally human, freed
of every conventional element."

What elevates the piece beyond demonstration to a
rhetoric of passion is its keening note of *voracity*—this,
and the unmediated dialogue on modes of Christian ex-
tremity which rustles through its scenes, as do these nuns
through their harassed corridors. Montherlant's tone is
supremely his triumph, to the support of which he invokes
the Greek example, and for the reinforcement of which
he would ideally have the work played without interval.
Its harrowing asceticism is congruent with, and brilliantly
equilibrated to, the play's most terrible image, drawn
from nature, in which the marshaled powers of church
and state, brilliant and glittering in their cold splendor,
are likened to a fearful army of gleaming insects—"enormous insects of the virgin forest"—hypnotizing a group
of terrified birds.

And it evokes, too, the special mode of Montherlant's
Catholicism, that body of his heritage towards which, he
writes, his attitude "has always been like that of the Medi-
terranean towards its beaches, now caressing and now
retreating . . . or of a cat, biting and licking at one and
the same time." Like the Don Alvaro of *Le Maître de
Santiago*—Castilian noblemen "complete with their decisive faith, their contempt for external reality, their taste
for ruin, their furious desire for annihilation"—his temperament draws him strongly towards "the first impulse
of Christianity: renunciation, the *Nada*; he has little feeling for the second: union, the *Todo*." His God is always
the God of transcendence, never of immanence.

If it happened to me one day [he writes] to be thunderstruck
by "grace," I should put myself in the line that I am tempted
to call the line of the heart of Christianity, because I seem to
see it running, like sap in a tree, through the heart of Christianity: it is a tradition that goes from the Gospel to Port-
Royal by way of St. Paul and St. Augustine (and does it not
skirt Calvin?). The motto I give it is Bossuet's cry: "Doctrine

of the Gospel, how severe you are!" and its form is that of the
ever narrowing way.

Hence the "scandal" of Montherlant's Christian senti-
ment to charity and to reason: an offense some would
take as but another variant on the "principle of alternation." Mme. Simone de Beauvoir, as an instance, rather
shrilly—and not, to be sure, in the role of *Fidei Defensor*
—indicts him (in *The Second Sex*) for neglecting "co-
existence . . . the great drama of living"; for allowing
in his work as in his life "only one mind" and for de-
claring—she would have it—"that by the very fact that
nothing is worth anything, everything is of equal value."

Perhaps: Montherlant has long since rejected the im-
plication that a writer should be "a slave in his creations
to the mistakes people make about him and his work."
Still, is it not ironic that a Catholic sensibility of such
subtle contradictions as Montherlant's—whose ambiguity
must at the last be readable only to God—should be the
agent to compel his fellow Christians to recognize one of
their faith's darkest and most tenacious roots: this ancient
habit and hazard he defines, in his role of moralist, as
the knowledge that "one has no rights except to those
things one is prepared to risk"?

*   *   *

The Old Testament must be given back to the Christian people.
Their pressing need for it outweighs all else. Christians must not
be deprived of half of their heritage; they must not be driven
from the Promised Land flowing with milk and honey. They
must be given back for their own use their great edifice of the
Bible . . . not a shapeless mass of unrelated materials half
eaten away by time, but a superb monument untouched by the
centuries and still available to us, intact and virginal, in its profound and sublime composition, in its original meaning and in
the invitation—just as compelling today as it was then—that it
extends to our intelligence, our imagination, our feelings, and
our needs for love and beauty.

So Paul Claudel (in *The Essence of the Bible*), and before the turbulence of such prophetic incantation who
would be idle or trivial enough to observe that it has
never, of course, that Old Testament, been taken away—
that it stands now, and has ever, "flowing with milk and

honey," nourishing still our needs for love and beauty.

Yet no complacency is possible before the phenomenon of Claudel: he imposes the intolerable weight of one's own insignificance; only the most dialectically sinuous (Gide is the classic instance) have been able to elude him—and even that austere prodigal, herald of *inquiétude* and *disponibilité*, confessed his inhibition in the presence of Claudel's mastering physical intimidation. He carried about him, the poet, and consciously, something of the "passion of the universe," of that exultation he derived from contemplating the millions of things which exist at the same time. *Que j'aime ce million des choses qui existent ensemble!*

And his theatre, too, flows with the same sweet and willful emotion of multitude, buckling almost—but gloriously, never quite—under the burden of immanence he would have it bear: the intricate pavane of eroticism and spirit in *Partage de Midi;* the abolishing scope of *Le Soulier de Satin,* in which not only traditional modes of comic and tragic, but time itself, and space, and history, drown in the dissolving vision of ecstasy and persuasion. Even so gentle a work as *Tobias and Sara*—a dramatic fable of Claudel's old age, prompted by his loving immersion in the testimony of the Bible—reveals his persistent meditation on the mystery of sacrificial charity; the symbolic investiture with which he clothes the visible world, and his joyful metaphor of the human soul—of which Sara, here, is surely the symbol—called to participate through time in a drama the climax of which lies beyond time.

In an extended comment on the poet at his death in 1955, Mr. Helmut Hatzfeld suggested as a central instance of the Claudel vision the lyrical *Cantate à Trois Voix,* in which "three beautiful young women sing about love in festive mood on a balmy summer night":

The unmarried brunette Laeta, unaware of love's bitterness and thinking only of her personal happiness in hope and desire, is jubilant about her youthful body ready to be conquered by a daring suitor, violent like the Rhône river, and whose arms never would appear too strong to her. She recognizes in love "the force which fastens the stone to its base." The married blonde Fausta full of regret and remembrance, but full also of strength and faith, has learned through a temporarily necessary separation from her husband that concern for the endangered beloved one and forgetfulness of self have become the decisive element in her love and that the gold of love is a kind of renunciation. She has understood that she has to be for her husband not a prison but a harbor, an arsenal, a tower. The young widow Beata, mild and charitable, has experienced that love must be renunciation, even radical renunciation, and she praises her husband's death as her liberty for the invasion of God. Beata has learned "that the word has to expire so that the sentence exists, that the meaning prevails," that "the face of the beloved man as hindering the Vision of the True Face has to disappear like the froth on a glass of wine." *

Claudel never ceased to meditate on his trinity of loves, rendering—in *Partage de Midi*—their colors of disaster, and in *Le Soulier de Satin* their terrible exactions of triumph. In *Tobias and Sara* he is milder: the pressure of actual experience is less insistent. He releases the motif into a gentle fantasia of spirit and liturgy and symbol, none the less profound for all its sweet air of *plaisance*. Yet even here one sees woman as the instrument and accomplice of grace; one grasps the urgency of Claudel's sacramental vision of the earth as "a text which teaches jubilation"; one is compelled by this drama of the man who, as poet and Christian, "has nothing with which to reproach the work of Almighty God, who, rather, finds it good and very good, and to whom the flesh never appears more beautiful than when, like a generous flower . . . it serves to glorify the spirit."

*   *   *

Jacques Copeau's *The Little Poor Man* is perhaps the loveliest of the plays in this collection, the one we should need least to trouble: open and unstressed and accessible as the Italian landscape across which it moves, and whose light falls on it with a kind of passionate benediction. It is also the most surprising, most contradictory: the creation of an intellectual who, with Gide and Jean Schlumberger, had founded that forum of French letters,

* "A Critical Revision of Claudel as a Catholic Poet," by Helmut Hatzfeld, *Cross Currents*, 5:2, Spring, 1955, p. 103.

the *Nouvelle Revue Française*; of an *animateur* whose theory and practice have left perhaps the most decisive impress on the modern French theatre; and of an ascetic, involved in the worldliest of arts, compelled at last, by his thirst for an ideal perfection, to solitude and to silence.

Yet the attraction for Copeau of the Franciscan image and experience—of its purity of line and first fresh impulse, and not least, of its gentle relevance to the moral and the social—may be seen as deeply congruent with the nature of his temperament: the flowering of what was most rigorous, sacred, and profound in all his secular energies. When he founded, in 1913, the Vieux Colombier, that greatest and most dedicated of all "little theaters," Copeau wanted, so Mrs. Helen Krich Chinoy writes in *Directing the Play*, to bring together

. . . under the direction of one man, a troupe of young, disinterested, and enthusiastic players, whose ambition was to *serve* the art to which they had devoted themselves. The creative director was essential for the unity of which Copeau so frequently spoke. In a letter to Louis Jouvet, his co-worker and *régisseur* (stage manager), Copeau wrote: "I would put all the books under lock and key, to forbid you to use them (that bothers you, eh?). . . . The science of the past, it is I who will absorb it, who will direct it, who will clarify it and who will transmit it to you little by little, all fresh, all new, pell-mell with the personal godsend of my unpublished science. No substitution. A creation. Life.

The poet alone he saw as "the true origin and life of all drama as Aeschylus was of Greek drama." To the director he assigned the honor not of the *trouvère*, of one who invents ideas, but of one who recovers them. In stagecraft, he insisted on *un tréteau nu*, the bare, ascetic space. Of the actor, debilitated by malice, egotism and insincerity—everything the French theatre understands by the word *cabotinage*—he demanded a moral renovation of sensibility and technique, a new and total simplicity. Behind all his labors lay the dream, romantic yet built on the real anguish of all nostalgia, of a theatre of communion, through which—as in the analogous liturgy of the Church—the discords and divisiveness of men would be reconciled, the rites of their nature, and the bond to what lies beyond that nature, celebrated.

What should there be, then, of surprise in Copeau's being drawn by imaginative sympathy to so unique a sanctity—the reality of which Claudel claims art is only a pale duplicate—as that of Francis of Assisi; to a holiness which would make new again the world by its exemplary revolution of poverty and simplicity; which counseled always against the subtler deceits of power, and saw as its only task the ceaseless annunciation of joy, the celebration of love's communion?

Art is not made, of course, with either sentiments or sympathies—alone—yet there is a kind of beauty fluent throughout *The Little Poor Man* that is not to be had by taking thought. It is a beauty wrought by that Gallic equilibrium which excludes neither the dark valors of Mauriac and Montherlant nor the prophetic jubilation of Claudel, but reconciles them, rather, within the pattern of its old and loving human wisdom: a wisdom of nature built upon by grace, the sum and power of which is to quiet in us that persistent craving Mr. Wallace Fowlie calls "our deepest desire to know the real." For one moment, the clamors of time and self are stilled, and we are released into a light we have known before only in reverie, in dream and in passionate memory.

RICHARD HAYES

ASMODÉE

by

FRANÇOIS MAURIAC

Translated by

BEVERLY THURMAN

CHARACTERS

MARCELLE DE BARTHAS, 38
EMMANUELE, *her daughter,* 17
MADEMOISELLE, *the children's governess,* 30
BLAISE COUTURE, *the tutor,* 40
HARRY FANNING, 20
FATHER BRUNET, *parish priest*
FIRMIN, *old servant*
ANNE, *Marcelle's daughter,* 13
JEAN, *Marcelle's son,* 12

ASMODÉE

ACT ONE

SCENE I—*The great hall of an old house in the moor country south of Bordeaux—a country of sandy soil and pine forests. You must feel that the house belongs to an established family of both wealth and tradition. The room opens directly on to a huge terrace beyond which you feel the presence of the pine forest. You must be able to see and hear what takes place on the terrace as well as in the great hall.*

A stairway leads to the bedrooms. It is so constructed that asides can be easily managed on it. People near the fireplace at the rear of the room cannot see the persons on the stairs.

A door leads to the dining room.

Although the scene remains unchanged throughout the play, it must seem different in each scene. This important role is played by light.

THE TIME: *A fine summer morning.*

MADEMOISELLE [*to* EMMANUELE *who is playing a Mozart rondo at the piano*]. Keep time! Wrists limber! Sit up straight! Don't look at your hands!

Enter JEAN and ANNE.

Jean. Let her go, Mademoiselle. Her half hour's up.
Mademoiselle. No. Five minutes more.
Anne. The English boy will be here any minute. If the train weren't late he'd be here now!
Emmanuele. Of course, but the train's always late.
Mademoiselle. So much the better. Your mother's not back from her ride. She should be here to meet the stranger.
Jean [*slapping at his leg*]. Oh, she won't be long now. It's getting hot and the flies bite like devils.
Emmanuele. I hope Fra Diavolo won't run away with Mama. I certainly wish she were back.

3

Mademoiselle [*kissing her*]. Don't worry, my dear.
Your mother never gets home before ten.

Anne. But what if the English boy comes?

Mademoiselle. Well, we don't all have to be on hand
to meet him. The English boy isn't as important as all
that . . .

Jean. What's his name anyway?

Mademoiselle. Fanning . . . I don't remember his first
name.

Anne. That's a funny name, Fanning.

Jean. What's funny about it, idiot?

Emmanuele. Now, now, Jean!

Anne. Idiot yourself!

Jean [*to* EMMANUELE]. We'll be watching for him at
the big hedge beside the gate. Come with us, Emmanuele.

Anne. I made a bet he's blond. Jean bet red hair.

Emmanuele. Why not brown?

Anne. All the English have blond or red hair, don't
they, Mademoiselle?

Mademoiselle. Not necessarily.

Jean. What do you think he'll be like? [MADEMOISELLE
is obviously thinking of something else.] I say, Mademoiselle, what do you think he'll be like, this Fanning
fellow?

Mademoiselle. Since he's changing places with your
brother Bertrand, I expect he'll be pretty much like him
—about fifteen but more fair, and his eyes will probably
be more blue or gray.

Emmanuele. It's funny to think that today the Fanning family's waiting for Bertrand, the French boy, just
as we're waiting for the English boy and trying to imagine
what he'll be like.

Jean. The English are stuffy. They never try to imagine
anything!

Emmanuele. What makes you think so?

Jean. Monsieur Couture said so at dinner last night.

Mademoiselle. You silly goose. You understand nothing
the grownups say!

Jean. Oh no? Didn't Monsieur Couture say the English
never try to imagine anything?

Enter BLAISE, *creating an immediate defensive silence in the room.*

Blaise. No, my child. I said the English were not strong on logic. Now you'll have to write this sentence fifty times this afternoon: "I listen to the grownups but don't understand them."

Jean. In the first place you're Bertrand's tutor, not mine. Mademoiselle is my teacher.

Blaise. You see, my child, I don't lose my temper. I could double your punishment but I simply tell you not to say another word.

Mademoiselle [*kissing* JEAN]. Go along and play and don't be rude . . . Well, what are you waiting for?

Jean [*going toward terrace with* ANNE]. Anyway, I'm sure he said it.

Emmanuele [*pensively, thinking of her favorite book*]. Anyway, David Copperfield is not stuffy.

Anne. Every time Monsieur Couture turns up, Mademoiselle sends us away. Have you noticed?

Jean. No. Why?

Anne. You're as stuffy as an Englishman.

EMMANUELE, ANNE *and* JEAN *run out into the garden.*

Mademoiselle. The children are all excited about the arrival of the little English boy.

Blaise [*nervously*]. Isn't Madame here yet?

Mademoiselle. She won't be long.

Blaise. Did you know yesterday that she was to go riding today?

Mademoiselle. No, it was arranged early this morning. Count de Coustous phoned.

Blaise. You should have told me.

Mademoiselle. I thought you heard the phone ring.

Blaise. You know I don't get any sleep until dawn and then it's heavy sleep.

Mademoiselle. All the more reason to let you sleep.

Blaise. Don't bother about my health. Just do as I say.

Mademoiselle [*bitterly*]. If I had waked you, you would have prevented Madame from going . . .

Blaise. That's no concern of yours.

Mademoiselle. I was just making an observation.

Blaise. Keep your observations to yourself.

Mademoiselle. You're so hard. It's terrible.

Blaise [*going toward terrace and returning*]. What time is it? It simply won't do for a young woman—a widow—to go trooping about like this with a lot of elderly playboys . . . Not only because of the scandal . . . Why are you smiling?

Mademoiselle. No reason . . .

Blaise. I know what's in your mind . . . you think I'm thinking something I ought to be ashamed of.

Mademoiselle. Jealousy is nothing to be ashamed of.

Blaise. I won't even answer that. How is it possible to live in the same house with you? You distort everything good! You throw mud on everything noble and unselfish. All right. Yes, I am jealous of the purity of a woman who's in my care. But you couldn't possibly understand such a feeling—a fool like you!

Mademoiselle [*bursting into tears*]. Yes, a fool like me!

Blaise [*with repressed violence*]. Oh no! None of that! I've warned you. As far as I am concerned, I can stand all this. I don't matter. But if my presence is a temptation to you and you insist on keeping a guilty passion in your heart, then it will be my duty, you understand, my strict duty . . .

Mademoiselle. To have me fired! Go on, say it!

Blaise. What do you take me for? That would be for Madame to decide. One of us would have to go and it might be me. After all am I any more important in this house than you? I'm used to that humiliation. I'm only Bertrand's tutor, just as you're Emmanuele's governess.

Mademoiselle. But Bertrand's gone away and you're still here.

Blaise. Because I'm supposed to teach the English boy that's coming to take Bertrand's place.

Mademoiselle. Oh come, come. Madame offered you a vacation, but it was just a formality. You know very well she can't get along without you.

Blaise [*mollified*]. You really think so?

Mademoiselle. So at last I've found a way to please you!

Blaise. I have boundless patience!

Marcelle. And I have boundless love!

Blaise [*in a low voice*]. I forbid this intimacy!

Mademoiselle [*also in a low voice*]. But I've earned the right to it.

Blaise. It was only once! I've suffered enough, I've paid enough, for that shameful, wretched moment. God knows it was you that led me on!

Mademoiselle. It was you! You started it! You started analyzing my soul, as you said—my soul! I wish I had the strength to laugh!

Blaise. Was it my fault if you're one of those girls who can think of only one thing? You don't know exactly what it is but you're dying to find out . . .

Mademoiselle. I love you, that's all.

Blaise. You'll never make me yield to temptation again. Never again!

Mademoiselle. No credit to you! It's just that I'm no temptation, am I? Isn't that what you mean?

Blaise. Why do you force me to say it?

Mademoiselle. You need me just the same. If only because I am the proof that you can make a woman suffer . . . a woman can suffer because of Monsieur Couture!

Blaise. If you think I need you to prove that . . . [*Breaking off before completing the thought.*] Ah! I hear the horses!

Runs to the terrace. Sound of horses and MARCELLE'S *voice offstage.*

Marcelle. Good-by Coustous! See you tomorrow, Monsieur Filhot! Yes, tomorrow morning. Go on home. Don't keep the horses.

Enter MARCELLE *in riding clothes.*

These flies! What a plague! Fra Diavolo is bleeding with bites. Hello, Monsieur Couture. Hello, Mademoiselle. Where are the children?

Mademoiselle. They're waiting for the Fanning boy. They're very excited!

Marcelle. Oh of course! The English boy. What a

bore! Why, you've left the windows open! Close them,
all of them! The heat will get in!

Mademoiselle. It's not even eleven o'clock!

Marcelle. But it's already scorching. And the little
stranger will be here any minute. Mademoiselle, be a
dear. Go see if his room is ready. See that all the shutters
are closed.

Mademoiselle. The windows too?

Marcelle. Certainly the windows too! And tell Firmin to come and lower the blinds.

MADEMOISELLE *goes out.*

These northerners don't know how to protect themselves from the heat. [*To* BLAISE.] Why don't you say
something?

FIRMIN *enters and lowers the blinds. The room is dark-
ened but a ray of sunlight knifes into the great hall.*
MARCELLE *and* BLAISE *silent until* FIRMIN *exits.*

Why don't you say something to me? [BLAISE *shrugs.*]
You could ask me if I had a good ride.

Blaise. Did you have a good ride, Madame?

Marcelle. Coming back it was frightful because of
the flies. But when we started out the mist was almost
cold. We went through the wood as far as Tartehume.
I stopped for a minute at the tenant farmers'. The oldest
son, Gaston, still can't get his social security payment.
They owe him money for his wife's having a baby.

Blaise. Why don't they give it to him?

Marcelle. It's all too much for me. I can't understand
these new laws!

Blaise. But you have an overseer, don't you?

Marcelle. Martin is almost illiterate. You know that
perfectly well.

Blaise. Do you have Gaston's file?

Marcelle. Yes, I've brought back all the papers.
Would you be kind enough to look them over?

Blaise. I suppose, Madame, that since you've mentioned it to me, you want me to do something about it.

Marcelle. Actually I hoped you would. But I don't
want to ask you to. After all, it's not your job.

Blaise. My only job in this world, Madame, is to serve you.

Marcelle. Ah! dear Monsieur Couture. What would I do without you? Wonderful! Then I may ask Martin to give you the file? Thank you. [*Sits down, very relaxed, in an armchair.*] Any news this morning in the paper?

Blaise. Excuse me, I left the paper in my room. I'll get it.

Marcelle [*stopping him*]. Don't bother. I've never learned to read the paper, remember? I only read the crimes. The rest is over my head. You give me the news.

Blaise. That's not my job either . . .

Marcelle. Oh, come now. That isn't a job. You enjoy it—giving me a summary of the news every morning. Everything seems so clear and simple when you explain it.

Blaise. I don't feel in the mood this morning, Madame. May I go now?

Marcelle [*laughing*]. You're furious and I know why. You're furious because I went riding.

Blaise. I have no reason to be furious. It's only that I hate to see you make an exhibition of yourself with that fast crowd.

Marcelle. Coustous, Floirac, old Filhot. A fast crowd? Those poor old fellows!

Blaise. Count Coustous is not yet sixty and his conduct toward women is disgusting! What do you suppose the country people think when they see you galloping through the woods with all those men after you?

Marcelle [*haughtily*]. I beg your pardon, Monsieur Couture! That's going too far, really!

Blaise [*suddenly humble*]. Please forgive me. It was interest in your welfare. I know you're above suspicion. You soar far above such miserable things.

Marcelle. I soar . . . I soar . . . What do you mean?

Blaise. I mean you're not very . . . very . . . How shall I say? Very passionate.

Marcelle. You *are* amusing, Monsieur Couture! Who told you I soar so high?

Blaise. Oh, I have no doubt about that. Thank God, you told me several times you had a horror . . .

Marcelle. Horror of what?

Blaise. You know perfectly well what I mean.

Marcelle. No, I don't know.

Blaise. You loved your husband, and yet your . . . duty as a wife . . . was really a chore for you in the strictest sense of the word . . .

Marcelle. You certainly can hurt people! Why should you feel the strange need to go over all that again?

Blaise. Forgive me for insisting. But I didn't dream it. You never did anything but submit passively.

Marcelle. I forbid you to say another word! [*Turns away from him, goes to the window and back.*] Try to forget my secrets. The fact is I didn't tell them to you. You pried them out of me. [BLAISE *makes a move of protest.*] Yes, yes, you stole them from me. Simply because you were the only human being here that I could talk to . . .

Blaise. I who put you on a pedestal . . .

Marcelle. But it's wrong to put me on a pedestal and to have illusions about me. I'm only a poor woman, Monsieur Couture. And if I didn't have to look after this big estate, this house—if I didn't have the children, it seems to me sometimes I'd die of loneliness.

Blaise [*ardently*]. No, no. You know you're not alone.

Marcelle [*looking into his eyes*]. That's true. I'm ungrateful. There's God.

Blaise [*disappointed and bitter*]. Yes, yes, there's God.

Marcelle. Unfortunately, Monsieur Couture, I am not a person for whom God is enough.

Blaise [*changing his tone*]. Believe me, there are very few women for whom God is enough. Perhaps there is no one for whom only God is enough. This shocks you a little?

Marcelle. It surprises me a little.

Blaise. Maybe I don't make myself clear. I believe two people must be *together* in order to reach God, and that the best place to find Him is in the heart of someone we love who loves us.

Marcelle [*laughing*]. That's an odd sort of creed you're teaching me!

Blaise. For many women the shortest road to perfection is . . . love. That doesn't mean you should give free rein to all your instincts, of course.

Marcelle [*mockingly*]. This surely wasn't the instruction they gave you in the seminary?

Blaise [*angry*]. I hate you to remind me I was in the seminary. You do it on purpose.

Marcelle. You don't have to apologize for the seminary.

Blaise. I didn't stay there long, you know. After six months I ran away.

Marcelle. Did you though? I thought your superiors decided not to keep you.

Blaise. Oh, I would have left anyway, believe me. They hated me and I didn't want to stay.

Marcelle. Dear Monsieur Couture! You always imagine you're being persecuted! The truth is they simply decided you weren't cut out to be a priest. How could your superiors hate you, I ask you?

Blaise. How could they? Because I had too much influence over the other students. I took our spiritual directors' clients away from them, do you see? They threw me out because they were jealous.

Marcelle. Couldn't it be that they were disturbed by the doubts you were spreading? I'm afraid you're not being fair.

Blaise. They kicked me out into the street. I hate them!

Marcelle. See here, Monsieur Couture. The fact is they left no stone unturned to find you a job. Remember, I brought you here on their recommendation.

Blaise. But of course. I tell you they would have done anything to get rid of me. I know them . . . The fact that they didn't hesitate to send a man of my age into a young widow's home proves how anxious they were to get me off their hands.

Marcelle [*laughing*]. There's absolutely nothing to this story, Monsieur Couture. They were convinced there wouldn't be the slightest danger here. I pledge you my word no one would ever have dreamed of such a thing!

Blaise [*bitterly*]. Yes of course. I see what you mean.
We belong to two different worlds, you and I—two different planets. No meeting between us is possible or
even imaginable. Then there's my face—my unfortunate
face!

Marcelle. Your face has nothing to do with anything.

Blaise [*still bitter*]. You don't have to be good-looking
to be loved.

Marcelle. Quite right, Monsieur Couture. On second
thought, I'll confess that your living in my house might
have caused some gossip. I remember now our priest
thought so. The year you came here Father Brunet insisted repeatedly that I part with you.

Blaise [*pleased*]. Really? I didn't know that! You
kept me in spite of him? That's wonderful. I know
Father Brunet. When he wants something he sticks to
it. You were marvelous to stand up to him!

Marcelle. Marvelous? Oh, not so marvelous. You're
not a man that one gives up without a fight, Monsieur
Couture.

Blaise [*laughing*]. Oh Madame, it's wonderful to hear
you say that!

Marcelle. I can tell you now that you were quite a
find for me. You know how hard it is to get a tutor
proficient in Latin and willing to live in the country
the year round. Even Father Brunet finally agreed that
your age and your . . . difficult nature . . . should
be ignored. Because frankly, you are indeed a rare bird!

Blaise [*angry*]. That isn't true!

Marcelle. What isn't true?

Blaise. It's not only because you had trouble finding
a tutor or because I'm proficient in Latin that you kept
me. Everywhere I've been, women have come to me.
Why, in the Guyenne school where I filled in for the
philosophy teacher for a few weeks before coming to
your house, my pupils' mothers thought up all kinds of
reasons to talk to me. And I saved the souls of several
of them. How often have I heard them say: "I gave up
my lover because of you."

Marcelle [*laughing*]. I'm very sorry, Monsieur Cou-

ture, but I have no one to give up because of you—
no one.

Blaise. You deliberately misinterpret what I say. I've
never asked anybody to give up anything because of me.

Marcelle [*significantly*]. Really? Have you never noticed that Mademoiselle's eyes often look as if she had
been crying?

Blaise [*furious*]. Why bring Mademoiselle into this?
You never listen to me. It's impossible to talk to you.

Sound of car offstage.

Marcelle. Not at all, Monsieur Couture. I'm listening
to you.

Blaise. I've nothing more to say. Mademoiselle has
nothing to do with it.

Marcelle. Did you hear the car? I mustn't let the English boy catch me in this outfit. I'll run and put on a
dress.

Blaise. Even for a child, your first thought is to please,
to charm.

Marcelle. Well, you certainly wouldn't want me to
keep my riding clothes on all day.

Enter MADEMOISELLE.

Mademoiselle. I heard the car.

Marcelle. Yes, I must go dress. Take care of the English boy. Show him his room. He'll probably want something cool to drink.

Mademoiselle. I've got a tray ready.

MARCELLE *goes upstairs and* BLAISE *remains seated.*
MADEMOISELLE *goes to meet* EMMANUELE, JEAN *and*
ANNE *who enter from terrace, excited.*

Emmanuele. The car is here. We heard it coming
through the village.

Jean [*to* ANNE]. If you think he'll play tennis with a
duffer like you, my poor girl! My word! An Englishman!

Emmanuele. He'll play with Anne if he's nice. And he
probably is nice.

Jean. The English don't like girls. That's what Mademoiselle said.

Mademoiselle. I never said anything of the kind.

Anne. You think he'll wear long pants?

Jean. Well, you certainly don't expect a fifteen-year-old to wear short pants!

Enter CHAUFFEUR *and* FIRMIN *carrying handsome but battered luggage, golf clubs, tennis rackets, etc.*

Blaise. Close the door. You're letting the heat in.

Jean. Too late. Here he is.

Enter HARRY FANNING, *big and handsome.*

Blaise. Did you come with the Fanning boy? We thought he'd be alone.

Harry. The Fanning boy? Why I'm Harry Fanning!

Blaise [staring at him in amazement]. You?

Harry. How are you? I suppose you're the tutor I'm to work with?

Blaise. I don't teach grown men, sir.

Harry. I don't understand.

Mademoiselle. You must pardon us for being surprised. We sent a boy of fifteen to England and we were expecting an English lad of the same age.

Harry [embarrassed]. Oh I see. Forgive me. I'm twenty, though it's true I look a little older. But I'm sure Madame de Barthas didn't mention any age limit, did she?

Mademoiselle. Of course she didn't. And there isn't any. It doesn't matter at all.

Harry [laughing]. Furthermore, when you exchange a young Englishman for a young Frenchman, you must expect to get a little extra weight!

The children laugh.

Blaise. Anyway sir, I'm surprised that you came to learn our language. You speak it perfectly.

Harry [bowing]. I'm very glad to hear you say so.

Blaise [sarcastically]. However, you're going to spoil your French. The people in this area have an accent—a frightful accent, if I may say so.

Harry. Yes, I know. But that's just it. I wanted to counteract what remains of my English accent by a soupçon of Gascon accent. Just as you put a touch of garlic in the leg of lamb, you know.

The children laugh.

Blaise [*still sarcastic*]. You chose our Gascony because we speak badly?

Harry. Exactly. You're going to think me odd. You'll say to yourself: "It's just like the English."

Blaise [*displeased*]. I try to avoid jumping to conclusions about people. [*Turns on his heel and exits.*]

Harry. Did I offend him? I'm making a bad start. I'm terribly sorry. But he wasn't very nice either.

Mademoiselle. Please forgive him. He's a fine person but hard to get to know.

The children laugh.

Anne. Getting to know him doesn't help at all.

Harry [*laughing*]. These children are charming! Is this Jean? And you're Anne?

Mademoiselle [*to the children*]. No more foolishness or impertinence. Take Mr. Fanning to his room.

Jean. Our big sister over there is Emmanuele.

Harry. Now I'm the one to be surprised. I didn't expect to find a young lady here.

Anne. Oh she's as old as the hills! She's seventeen!

The children fight over the luggage.

Harry [*to* EMMANUELE]. Is Madame de Barthas well, Mademoiselle?

Emmanuele. Yes, thank you, sir. She'll be down in a minute. Would you like something cool to drink?

Harry. No thank you. I'll wait for lunch if you don't mind. [*Aside to* MADEMOISELLE.] But I'd like a bath if it's all right.

Mademoiselle. I hope there's some warm water.

Harry. I'm not afraid of cold.

Exits with children who are loaded with baggage. Enter
BLAISE.

Blaise. This must be the boy she played golf with last year at Font Romeu.

Mademoiselle. What boy?

Blaise. You know. The one that sent her postcards for several weeks.

Mademoiselle. Oh, I wouldn't think of spying on her mail.

Blaise. No, I remember now. The fellow at Font Romeu was an Argentine.

Mademoiselle. Don't worry. Two months ago Madame didn't even know the Fannings existed.

Blaise. I tell you she's met that fellow before. But where?

Mademoiselle. As if she could meet anyone without your knowing it!

Blaise. She can, all right.

Mademoiselle. You're imagining things.

Blaise [*shouting*]. She's fooled us!

MARCELLE *appears at top of stairs. She has on a summer dress.*

Marcelle. Who's fooled you?

Blaise [*raging*]. We've seen little Fanning!

Marcelle. So?

Blaise. You should have let us in on the secret.

Marcelle. What secret?

Mademoiselle. Monsieur Couture and the rest of us were expecting a school boy but he's a young man.

Blaise. Yes. A man of twenty. But he looks twenty-five.

Mademoiselle. Why, he doesn't look a day over twenty-two.

Blaise [*furious*]. When will you stop contradicting me?

MADEMOISELLE *backs up, startled.* JEAN *and* ANNE *rush in.*

Anne. Mama, he gave us a box of chocolates.

Jean. And some ginger candy. He says it burns your mouth. Wow!

Marcelle. That's nice. Leave the boxes here. You mustn't open them till after lunch.

JEAN *and* ANNE *go toward terrace.*

Mademoiselle. Don't go too far and don't get overheated. It's almost noon.

Jean and Anne. The bell hasn't rung yet.

They go out and MADEMOISELLE *leans on balustrade.*

Blaise. Twenty years old. As if a twenty-year-old weren't a man!

Marcelle. It's a pity of course, I thought it was understood that in an arrangement of this kind you exchanged boys of the same age. What shall I do?

Blaise. Talk it over with him. If he's the right sort he'll understand and go back to his island.

Marcelle. You're strange, Monsieur Couture. How could this boy be the wrong sort?

Blaise. He speaks French too well. I don't fully understand why he's here. Are you sure you've never met him?

Marcelle. How do I know? I'll tell you after I've seen him.

Blaise. I'm beginning to think you're not mixed up in this plot.

Marcelle. My poor dear friend. What did you suspect me of?

Blaise. I'm uneasy about you and sensitive to the slightest threat to you. I feel responsible for your welfare. I am, in fact. I quite definitely want to take care of you.

Marcelle. I'm very grateful. But aren't you unduly alarmed?

Blaise. No. My instinct never fails me.

Marcelle. Your watchdog instinct. You're so pale suddenly!

Blaise. It's this hellish heat.

Marcelle. The house is cool though.

Blaise. Yes, but the doors and windows are sealed. It's cool but there's no air. I hate this climate. I hate your country. It's the country of thirst.

Marcelle. Every time I've suggested that we spend August at the beach or in the Pyrenees you've opposed it. The children haven't forgiven you.

Blaise. You say yourself that Bertrand only feels well here in the pine country since his pleurisy. And I'm afraid of life in hotels for you. A woman alone runs too many risks in summer resorts. You have a quiet life here, a chance to think and yet enough to do to keep you from being bored. At least it *was* so until today. [*Beseeching her.*] You'll get rid of this outsider right away, today, won't you?

Marcelle. Don't forget that Bertrand is already living with the Fannings.

Blaise. We'll find another place for Bertrand.

Marcelle. Do you think that's easy? We looked for weeks and weeks.

Blaise. I tell you it must be done by tonight!

Marcelle [*offended*]. It must be?

Blaise. Forgive me. It was only my eagerness to help. But don't you see that if that fellow stays here in the home of a woman alone, a widow, it would be simply crazy and the scandal would be tremendous?

Marcelle. Is he as good-looking as all that?

Blaise. Who told you he was good-looking? He's just a big brute, of course.

Luncheon bell rings.

Mademoiselle [*calling from terrace*]. Children!

Enter ANNE *and* JEAN, *shouting.*

Anne and Jean. Let's eat! Let's eat!

Anne. Has the young man come down?

Mademoiselle. No, not yet.

Jean. Yes, there he is.

HARRY *appears at top of stairs, radiant with youth, and comes slowly down. All eyes are on him.*

It's too bad he's so old. We were counting on him to play with us.

Anne. The English boy will only play with the grown-ups, I'm afraid.

CURTAIN

SCENE II—*Three days later. Moonlight on the terrace. The family has just dined.* EMMANUELE, JEAN, *and* ANNE *come out of the dining room, followed shortly by the grownups, and sit down on the stone steps of the terrace.*

EMMANUELE. The night is beautiful!

Anne. Bright as daylight.

Jean [*turning back toward the dining room*]. Mr. Fanning, come and see the moonlight on the pine trees!

Enter MARCELLE, *followed by* HARRY *and* MADEMOISELLE.

Marcelle. Let Mr. Fanning alone. He must want to rest.

Anne. He's had three days to rest.

Jean. Last night we couldn't go out because of the storm. But tonight we want him to see the grounds.

Harry. I'd like to very much. The moonlight on the pines is splendid.

Emmanuele. And you'll like the smell of the woods at night.

Mademoiselle. Now children, don't be foolish. Mr. Fanning has travelled around the world and you expect him to admire our grounds.

Marcelle. They think their country is the most beautiful in the world.

Harry [*turning toward terrace*]. It's quite true that the moor here is different from anything I've seen and the fragrance is amazing. A mixture of resin, mint and scorched bark.

Emmanuele. There must have been a forest fire.

Jean. Yes, but very far away toward the sea. The wind's blowing from that direction.

Marcelle. You'd better put something on, Mr. Fanning. We're on low ground here and at night it's very damp.

Jean [*eagerly*]. I'll go get your coat.

Harry. No, thanks, old man. What I'd like is my scarf and you wouldn't be able to find it.

Anne. Hurry up. We'll be here on the steps. We'll sing while we wait.

Marcelle. You must forgive them. They don't stand on ceremony.

ANNE, JEAN *and* EMMANUELE *gather round* MADEMOI-
SELLE *on the steps and sing* "Resplendent Night" *from
Gounod's opera* Cinq-Mars.

> Oh, night resplendent,
> How deeply silent,
> Thou fillest my heart
> With peace and sweetness.
> Through thy far spaces,
> Oh, radiant night,
> The glittering stars
> Sleep in heaven so blue.
> Soft breezes murmuring,
> Tenderly sighing,
> Under the clear sky
> Glide through the branches
> Without awak'ning the quiet forest.

Harry [going upstairs for scarf]. I think they're adorable!

Enter BLAISE.

Blaise. Have you spoken to him?

Marcelle. No, not yet. How could I?

Blaise. He's made the most of his time these three days.
He's already become great friends with the children, and
by the most contemptible methods.

Marcelle. Surely you're mistaken.

Blaise. Get it over with tonight while you're taking your
walk.

Marcelle. We won't be alone.

Blaise. Mademoiselle and the children shouldn't pre-
vent you from taking him aside. I advise you to go right
to the point and be very clear, very positive. Let him see
that your decision can't be changed.

Marcelle. It won't be easy. After all it's not the boy's
fault. He's not to blame for being twenty and looking
older.

Blaise. You're already weakening. You already like him.

Marcelle. I don't care whether this boy stays or not, I
assure you. But I wouldn't hurt his feelings for the world.

Blaise. You're already making excuses.

Marcelle. Be careful. Here he is.

Enter HARRY

Harry. Sorry I kept you waiting. I couldn't find my scarf.

Marcelle [*turning toward terrace*]. Emmanuele! Come back in, dear!

Emmanuele [*returning to room*]. Oh Mama, I want so much to show Mr. Fanning round.

Marcelle. No, I'm afraid the dampness from the brook wouldn't be good for you. You've been coughing today.

Emmanuele. Oh Mama. Please!

Marcelle. Come now, do as mother says, little Emmanuele.

Emmanuele. I'm sorry, Mama. [*Sits down at small table and takes up a book.*]

Blaise. I'll keep you company, Emmanuele.

Emmanuele. I'm not afraid to stay by myself.

Marcelle [*to* HARRY]. Have you everything you need in your room?

Harry. I wonder if I might have a siphon and some ice?

Marcelle [*as they go out*]. I'll have some ice brought up for you when you go to bed. And tomorrow you shall have a siphon. There's brandy in your room.

Harry. I'm expecting a case of whisky.

HARRY *and* MARCELLE *go out.*

Blaise. The English! They're all drunkards with their whisky. So you're not going out, Emmanuele?

Emmanuele. Mama doesn't want me to, because of my cold. [*Returns to her book.*]

Blaise. What are you reading?

Emmanuele. I'm reading *David Copperfield* for the second time. I almost know it by heart. I only need open the book at any page . . .

Blaise. It's about time for you to do some more serious reading.

Emmanuele. I agree, Monsieur Couture.

Blaise. I can advise you.

Emmanuele. You're very kind. Father Brunet lends me books.

Blaise. Father Brunet is a fine man but he's a simple soul.

Emmanuele. Well, he's smart enough for me.

Blaise. Beware, little Emmanuele. You think you're humble but beware of false humility. Virtues are like mushrooms. You always find poisonous ones that look enough like the good ones to fool you.

Emmanuele. It's only too true that I'm proud.

Blaise. I didn't mean that you're proud, child. But I fear that although you don't realize it you may be a little inclined to put on airs. What do you think?

Emmanuele. It's possible, Monsieur Couture. [*Returns to her reading.*]

Blaise. I haven't offended you, I hope.

Emmanuele [*giving up and closing her book*]. Certainly not.

Blaise [*leaning against her armchair.* EMMANUELE *too embarrassed to get up*]. Because I must confess, Emmanuele, that I admire you.

Emmanuele [*laughing*]. Admire me? You don't mean it!

Blaise. I know a lot about the human soul, you know. I see that yours is exquisite. I have insight into these things, a divine gift, if you will. I see your soul as clearly as I see your neck, your little round shoulder under your shirtwaist. [*Touching her shoulder.*]

Emmanuele [*getting up*]. I have a very ordinary soul, Monsieur Couture.

Blaise. You could go far, little Emmanuele, if you listened to me . . . Very far, very high.

Emmanuele. Oh, it would be too far and too high for me. Father Brunet tells me: "Stay as you are, a little child." He says that's what God wants me to do.

Blaise. God's will isn't always as plain as that good man thinks.

Emmanuele. Maybe you'll consider me proud again, Monsieur Couture. But I think that even in the most ordinary daily matters I know what I ought to do so that God will be pleased with me. That doesn't mean of course that I always do it or even do it very often. But believe me, it's as simple as if He held me by the hand or whispered in my ear . . .

Blaise. How do you know you're not deceiving yourself? Furthermore you're growing up, little Emmanuele. You're growing fast. You're all of seventeen years old. Seventeen! Think of that! Everything will be more complicated. Why, you're not a little girl at all any more. Just look at yourself. There will be times when God's voice will be silent. It will be drowned out by another voice. Perhaps already at times you feel some uneasiness, some emotion?

Emmanuele. Why no. What about?

Blaise. Everything or nothing at all. How should I know? A desire to confide in someone. For example at night when you can't sleep. A desire not to be alone.

Emmanuele. I'm never alone.

Blaise. That may be. But your mother, brother, sister, they won't always be enough.

Emmanuele. Even when there's no one, I've always someone with me.

Blaise. I understand. But it's my duty to warn you. It won't always be so. On a beautiful night like this, wouldn't you like this presence to take the form of another person with a face and eyes?

Emmanuele. I know, I know. I'm deeply devoted to the Virgin's face. I'll tell you a secret. You know the little lamp that shines before her statue in the Church? Well, I'm the one that keeps it burning. Father Brunet gave me permission. I buy the oil myself.

Blaise. You're a little girl.

Emmanuele [*smiling*]. A little goose?

Blaise. I didn't say that.

Emmanuele [*suddenly serious*]. Anyway Monsieur Couture, there are things that I understand.

Blaise. What things?

Emmanuele. You won't be angry if I tell you?

Blaise. Why should I be?

Emmanuele [*hesitating*]. For instance, I see that Mademoiselle isn't happy.

Blaise [*curtly*]. Don't worry about Mademoiselle.

Emmanuele. Can I fail to worry when someone I love is suffering?

Blaise. In any case you can't do anything about it. Let's speak of something else.

Emmanuele. You could do a lot about it, Monsieur.

Blaise. You're simply extraordinary! My word, don't meddle!

Emmanuele. You're hard with her. You're merciless.

Blaise [beside himself]. What will I hear next? You dare to lecture me? Me! And on such a subject! Don't be absurd!

Emmanuele. I understand why you're displeased with me. The reason I insist is that I know Mademoiselle. She's been miserable a long time but, because she had me to comfort her, she was miserable in a quiet way. I was with her, do you understand? Now for several weeks she has been going away from me, as if she were disappearing into a dark forest where I can't follow her—except in my prayers. I try to imagine what despair is like.

Blaise. Not another word! I excuse you because you haven't even the faintest idea of why I treat her as I do. It's because I have self-respect and a sense of duty to God and to her that the poor woman suffers. It embarrasses me to discuss such things with a young lady, but your indiscreet remarks make it necessary.

Emmanuele. You needn't be embarrassed. I understand the situation.

Blaise. No more, please!

Emmanuele. I must say something more. I have no experience in such things. But isn't it possible when someone loves you to save her from despair and still keep God's love and stay close to Him? It's terrible to hate and torture a person whose only crime is not to be able to live without you!

JEAN *and* ANNE *are heard singing and their voices gradually come nearer.*

Blaise. For a little girl who claims to be religious this is bold talk. Do you discuss these strange ideas with Father Brunet?

Emmanuele [with despair]. You don't understand, Monsieur Couture. You don't see the danger. There are times when I see Mademoiselle going toward a precipice —running toward it with her eyes closed. And you are pushing her over the edge! Yes, you!

Enter MADEMOISELLE, JEAN *and* ANNE.

Blaise [*aside to* MADEMOISELLE]. Where is Madame?

Mademoiselle. She stayed behind with Mr. Fanning.
They said it was too beautiful a night to come indoors.

Blaise. Are you mad? Why did you leave them alone?
Did you do it on purpose?

Mademoiselle. Madame asked me to bring the children
in. It's their bedtime.

Blaise. Emmanuele will take care of them. Try to find
Madame and that . . . that . . . fellow. At once!

Mademoiselle. They went off toward the mill. How can
I possibly find them?

Anne. Mademoiselle, will you come and tuck me in?

Mademoiselle. Yes, yes, go up quickly.

Anne. Will you tell Mama to come and give us a good-
night kiss?

Jean. Tell her we won't go to sleep until she comes.

Mademoiselle. Emmanuele, see that they say their
prayers.

Emmanuele. Yes, Mademoiselle. Good night.

Mademoiselle. Good night, dear.

Emmanuele. Will you come and give me a kiss when
I'm in bed?

Mademoiselle. I will if you're not asleep.

Emmanuele. I won't be asleep.

EMMANUELE, JEAN *and* ANNE *go upstairs.*

Blaise [*going to terrace and back*]. You must go get
them right away!

Mademoiselle. It's as if I saw you bleed. Look at yourself in the mirror.

Blaise. I bleed? You have hallucinations, poor thing!
I'm uneasy of course. How could I be otherwise? [*Going
to terrace and peering into darkness.*] Where can they be
now?

Mademoiselle. Would you really like to know? I left
them sitting beside each other. Yes, very close to each
other on the bench under the old oak.

BLAISE *makes a move to go out but* MADEMOISELLE *restrains him.*

No, it's no use running out there. You won't find them because as I was leaving they were already getting up. I turned around and saw them disappear through the brushwood toward the mill. On the way back they have a choice of several paths. I doubt they'll take the shortest one.

Blaise. Keep still! I hate you!

Mademoiselle. Hate me? Even so, believe me, I get no consolation from seeing you suffer.

Blaise. If I suffer it's because I love her soul ardently.

Mademoiselle. Her soul? Come, come! You hover over the soul of everyone here!

Blaise. No later than tomorrow one of us must leave this house. I won't spend another night under the same roof with you.

Mademoiselle. No, Blaise, be merciful! I'm a poor mad thing! Forget what I've said. You couldn't know how awful it would be for me not to see you any more. You may hate me but at least I see you! To be hated by the one you love—do you understand what that means? And yet I bear it because I live only in your shadow. The air you breathe, I breathe. You're here. Sometimes I touch your hand.

BLAISE *moves away from her toward terrace and looks out.* MADEMOISELLE *speaks as if to herself alone.*

Sometimes I get up at night and stand beside your door to hear you breathing as you sleep. And then I never let you two out of my sight, you and her. I watch you. If you have me sent away! Oh! If you have me sent away!

Sound of voices.

Blaise. There they are at last! How slowly they walk!

HARRY's *voice.* MARCELLE *laughs.*

He makes her laugh! [*Suddenly* BLAISE *switches off the chandelier and the wall lamps. The only light remaining is that of the lamp on the center table.*]

Mademoiselle. Why did you turn off the lights?

Blaise. At last I'm going to find out what that fellow came here for.

Mademoiselle. No, Blaise, no! That's unworthy of you. Don't betray her!

Blaise. You'll betray me if you say a single word! Don't make a sound and then maybe I'll forget your outrageous conduct. [*He pulls her into the dining room.*]

MARCELLE *enters from terrace with* HARRY. *They lean against door side by side.*

Marcelle. They've all gone to sleep.

Harry. How can anyone think of sleeping on such a night?

Marcelle. Do you feel the coolness of the brook?

Harry. I smell its fragrance. Water has a fragrance, you know.

Marcelle. It's not the water you smell but the plants growing on the banks . . . the smell of the mud.

Harry. I like rather to think it's the smell of the water.

Marcelle. But if it's not true, why pretend to believe it?

Harry. How French you are, Madame! I mean, how realistic!

Marcelle. I take care of everything here—the people and the animals. I have no time for dreaming.

Harry. You're the only person in the house who doesn't dream, whose head isn't in the clouds, as we say in my country.

Marcelle. You've discovered this in so few days!

Harry. I always see everything very quickly, as if I were French.

Marcelle. Well then, you must know what I've been trying to tell you since we started our walk.

Harry. Oh, that's not hard to guess. For three days you've been beating about the bush. How do you say it in French?

Marcelle. Yes, because I was afraid of hurting you.

Harry. I would be hurt, Madame, if *you* wanted me to leave.

Marcelle. Who told you I don't want you to?

Harry. No, Madame, *you* don't want me to.

Marcelle. I thought conceit was a failing of young men in our country.

Harry. You don't understand. I mean that someone is insisting that I go and it isn't you.

Marcelle [*vexed*]. Let me say that no one here but me has the right to insist on anything.

Harry. Really? Except the tutor who must be raging at this moment somewhere in the house.

Marcelle. Mr. Fanning. I ought not to answer your innuendo. But impudence from a boy of your age doesn't bother me.

Harry. No, I'm not impudent. I'm truthful.

Marcelle. Don't raise your voice. The children are sleeping.

Harry [*gently*]. I love this house full of sleeping children.

Marcelle [*suddenly serious*]. Listen to me. You must understand. Eight years ago they brought my husband home. He'd fallen from his horse. His foot caught in the stirrup.

Harry. He was dragged? That happened to me once.

Marcelle. His head struck a pine tree.

Harry. Oh Madame! Was he killed outright?

Marcelle. He was unconscious. The doctors say he didn't suffer.

Harry. Do you have a picture of him?

Marcelle [*going to the center table where the lamp is lit*]. Yes, here in the album. [*They bend over it together.*] Here he is and this is Bertrand. They look extraordinarily like each other, don't they?

Harry. What faces! How handsome they are, both of them.

Marcelle [*looking pleased*]. Yes, he was very handsome. And I must say that Bertrand, even if he is my son . . .

Harry [*still looking at the photos*]. I may seem naïve but don't you think that all the disputes about whether there is a God and eternal life should be solved just by the sight of this marvel: a human face? This line of the forehead, this arch above eyes full of tenderness and pride. And the mouth most of all . . .

Marcelle. I had never thought of it . . . so what was I saying?

Harry. You were telling me about your husband . . . the accident.

Marcelle. I found myself alone here. There's no one to see—except a few country gentlemen, a few land-owners, all of them old. The young people go away, you may be sure. No one ever comes this way. The roads from here go nowhere.

Harry. Have you no other family?

Marcelle. To be sure, we have family. On the moor everyone is cousins. But I've lost nearly all my close kin. I still have a sister who lives in Bazas. Only we quarreled over the inheritance after my father died. We'll never see each other again, I fear. My mother-in-law lives in Bordeaux in a convent as a paying guest. She has never forgiven me for marrying her son. I take the children to see her every two or three months but she's vowed never again to set foot here.

Harry. God, you're even lonelier than I thought!

Marcelle. Foutunately I was saved immediately by the responsibilities I had to take over. We have nearly fifteen thousand acres, you know.

Harry. It's a magnificent estate.

Marcelle. Yes, truly magnificent. I'll take you over it on horseback. It's a marvelous country for riding. Miles and miles of sandy paths. But think of the loneliness at night when my children were in bed . . . the silence of the moor!

Harry [*gloomily*]. Yes, and the tutor was here . . .

Marcelle [*laughing*]. I loathe misunderstandings and I've nothing to hide from you. My children's tutor is a poor boy brought up in a seminary on charity. His mother was a scrubwoman in Bordeaux. He was dismissed from the advanced seminary for insubordination and I took him in seven years ago at the urgent request of his superiors, who didn't know what to do with him. I was look-ing for someone for Bertrand who had just had pleurisy, and had to be brought up in the country. I took what I could find.

Harry. In any case he's not a monster. He must have

a kind of charm. So far as I can tell he's able to please
Mademoiselle anyway.

Marcelle. What an idea! Mademoiselle is just Mademoiselle. It's true, though, that he has charm. The charm of
a witch doctor! He gets a sort of hold over people. Let's
say no more about him. Tell me about yourself, Mr. Fanning.

Harry. I'm twenty, Madame. I'm not a witch doctor
and I'm preparing for the Foreign Office. That's my story
in a nutshell.

Marcelle. You're twenty years old?

Harry. And have been for two months.

Marcelle. Twenty years old! . . . We must get some
sleep. At dawn I must count pine trees with the overseer.
Also, I'm beginning to feel the damp.

Harry. Let's stay a little longer. Take my scarf.

Marcelle. Then you'll be cold.

Harry. I'm very warm now. I'm burning up. Here, feel
my hand.

Marcelle. Your scarf smells good.

Harry. What is there about moments such as these
when nothing special happens and yet we know very well
that they are very precious?

Marcelle [*after a pause*]. The moon is going down. I
can hardly see you.

Harry. I'm here. I'm touching your arm.

Marcelle. Take your hand away. [*Another pause.*] And
this secret you were going to tell me?

Harry. What secret?

Marcelle. You know. Why you came here. I want to
know before I go to sleep.

Harry. Oh, that was to keep you guessing. There is no
secret. Or at least it's hard to put into words. My father's
a diplomat, you know. He was stationed in Madrid a
long time. Those endless journeys across France when I
was a child made a deep impression on me. During those
night trips I'd look through the train window at your
sleeping countryside. I wanted to be the demon Asmodée.
You know, the demon that lifted the roofs off houses to
see what went on inside. Nothing in the world has ever
seemed so mysterious to me as one of your old houses,

doors and shutters closed, under the stars. I imagined
strange dramas, terrible, dark passions. I always had a
secret yearning to get inside one of those houses.

Marcelle [*laughing*]. You're out of luck, Mr. Fanning.
If Asmodée could lift our roof, the poor demon would
be sadly disappointed. Fate has brought you to a house
without a story, where nothing has ever happened, where
nothing does happen.

Sound of body collapsing onto floor. A stifled cry. The
lights go up.

Who's there? What is it? Is it you, Mademoiselle?

Mademoiselle [*pointing to* BLAISE *lying on floor*]. He's
fainted! [*To* HARRY.] Help me carry him to his room!

CURTAIN

ACT TWO

The next day. A fine summer morning. ANNE *and* JEAN
come out of dining room, breakfast just finished, and run
to meet HARRY *coming downstairs.*

JEAN. Hurry up, Mr. Fanning. We're going to set traps
in the brook.

Harry. Traps? What for?

Anne. To catch crayfish.

Jean. We set out little nets with bait inside.

Anne. The bait's a piece of old sheep's head.

Jean. Old sheep's head sprinkled with basil juice. The
crayfish love it!

Harry. You little monsters! Has Emmanuele come down
yet?

Emmanuele [*coming from dining room as* JEAN *and*
ANNE *go to terrace*]. Of course! I came down long ago.
You should have seen the fog this morning. It smelled
like autumn.

Harry. Are you always the first one up?

Emmanuele. Yes, Mr. Fanning, because I go to seven o'clock mass.

Harry. Oh, Emmanuele, you promised to call me Harry!

Anne and Jean [*from terrace*]. Oh, there's the postman! the postman! the postman! [*They run offstage.* MA-DEMOISELLE *comes slowly downstairs looking miserable.*]

Emmanuele [*embracing* MADEMOISELLE]. Mademoiselle!

Harry. Good morning. How's Monsieur Couture this morning?

Mademoiselle. He spent a restless night. But he feels much better now.

Harry [*going into dining room*]. I'll eat breakfast quickly so as not to keep the children waiting.

Emmanuele. Oh, no, Harry, take your time.

MADEMOISELLE *sits down as if overcome.* EMMANUELE *puts her arms around her.*

What's the matter, Mademoiselle? What's the trouble, dear Mademoiselle?

Mademoiselle. Nothing at all. I'm just a little tired. I didn't sleep last night.

Emmanuele [*intensely*]. It hurts me so not to be able to do anything for you. If I weren't such a bad girl, God would help you. I've been praying for you every morning for such a long time.

Mademoiselle. Emmanuele! My little girl! [*Gently strokes her hair.*] It's strange that you should love me!

Emmanuele. Why strange?

Mademoiselle. You don't really know me, Emmanuele. You can't.

Emmanuele. But suppose I say I can read your thoughts?

Mademoiselle. I wouldn't believe you.

Emmanuele. Then who would have taught me about despair . . .

Mademoiselle. Emmanuele!

Emmanuele. . . . if I couldn't read your thoughts?

Mademoiselle. My little girl. Since we've said this, I feel I can tell you, confess to you . . . Yes, sometimes

I've wanted to die so much that there was really nothing to hold me back. I had only to lift my hand and pour water into a glass. I could have done it as quickly as you would throw yourself into the sea if you were on fire.

Emmanuele. I knew it.

Mademoiselle. At those times, at the very last moment, I feel your presence. I don't see you, yet I know you're there, so weak, so little and yet able to do miracles.

Emmanuele. Oh, Mademoiselle, it's not me!

Mademoiselle. It's you and yet it's not you.

JEAN *comes in from terrace followed by* ANNE.

Jean. There was nothing but a letter from England.

HARRY *emerges from dining room.*

Anne [*to* HARRY]. But it's not for you, Mr. Fanning. It's for Mama. It's Bertrand's writing.

Emmanuele. Quick. Take the letter to Mama!

Jean [*from stairs*]. The stamp's for me!

Anne. No, it's mine!

Jean. Oh, English stamps are nothing much. You can have it.

Anne. Thanks. I don't want it any more.

JEAN *and* ANNE *go upstairs.* EMMANUELE *follows.*

Emmanuele. Don't quarrel! Mr. Fanning will think you don't love each other. You don't think that, do you, sir? If only you knew how much they miss each other when they're apart.

HARRY *watches* EMMANUELE *disappear upstairs.*

Harry. Little Emmanuele! As a rule I don't like girls. I must admit they bore me stiff. But she's wonderful!

Mademoiselle. She certainly is.

Harry. To me she doesn't seem pretty. No, she's not pretty. She has—I don't know how to say it—an inner light.

Mademoiselle. Yes, she shines with inner light.

Harry. I haven't said ten words to her and yet I know her. Just to look at her makes you believe in something again!

Mademoiselle [*looking closely at him*]. I like you very much, Mr. Fanning. Yes, very much. So you must do what I'm about to ask you.

Harry. Is it so hard?

Mademoiselle. No, you only need see Monsieur Couture for a few minutes. He wants to talk to you.

Harry. Does he?

Mademoiselle. Yes, as soon as possible.

Harry. You know what it's about?

Mademoiselle. He hasn't told me.

Harry [*worried*]. Really? But I expect you can guess. If he thinks I'm an easy mark . . .

Mademoiselle. Come, come, Mr. Fanning. Don't get excited before you know.

Harry. When will he be down?

Mademoiselle. Any minute. As soon as the children have gone.

Emmanuele [*coming downstairs with* ANNE *and* JEAN]. We haven't read Bertrand's letter. Mama has her door locked.

Jean and Anne. Well, Mr. Fanning. Are you ready?

Harry. You go ahead. I have to write a letter.

Jean and Anne [*surrounding him*]. Oh no, Mr. Fanning. Come with us.

Harry. I'll be with you in fifteen minutes.

Jean and Anne [*running to terrace*]. Right! Fifteen minutes. No more.

Emmanuele [*to* HARRY, *from terrace*]. Cut through the meadow. You'll get your feet wet but that doesn't matter.

Jean and Anne. Just give a yell. You know our signal. [*They utter their rallying cry.*] We'll answer.

HARRY *imitates the yell.*

That's right! Just like that!

Harry. Right!

JEAN, ANNE *and* EMMANUELE *go out.*

Mademoiselle. I'll leave you now. Monsieur Couture is coming down. Be kind and patient.

Harry. I'll do my best.

MADEMOISELLE *goes to stairs and signals to* HARRY. BLAISE *appears. She steps aside to let him past and goes upstairs.*

Blaise [*very gently*]. Mr. Fanning, I thank you for agreeing to talk to me.

Harry. No need to thank me. I'm glad to.

Blaise. I've something to tell you about what happened last night. I hardly know how to say it. Well, it's this: I wouldn't want you to think me capable of listening behind doors.

Harry. Oh no. I don't think you could possibly do such a thing. Just because you did it once doesn't mean you make a habit of it.

Blaise. No, no. Not even once, Mr. Fanning. I often have these fainting spells. They're not at all serious. But for a few moments before they hit me, it's hard for me to move or even make a sound.

Harry. This must be frightfully unpleasant.

Blaise. Yes, very unpleasant. So if I overheard part of what Madame and you said last night, I pledge you my word it was in spite of myself.

Harry [*courteously*]. I'm glad to hear it, Monsieur Couture. And I hope you won't hold against me anything slightly unkind I may have said about you.

Blaise. I'll forget it. I've already forgotten it, provided you won't take me for an eavesdropper.

Harry. Far be it from me even to suspect such a thing.

Blaise. You're sure?

Harry. Perfectly sure.

Blaise. Thank you, my boy. You lift a great weight from my shoulders. I'll go away with an easier mind.

Harry [*surprised*]. Go away?

Blaise. Yes, I'm leaving this house, Mr. Fanning.

Harry [*laughing*]. Really?

Blaise [*displeased*]. That makes you laugh?

Harry. I'm laughing because this time . . . Forgive me if I offend you, but I don't believe a word of it.

Blaise [*angry*]. Of course. After what Madame told you, you think I want to keep my job. Nevertheless, by tonight at the latest, I'll be far from here. And when

I say good-by you'll see whether Madame or I will be sorry.

Harry [*sharply*]. Please leave Madame de Barthas out of this.

Blaise [*shouting*]. I'll talk about her if I like. Did she hesitate to talk about me last night? [*Getting hold of himself.*] Excuse me. I'm hot tempered. Furthermore, I have a lot on my mind. You couldn't imagine what I've had to put up with. She can be pretty heartless sometimes. You don't mind my saying so?

Harry [*sarcastic*]. Oh no, Monsieur Couture.

Blaise. You know what Madame means to me and I to her. You know if I leave her it's not for revenge. No, it's simply weakness.

Harry. Weakness?

Blaise. It's more than I can bear to see certain things that are going to happen here. Do you understand?

Harry. No. I confess I don't understand.

Blaise [*in a low voice*]. What began between you two last night . . .

Harry [*laughing*]. But there's nothing, Monsieur Couture. What are you talking about? Less than nothing!

Blaise. Nothing? Is it nothing to make a woman's salvation the goal of your life? To protect her for years against all dangers and threats, then see in a moment the work so carefully, painfully done, about to be destroyed? Excuse me for showing my feelings. I'm keeping nothing back.

Harry [*moved*]. I assure you I'm awfully sorry, really. I certainly didn't expect you to talk to me so frankly. But you're misled by your anxiety about Madame de Barthas. Don't jump to conclusions. I'm just an English boy who's come to France for six weeks to improve his accent.

Blaise. No. Remember what you said last night. You've come to meddle in the life of one of our homes and pry into its secrets.

Harry [*embarrassed*]. It's not a crime to want to see what goes on in a French family. Anyway, in two months I'll be gone.

Blaise. Yes, in two months. But in three days you've destroyed the tranquility of this house.

Harry. How can you think such an awful thing? I mean nothing to Madame de Barthas.

Blaise. Of course you mean nothing to her. But you awaken dreams and longings in her. Your presence has reopened a door I thought I'd closed forever. It's all going to start over again: regret for what might have been, for the passing of her youth. Ah, you have no idea what you've done!

Harry. Since I've been here I haven't had a single thought I need be ashamed of, believe me.

Blaise. I believe you, my boy. I know young people. It's my business to know them. I sized you up right away. You're honest and sincere. There's nobility in you and a kind of innocence.

Harry. Oh, I'm not so fine as you think. But it's true I hate to make people suffer.

Blaise. Yes, you're a good lad.

Harry. Well then, Monsieur Couture, what is it about me you're afraid of?

Blaise. You're a good lad but you're also a twenty-year-old man.

Harry. A twenty-year-old man's nothing much.

Blaise. No, but women are terribly weak.

Harry. What do you mean, Monsieur Couture?

Blaise. A twenty-year-old is dangerous because of his charm and the feeling it stirs in women's hearts. You don't realize the harm you do.

Harry [laughing]. You certainly manage to complicate things. If you knew anything about my life! Don't worry. I've no crime on my conscience.

Blaise. Are you quite sure?

Harry [laughing]. Perfectly sure.

Blaise. Could you swear before God that in school and in the world outside you've never hurt anyone? Perhaps it would have been better if some friend or girl had never met you? Have you nothing to say?

Harry [somberly]. What can I say? No one can be sure.

Blaise. I'm certain that at this very moment you're thinking of someone—perhaps several people—who'll never entirely get over the unhappiness you've brought them.

Harry [*deeply moved*]. If I've made anybody unhappy it was without wanting to.

Blaise. Anyway, I imagine that in your country you move in a society where any effect you have on a person is counteracted by others. But here you're faced with a tight little world, a virgin soil and hearts sheltered and protected that react violently.

Harry [*worried*]. But you're here, Monsieur Couture. You'll be here.

Blaise. Didn't I tell you I was leaving tonight?

Harry [*frightened*]. No, you mustn't.

Blaise. Do you believe me now? Do you believe I'm telling the truth?

Harry. You can't possibly go! I felt from everything Madame de Barthas told me yesterday that she can't do without you.

Blaise [*triumphant*]. She'll miss me even more than she knows. I've filled her life so completely I don't know how she'll be able to live without me. You'll have to be very good to her, Mr. Fanning.

Harry. I'll try. And anyway six weeks pass quickly. You'll find her again just as you left her.

Blaise. Find her? You don't understand. If I leave this house tonight I'll never return. I'll go without looking back and, I must say, without regret.

Harry. Without regret? Oh, Monsieur Couture!

Blaise. I can't help it. I can't bear to see someone that's dear to me influenced by anyone except myself. It's hateful to me. It disgusts me. Like finding smudgy finger marks on a white page. I wish I were going already!

Harry. You're a terrible person, you know. [*A pause.*] But suppose I were to go, Monsieur Couture?

Blaise. You, oh no. I couldn't ask that, although I know it would be easy for you.

Harry [*quickly*]. Not as easy as you think. You don't know how fond I am of all of them.

Blaise. Already?

Harry. Yes, already. There are families that have charm, aren't there? A mystery? It's hard to say. I felt that so strongly last night when the children were singing on the terrace. You'll think me foolish. I could hardly keep from crying.

Blaise. You see, it's too late for you to leave them.

Harry. Oh, I can make myself go.

Blaise. I understand you better now. I'll be able to leave with peace of mind. I'm sure you'll do the least harm possible. Only promise me not to abandon Madame when you're back in your own country. Even when you're gone you'll think of her very often, won't you?

Harry. The responsibility is frightening. See here, Monsieur Couture, I see you can't stand my being here. But it would be so easy for you to come back to your place when I'm gone—so easy.

Blaise. You must see I don't dislike you, Mr. Fanning. Far from it. I have more friendship for you than you can know. Don't you understand that what I can't bear is the thought of the wreckage you'll leave behind in a creature that was my creation? Yes, I'm not afraid to say so—my masterpiece!

Pause.

Harry [*hesitantly*]. If I decided to go, I'd have to find some excuse. I could tell Madame de Barthas I'd received a telegram—that my father told me to come home. The children would be sorry, you know. And Emmanuele too.

Blaise. You know they'll all insist on keeping you and you'll finally agree to stay.

Harry. I believe I love them enough to give them up.

Blaise. That's an admirable thing to say, my boy.

Harry. I didn't mean to say anything admirable.

Blaise. I see now you're strong enough to do it. You're a fine person, very fine.

Harry. Oh, I'm weaker than you think.

Blaise. No, I see your mind's made up now.

Harry [*dejected*]. Yes, Monsieur Couture.

Blaise [*pressing his advantage*]. Well then, you'd better hurry. It will hurt less if you act quickly.

Harry. Yes, Monsieur Couture.

Blaise [*still urging*]. Tell Madame as soon as possible.
I advise you to conceal your plan from the children.
Take French leave, as you say.

Harry [*noticing* BLAISE *is too happy*]. French leave?

Blaise. Yes. That is, go without saying good-by to
any of them.

Harry [*curtly*]. As for that, I won't make any
promises.

Blaise. Just as you like, of course.

Harry. Yes. The main thing is for me to clear out,
isn't it?

Blaise. Why wait, since your mind's made up? [*Insistently.*] There's a train this evening, you know. At six
o'clock.

Harry. In any case I'll have to say good-by to Madame
de Barthas and pack my bags.

Blaise. You have all day and Mademoiselle will help
you. [*Clasping* HARRY's *hand.*] I know I can count on
you.

Harry. Yes, Monsieur Couture.

Blaise. They'll all hang on to your coat tails and try
to keep you but you won't give way. A boy like you,
an English boy, is true to his word, I know. I'm sure of
it. I'll see you again before you leave. If you need any
advice or help you can find me. I won't leave my room.

BLAISE *goes upstairs.* EMMANUELE *enters quickly from
terrace.*

Emmanuele. Well Harry, what happened to you? I
was afraid you'd lost your way. Hurry up.

Harry. I'd like to go with you, Emmanuele, but I must
pack.

Emmanuele. Pack?

Harry [*sadly*]. Yes, I'm leaving.

Emmanuele. For good?

Harry. For good.

Emmanuele [*upset*]. But it's not possible, Harry.

Harry. Will you miss me?

Emmanuele. Oh Harry! You haven't had bad news
from home, I hope? There wasn't any mail for you
today.

Harry. No. I got a telegram. I have to go home . . .
about . . . a lawsuit.

Jean [from terrace]. Well, is Mr. Fanning ready? Are
you coming or not?

Emmanuele [joining JEAN *on terrace].* Mr. Fanning's
leaving us.

Jean. Leaving? Did you say leaving?

Emmanuele. Yes, for good.

Jean. Oh, that's terrible! We can't let this happen.

Enter ANNE.

Anne. What's going on?

Jean. Didn't you hear? Mr. Fanning's going back to
England.

Anne. No! But why?

Emmanuele. He has some business to attend to. It's
about a lawsuit.

Jean. Mr. Fanning, we've decided you can't go.

Anne. We'll lock you up.

Jean. Does Mama know?

HARRY *shakes his head.*

I thought not. She'll arrange matters. You'll see.

Harry. You're so kind. Really I'm sorry. We would
have got along so well and had such a good time.

Jean. There will be moonlight again tonight, Mr. Fanning.

Anne. The moon rises late but we'll wait.

Jean. Tonight you must sing with us. We'll teach
you "Resplendent Night."

Harry. Tonight I'll see the moon from the train window. I'll see it running along beside the rails and I'll
know it's watching over all of you and shedding the same
light on the tops of the tall pines and your little heads.

Anne. No, Mr. Fanning. If you're not here it'll be
cloudy tonight. It'll rain.

Harry. I'll come back, I promise, I'll come back next
year. I'll look at the calendar so that I can get here
with the moon.

Emmanuele. Yes, but it won't be the same moon and
we won't be quite the same either.

Enter MADEMOISELLE.

Jean and Anne. Mademoiselle! Do you know Mr. Fanning wants to leave us? Don't let him, Mademoiselle. Please.

Mademoiselle [*to* HARRY]. Is it true you're going to leave?

Harry [*tense*]. I expect Monsieur Couture has already told you. No?

Mademoiselle [*to the children*]. Don't bother Mr. Fanning. Go and play.

Jean. We don't feel like playing.

Anne. We're much too sad.

Mademoiselle. Well, you have half an hour before lunch so go and finish your lessons. You'll be free this afternoon.

Anne. Good idea. We can enjoy Mr. Fanning till the last minute.

Mademoiselle. Off with you then.

Jean [*to* EMMANUELE]. Are you coming with us?

EMMANUELE *nods.*

You can help with my composition.

Jean and Anne [*from doorway*]. You'll stay, Mr. Fanning? Right? You won't go?

Mademoiselle [*taking them away*]. Leave Mr. Fanning alone. He knows what he must do. [*To* HARRY.] Everybody here will be so sorry to see you go. But only I will know how much we owe you.

MADEMOISELLE, JEAN, ANNE *and* EMMANUELE *go off.* HARRY, *alone, looks round, goes to door and looks out. He turns round as he hears* MARCELLE *come downstairs holding open letter.* MARCELLE *looks very young and gay in summer dress.*

Marcelle. Oh, Mr. Fanning. I was looking for you. I got a letter from Bertrand this morning. He's deliriously happy with your family. He tells me about your mother. I'm not surprised to hear that she's kind and charming. Here, you must read it. He's already been riding your horse. He's really in seventh heaven!

Harry [*reading*]. What a fine letter! He's the only one of your children that I won't have known. That makes me sad, you know.

Marcelle. But you will know him. On your way home you'll meet in Paris and can have dinner together. You don't look very well this morning, my dear boy. I hope what happened last night didn't keep you from sleeping.

Harry. Oh, for something to keep me from sleeping! . . .

Marcelle. You're homesick.

Harry [*bitterly*]. No, it's when I go I'll be homesick.

Marcelle. Why do you speak of the time when you'll be gone? August has hardly begun and there's still all of September. That's the adorable season here. And surely you'll stay several days in October to go pigeon shooting?

Harry. Where will I be in October?

Marcelle. Why, here, I hope. Besides it's too early to talk about that. We have the whole long vacation season ahead of us.

Harry. The whole long vacation. Perhaps it won't be as long as you imagine.

Marcelle. Don't look so solemn. Think what a single night like last night means. We smelled the fragrance of the water. Remember?

Harry. Yes. A whole life can be lived in a night like that.

Marcelle. Then you have many more lives to live here!

Harry [*ardently*]. Even if I left tonight I would take you with me in my heart.

Marcelle [*moved*]. You're very sweet, Harry.

Harry. I'd take you all with me. Even Bertrand whom I don't know.

Marcelle [*disappointed*]. Ah, well. You're in love with the whole family then!

Harry. Yes. The children, you. You're not offended, are you?

Marcelle. How could I be offended?

Harry. It seemed to me you looked displeased.

Marcelle. On the contrary. I'm so glad you like the children! You'll grow fonder of them day by day.

Harry. Which is your favorite?

Marcelle. Do I have a favorite? I don't know. Bertrand, perhaps. He's the most mysterious of all, the most serious. Emmanuele is in a class by herself. She . . .

Harry [*with fire*]. I can't tell you how much I love Emmanuele!

Marcelle. Everyone loves her. But she frightens me. I'd like her to do something a little bad from time to time. I have a feeling—how shall I say?—that someone has already taken her from us.

Harry. Good Lord! But she's in good health, isn't she?

Marcelle. Of course. But for us there's another death which threatens our little girls when they're too pure. Death to the world.

HARRY *turns away suddenly and hides his face in his hands.*

What's the matter, Mr. Fanning? What is it?

Harry [*in despair*]. I'm so unhappy to leave you!

Marcelle. But, my child, you've two more months to stay.

Harry. No, no, I leave tonight. I'm taking the six-o'clock train.

Marcelle. This is nonsense! Who's forcing you to go today?

Harry. I do such damage here. That's what Monsieur Couture and Mademoiselle say.

Marcelle. Damage? Did you say damage? I hope you don't imagine . . . [*Sarcastic.*] No, that would be too funny!

Harry [*ashamed*]. I don't imagine anything, Madame.

Marcelle [*laughing*]. It's just that I know Monsieur Couture! He's quite capable of making you think you're a dangerous character!

Harry [*more and more embarrassed*]. I wouldn't have believed him. I'm not so foolish.

Marcelle. I should hope not. Then what is this damage?

Harry. Oh, it's very simple. If I stay, Monsieur Couture said he'd go for good and by tonight at the latest.

Marcelle [*laughing*]. By tonight at the latest. And you believed him!

Harry. Yes. And I still believe him. He means it.

Marcelle. Don't worry, my poor boy. The time is not yet for Monsieur Couture to fare forth into the wide world. For years he has threatened to go. I don't even pay attention any more.

Harry. I must warn you he seemed completely determined.

Marcelle. Really? He's never consented to take even a week's vacation since he's been here. Outside this house he can't breathe. That's the truth.

Harry [*looking at her intently*]. What if he actually goes?

Marcelle. I tell you he won't go.

Harry. You must admit that you can't even bear the idea of his leaving.

Marcelle. I hate to imagine the impossible. What can't happen doesn't interest me.

Harry. How very much you too need him.

Marcelle [*laughing*]. Next you'll say I'm in love with Monsieur Couture.

Harry. Oh, no, of course not. But perhaps he creates around you an atmosphere of adoration without which you can't breathe either.

Marcelle. I could very easily do without him. Only I'll never have to try. He'll not leave me willingly. If you have no better reason to part company with us . . .

Harry [*weakly*]. I've given him my word.

Marcelle. Your word! But he extorted it from you! I know him. For getting people worked up there's no one to equal him. My little Harry, don't you see that your being here is a lucky thing for all of us? You'll make the happiest change here. Living pent up together, we were all going stale. You're foolish to think you must go!

Harry [*in a low voice*]. It's not only on account of Monsieur Couture. I was thinking of myself too. I don't dare tell you.

Marcelle. My little Harry. Tell me everything.

Harry [*almost whispering*]. I become terribly fond of people, you know.

Marcelle. Well, it's not bad to become fond of people.

Harry. Yes, but afterwards?

Marcelle. You must never think of afterwards.

Harry. If I stay, how humiliating it will be for Monsieur Couture. How he'll suffer.

Marcelle. Oh that! That's of no importance. My word!

Harry. You're hard-hearted, Madame.

Marcelle. He'll suffer? Suppose he does. Everyone suffers.

Harry [*looking at her intently*]. It's true after all that you're cruel.

Marcelle [*gently*]. Cruel?

Harry. I wonder where Emmanuele gets her sweetness.

Marcelle. Oh, but she's violent too. Don't be deceived. You'll have time to see that.

Harry. If I stay.

Marcelle [*taking his head in her hands*]. You'll stay. You're my child for two months. You must obey me.

Harry [*like a little boy*]. Yes, Madame.

Marcelle. Well, then, we'll have no more talk about leaving?

Harry. No, Madame.

Marcelle. Good!

Harry [*going to dining room door*]. Emmanuele, I'm not leaving!

EMMANUELE *runs in.*

Emmanuele. You're staying? It's true? Jean! Anne! Come quickly! Mr. Fanning's not leaving.

Enter JEAN *and* ANNE.

Anne. What happiness! I knew Mama would arrange things!

Jean. We mustn't stay in the dark! The sun must be in on the fun! [*He starts to pull up the blinds.*]

Marcelle. Miserable child! You're letting the heat in!

Jean [*still rolling up blinds*]. Let the heat come in! Everybody's invited!

The sun gradually fills the room. MADEMOISELLE *is seen glued to the wall like a little dark bat and* BLAISE, *pale as a ghost, is visible at top of stairs but no one pays any attention. The bell rings.*

Anne and Jean. That's the first bell. We've time to go to the brook before lunch. Who wants to go to the brook?

Marcelle [taking parasol from umbrella stand]. Emmanuele, take a parasol, dear. Yes, yes, you must. The sun's dangerous.

Harry [to EMMANUELE *as they go out].* Well, are you pleased?

Emmanuele. I'm more than pleased. I'm very happy!

Harry. But Emmanuele. It's not possible! You don't know what you're saying!

HARRY, EMMANUELE, JEAN *and* ANNE *all disappear into the sunlight. Noise of voices and laughter receding.*

Marcelle [going to terrace with parasol]. Children! don't run! I can't keep up with you! Emmanuele, come back, dear! I've got something to tell you!

Re-enter EMMANUELE, *out of breath and joyous.*

Emmanuele. Quick, Mama. Harry's waiting!

Marcelle. No, stay with me. I wanted to warn you. You're seventeen, Emmanuele. You're too demonstrative. You must be more restrained.

Emmanuele [laughing]. Oh, Mama. With Harry!

Marcelle [curtly, opening parasol]. Just so, with Harry.

MARCELLE *and* EMMANUELE *go off together under parasol, their voices receding.* MADEMOISELLE *approaches* BLAISE.

Blaise. Tell the chauffeur. I've just time to catch the express at La Motte.

Mademoiselle [with despair]. Blaise, where are you going?

Blaise. I don't know yet. I'll write you.

Mademoiselle. But me? What's to become of me?

Blaise. Stay here. You must keep me informed of everything that goes on here.

Mademoiselle. I'll never see you again!

Blaise [*with repressed anger*]. Be still! You'll see me again soon!

CURTAIN

ACT THREE

SCENE I—*The middle of a fine October afternoon, at vacation's end. The sun is still bright but there is a coolness of autumn in the air. Enter* EMMANUELE *and* FIRMIN.

FIRMIN. Shall I light the fire?

Emmanuele. No, don't bother. The sun's still warm. Time enough to light it when the hunters get home.

Firmin. It's all ready. We need only put a match to it. Shall I wait for Madame and Monsieur Harry to serve tea?

Emmanuele. Yes, and Monsieur Harry will probably want sherry.

Firmin [*expansively*]. He certainly likes sherry. During the two months he's been here he's drunk several bottles —not to mention the whisky. Well, the English are like that. What about Mademoiselle? Will she be back from Bordeaux in time for dinner?

Emmanuele. Surely. But not before dark. She had some errands to do with the children and then she was to take Anne to her convent and Jean to his boarding school. And since they're not in the same neighborhood . . .

Firmin. Oh, with the car she won't be long. The house will be sad without the children.

Emmanuele. Won't it though! Already even the silence isn't the same.

Firmin. Yes, as we were saying in the kitchen, they

are a lot of bother but it's still more of a bother not to have them with us.

Sound of horses offstage.

Madame and Monsieur Harry are back so soon?

Emmanuele [*going toward terrace*]. Why, yes. No doubt the pigeons weren't flying over today.

Firmin [*lighting fire*]. They should have waited for sundown. That's when you bag a lot of them with the nets. I'll get the sherry.

Enter MARCELLE *and* HARRY *in hunting clothes,* HARRY *carrying two shotguns and* MARCELLE *autumn branches.*

Emmanuele. You're back early!

Harry. The pigeons weren't flying over. We were dying of boredom.

Marcelle. The pigeons weren't flying over? The truth is he has been unbearable!

Harry. I'm a hunter, not an angel! You need the patience of an angel to hunt your French birds.

Marcelle. He can't keep still. At about eleven there was a magnificent flight but Monsieur was looking for mushrooms around the cabin. We whistled for him to lie flat on the ground. Of course he didn't understand the signal although we had explained it to him carefully beforehand.

Harry. I understood but I didn't feel like sprawling in the gorse.

Enter FIRMIN *with tea tray.*

Marcelle. At one o'clock, while we were lunching, another flight came over. But would His Highness interrupt his meal? And to cap the climax he broke a dish. You can well imagine how high that sent the pigeons.

FIRMIN *serves tea, then exits with shotguns.*

Harry. Lunch is the only pleasant moment on this kind of hunting expedition.

Marcelle. That's not a very nice thing to say. It must be that my company bores you.

Harry. Your company! But I wasn't supposed to open my mouth!

Marcelle. That didn't keep you from doing it, though.

Harry. Well, tomorrow you can go without me. I'm getting up late.

Marcelle. I'll try to grin and bear it.

Harry. Oh, but the thing is you don't like to go by yourself. I know you! You must have company. Why don't you call back the poor exile? You know who I mean. The poor voluntary exile. [*Offers* MARCELLE *sherry. She declines.*]

Marcelle. My little Harry, you should be the last one to make fun of Monsieur Couture. Don't forget that he left because of you.

Harry. Oh, Madame. That's not fair. You're the one who . . .

Marcelle. Let's say no more about Monsieur Couture. [*Rising and crossing to arrange branches in urn.*]

Harry. I'd certainly like to know what Mademoiselle is telling him at this very moment in some little room in Bordeaux.

Marcelle. Really Harry, you shouldn't say such things.

Harry. Don't worry. You'll soon be rid of me. A week from now I'll be far from here.

Marcelle. Yes, that's so. You'll be far from here. And to think we're wasting the last days we have together quarreling.

Harry. Forgive me, Madame. I have a foul temper. I know it.

Marcelle. Well, at least you admit it. Friends again?

Harry [*kissing her hand*]. Once again.

Marcelle. I'm going to change. Will you come with me, Emmanuele?

Emmanuele. There's nothing for me to do upstairs, Mama. I'll stay with Harry.

Harry. Let's go out, shall we? After hours of keeping still I could walk till tomorrow morning.

Marcelle. You'll tire Emmanuele. She doesn't need to get any thinner. I advise you to stay quiet, little one. You've been running about all morning.

Emmanuele. Oh, I was only visiting sick people in

the village. That wasn't tiring. I'd love to take a walk.

Marcelle. All right, then. Wait for me. I'll just put on a dress and be with you.

Harry [*not very pleased*]. Only five minutes, please, Madame. Because it gets dark so soon now. Especially since we're off summer time. We'll barely have time to go beyond the gate.

Marcelle [*going upstairs*]. I'll be down right away.

Harry. Have you ever noticed? Women of your mother's generation always make you wait. But with you when I say "Let's go," you're always ready.

Emmanuele. You're a very impatient boy. And furthermore you're like a spoiled child.

Harry. Not spoiled by you, Emmanuele. No, you don't spoil me much.

Emmanuele. You're a funny one. What would you specially like me to do?

Harry. I don't know. But I'd like you to make a fuss over me—act glad to see me.

Emmanuele. I am glad to see you, Harry.

Harry. I'd like you to be sorry that we aren't going alone.

Emmanuele. I don't like you to speak unkindly of Mama.

Harry. I never speak kindly of my friends because I expect so much of them and they're always rubbing me the wrong way. Your mother didn't tell you that a little while ago when we were hunting, I made a scene. Now I'm sorry for it. That's the real reason we came back early.

Emmanuele. I'm sure you were disgusting.

Harry. Yes, I was disgusting, but I couldn't help it.

Emmanuele. What was it about?

Harry. About the children. I was amazed that she had Mademoiselle take them to Bordeaux to start school instead of going herself.

Emmanuele. You know what Mademoiselle is to us and how much the children love her. Mama preferred to say good-by here. It would have been much harder in the school office.

Harry. You don't expect me to believe that, do you?

Want me to tell you the real reason? She didn't want to leave us two alone.

Emmanuele. Suppose she didn't? Mama feels her responsibility. Maybe it wouldn't be good for us to be together all the time without a chaperon. I understand her concern.

Harry. You really think that's the reason?

Emmanuele. Well, of course. Why else would she be worried?

Harry. I guess you're right. [*Pause.*] But you know, little one, we're not doing anything wrong.

Emmanuele. You're not, Harry. You're not doing anything wrong. But I'm not so sure about me.

Harry. What do you mean? [*Pause.*] What are you thinking?

Emmanuele. I'm thinking about your going away so soon.

Harry. Yes, just as soon as I get a telegram from my father.

Emmanuele. And you expect it any day?

Harry. Any minute.

Emmanuele [*about to cry*]. You're leaving.

Harry. I hate to think of it.

Emmanuele. No, no, don't say something that's not true.

Harry [*insistently*]. Listen. I may be gone by tomorrow night. Perhaps this is the last walk we can have together. Since your mother hasn't come down . . .

Emmanuele. No, that wouldn't be right. We promised to wait for her.

Harry. She'll understand our being impatient. And we'll explain afterwards. Oh, Emmanuele, I see you want to go as much as I do.

Emmanuele. Maybe. But it wouldn't be right.

Harry. I've something to tell you that I can't tell you in the house. If you won't go out alone with me I'm afraid I'll never be able to tell you.

Emmanuele. Don't tell me! Maybe God doesn't want me to hear it!

Harry. Just the same, it's He who gave us our hearts!

Emmanuele. Harry, have pity on me!

Harry [*pulling her out to terrace*]. Come, beloved!

The stage is empty for a moment. Then MARCELLE *comes downstairs, throwing coat over her shoulders.*

Marcelle [*from stairs*]. Have I kept you waiting? Where are you? [*Goes to terrace.*] Now where have they gone? [*Calling.*] Emmanuele! Harry! Oh, this is too much! If they've gone without me!

To FIRMIN *who enters from dining room and picks up tea tray.*

You didn't see Mademoiselle Emmanuele and Monsieur Harry go out, did you?

Firmin. Yes, Madame, they went off toward the mill.

Marcelle. I'll try to catch up with them.

Firmin [*beaming*]. I hardly think Madame will be able to. They were running and Monsieur Harry was holding Mademoiselle's hand.

Marcelle [*brusquely*]. Very well. Take the tray.

FIRMIN *exits with tray to dining room.* MARCELLE *starts toward terrace and almost bumps into* FATHER BRUNET *who is about to enter. He is about fifty, small and self-effacing.*

Oh! Father Brunet!

Brunet [*just inside terrace door*]. I don't wish to disturb you, Madame. I was just passing this way and thought I'd stop in to see Emmanuele.

Marcelle. She has just gone out. May I give her a message, Father?

Brunet. I wanted to tell her I have a wedding mass tomorrow morning at nine. It's Coste's daughter, you know? So of course there won't be any seven o'clock mass. But Emmanuele may come as usual and I'll give her Holy Communion.

Marcelle [*trembling*]. Oh, Father! Your little Emmanuele!

Brunet. What's the trouble?

Marcelle. I hardly know her any more. She's changing fast these days—and not for the better, unfortunately.

[*Indicating chair by fire and putting coat over back of sofa.*]

Brunet [*sitting*]. You surprise me. She seems the same to me.

Marcelle. Well, that simply proves she doesn't tell you everything.

Brunet. Except for the confession of error, God doesn't require that she tell me everything.

Marcelle. Probably she hasn't told you there's a young man in her life.

Brunet. The young Englishman? Yes, I know.

Marcelle. I must say, Father, your indifference astonishes me. If someone had told you a month ago that your Emmanuele would fall in love . . .

Brunet. But Madame, why don't you want this child of seventeen to have the heart of a child of seventeen?

Marcelle. Why? Because for years she has been playing the little saint in our midst.

Brunet. Forgive me, Madame. But you astonish me.

Marcelle. I'm so annoyed, so disappointed. [*Going to terrace.*] Would you believe that she went to the mill with that boy without waiting for me? They did it on purpose. They didn't want me. They're by themselves and it's almost dark. In October night falls quickly. Of course I'm not afraid of anything serious. [*Sitting on sofa.*]

Brunet. Of course not. He seems a fine young fellow.

Marcelle. Nevertheless, he has a way of taking your hand, touching your arm. In fact, Father, I ask you. Are you or are you not my daughter's spiritual adviser? And if you are, isn't it your duty to do something about this?

Brunet. With this child, Madame, I need do less than you might think. Almost nothing. I try very hard not to interfere with God's will. After all, who knows whether it was not intended that Emmanuele should become attached to this boy? When I was a lad of twenty an old and saintly priest said to me in his simple way: "You've done nothing for your Heavenly Father until you've trod upon your heart." [MARCELLE *rises*.] But maybe Emmanuele will not have to tread upon her heart. Marriage is a great sacrament.

Marcelle. Well then, you consider it's God's will that a girl who takes communion every morning should go walking at twilight with a boy?

Brunet [getting up]. Madame, as your priest I must tell you you're going much too far.

Marcelle [angry]. You're indulgent with Emmanuele. That's the truth. There's nothing she can do that you don't consider admirable!

Brunet [starts out and turns back on terrace]. When you're alone in your room tonight, draw close to God and look straight at the emotion that makes you say these things.

Marcelle. I have no emotion I need be ashamed of, Father.

Sound of automobile stopping in front of terrace.

Brunet. Someone's here.

Marcelle. It's Mademoiselle back from Bordeaux. We'll talk about this another time. I don't want you to think . . .

Enter MADEMOISELLE. MARCELLE *and* BRUNET *meet her on terrace and during the next remarks* FIRMIN *takes* MADEMOISELLE's *packages, stirs fire and makes soft light in room.*

Brunet. Well, Mademoiselle? Were our little school-children brave?

Mademoiselle. They hardly cried at all. They know their mother will come to see them Thursday. We ran wild in the shops buying book satchels, pencil boxes and colored crayons.

Brunet [starting off]. I believe they'll be with friends. I know there's a little Coustous girl in Anne's class.

Marcelle. Good night, Father.

Brunet. Take care of yourself, Madame. Good-by.

FATHER BRUNET *goes out.* MARCELLE *and* MADEMOISELLE *come back into living room.*

Marcelle. So, did you see Monsieur Couture? Did you give him my letter? Was he willing to see you?

Mademoiselle. He not only saw me. He came back with me.

Marcelle. What? He came back with you?

Mademoiselle. Yes, Madame. He's here! I brought him back in the car.

Marcelle. You're joking!

Mademoiselle. Wasn't that what you wanted, Madame?

Marcelle. I didn't expect him to return so soon. Where is he?

Mademoiselle. He went straight to his room. He probably wished to avoid Father Brunet. As soon as he saw the cassock . . . You know he doesn't like priests.

Marcelle. So he's here!

Mademoiselle. And he wants to see you as soon as possible. And alone.

Marcelle [*picking up her coat*]. Ask him to wait a few minutes. I'm too upset. I'm going to look for Emmanuele.

Mademoiselle. Where is Emmanuele?

Marcelle. With Harry. They've been gone half an hour. That's strange, isn't it?

Mademoiselle. I've seen so many girls who seemed determined to take the veil suddenly change their minds. So many seventeen-year-olds who thought they were called but weren't. It's like the dawn mist on a hot day.

Marcelle. Anyway she certainly succeeded in fooling us. [*Putting on her coat.*]

Mademoiselle. Poor child! She's done no harm.

Marcelle. Let us hope so.

Mademoiselle [*bitterly*]. But of course she's done no harm! We simply failed to understand her. She's human like everybody else. Everyone's the same.

Marcelle. No, thank God, everyone's not the same. Where can they be now?

Mademoiselle. But Madame, why not wait for them beside the fire? It's pitch dark.

Marcelle [*hesitantly*]. Yes, that's so. It's pitch dark. Perhaps they've found shelter in some cabin or some abandoned sheepfold.

Mademoiselle. Monsieur Couture surely will be wondering why you haven't gone to see him yet.

Marcelle [*taking off her coat*]. Yes, you're right. It's better for me to go to Monsieur Couture first.

MARCELLE *goes upstairs.* MADEMOISELLE, *alone, goes to terrace door, opens it, looks out.*

Mademoiselle [*softly*]. That little Emmanuele! Who would ever have thought it?

MADEMOISELLE *goes into dining room. The stage remains empty a few moments.* EMMANUELE *and* HARRY *come in from terrace.*

Harry. Your mother isn't here?

Emmanuele. Maybe she went looking for us.

Harry. No, she must have gone up to her room.

Emmanuele. I'm afraid to go up. I'm afraid she'll scold me, or else say nothing.

Harry. How important little things seem to you, dearest.

Emmanuele. There are no little things.

Harry. You're not sorry you went with me?

Emmanuele. Oh Harry! But it was so dark on the way back.

Harry. Yes, it wasn't like the "resplendent night" of my arrival.

Emmanuele. Tonight we felt almost lost. You wanted to come in yourself.

Harry. Yes, because I felt you were uneasy. And especially because I didn't dare do the only thing we were both thinking of.

Emmanuele. No, no! I didn't want anything more!

Harry [*with despair*]. If I leave tomorrow I won't have kissed you. I'll never have held you close to me.

Emmanuele. Don't be sad. I can't bear it. Remember? The whole time you held my hand. You kissed it.

Harry. It was a drop of water and I was dying of thirst.

Emmanuele. Poor Harry!

Harry. I'll tell you something that will surprise you. All the time we were outside I was annoyed.

Emmanuele. Harry! Don't be cruel!

Harry. Let me explain. If lovers don't kiss it's useless for them to be near each other. A space separates them.

A gap that no word can cross, that only a caress can bridge.

Emmanuele. I would have been so weak if you had dared!

Harry. Oh don't say so! It's unbearable!

Emmanuele. For me that happiness was enough. To be beside you in the night.

Harry. I need the night, dearest. Come, I can't bear to have you look at me. I love you so much. Come into the darkness. Only a moment. We'll stay close to each other without speaking. Only a moment. [*Pulling her onto terrace.*]

Emmanuele. It's cold and I've no coat.

Harry. Mine's big enough for both of us.

They lean against terrace railing lit dimly by lamps. Enter MARCELLE. *She sees them at once.*

Marcelle. Emmanuele, you'll get chilled!

Emmanuele [*coming into room followed by Harry*]. It's you, Mama?

Marcelle. You aren't chilled?

Emmanuele. Harry lent me his coat.

Marcelle [*sarcastically*]. Oh?

Harry. We looked for you. We ought to have waited for you. It's my fault. You know how impatient I am. I insisted on Emmanuele going with me. I thought you'd catch up with us.

Marcelle [*bitterly*]. Yes? I suppose that's why you started running?

Emmanuele. Mama, I swear to you. . . .

Marcelle. Why, little Emmanuele, you needn't worry. What you've done is completely unimportant.

Emmanuele. You sound displeased. I can tell.

Marcelle. It made me a little sad, but it's all over. Let's say no more about it. [*Kissing* EMMANUELE, *but without enthusiasm.*]

Harry. Madame, have I time to write some letters before dinner?

Marcelle. Yes, but listen for the bell.

Harry [*from stairs*]. I'll come down at the first stroke.

[*He throws a kiss to* EMMANUELE *as he exits, taking care that Marcelle doesn't see.*]

Marcelle. I forgot. Father Brunet came while you were out. There won't be any seven o'clock mass tomorrow.

Emmanuele. Yes, I know. There's a wedding mass.

Marcelle. But if you want it he'll give you communion.

Emmanuele. Yes, I want it.

Marcelle. I suppose you'll need to be waked earlier than usual? If you wish to go to confession.

Emmanuele. No, Mama, I don't intend to go to confession.

Marcelle. Oh, I thought . . .

Emmanuele [*distressed*]. What do you think? What do you imagine? We're not doing anything wrong. Or is it wrong?

Marcelle. What can I say? You don't tell me anything any more. You hide things from me.

Emmanuele. Oh, Mama, it's you who don't seem to love your little girl any more.

Marcelle. If I didn't love you would I be so worried? I didn't think you were so impulsive. Think a little, Emmanuele. This boy, who is he? A foreigner, a Protestant. We don't know his family. They're surely not our kind of people. He's very nice of course, in fact, charming, in spite of his poor manners. For he's been very badly brought up. Nevertheless, my poor dear, he'll have forgotten all about you by the time he's on the Channel boat.

Emmanuele. No, Mama.

Marcelle. I hurt you by saying this, but it's my duty.

Emmanuele. No, Mama, you don't hurt me because I know you're mistaken.

Marcelle. My poor child, so you take seriously the sweet nothings he tells every woman he meets?

Emmanuele. Every woman? How do you know?

Marcelle. I know. I've watched him. This kind of boy is an open book to me. It's quite simple. They can't even look at a woman without falling in love with her.

Emmanuele. Maybe that's true about the others. I don't know. But Harry loves only one girl.

Marcelle. And you're the one, my poor dear.

Emmanuele. Yes, he loves me.

Marcelle. For vacation time.

Emmanuele. For his whole life. He'll never forget me.

Marcelle. What makes you so sure?

Emmanuele. All he feels, I feel. I didn't know it was possible. As if we two had only one heart.

Marcelle. But dearest, if that's the way it is, why shouldn't he marry you?

EMMANUELE *starts as if wounded.*

Ah, I see I've touched a nerve! He talks to you about a lot of things, this young Harry. He talks about everything but marriage, doesn't he?

EMMANUELE *weeps, face in hands.*

I may seem harsh, but it's for your own good. You must be hurt to be cured.

Emmanuele. Mama, I know you're simply trying to do your duty as you see it, but you don't know how wrong you are. Harry would marry me right away if I asked him to. But there's something that keeps us apart.

Marcelle. I'd certainly like to know what excuse he's thought up.

Emmanuele. No, no, the obstacle doesn't come from him. It's inside me! Mama, do you think God wants people to be happy in love? I know He wants us to be happy. But this other kind of happiness? You know, when you say about somebody: "He's everything to me." I didn't know what that meant but I know now. Father Brunet tells me that married people love each other in God. I don't understand. If some day Harry were everything to me, there would be no more room in my heart or in my life for anyone—not even God!

Marcelle. Hush, you're excited. You're imagining things. You must get hold of yourself and then go to sensible people for advice. Father Brunet's a fine man but you realize he's no help.

Emmanuele. Oh, Mama, just the opposite. Thanks to him I don't lose confidence. I keep going even when I don't know the way. Where would I be if I didn't have him to lead me?

Marcelle. What you need is a guide less fond of you and not blinded by affection. [*She looks at ceiling, her attention caught by sound of footsteps overhead.*]

Emmanuele. But who could I turn to? [*Also looking at ceiling.*] Do you hear too, Mama? It sounds as if someone were walking in Monsieur Couture's room.

Marcelle. Yes. He's back.

Emmanuele. He's back?

Marcelle. I didn't expect him until after Harry Fanning had gone. He came ahead of time, but I'm not sorry.

Emmanuele. He's here!

Marcelle. You look as if you were afraid of him. Really, I wonder why. In spite of all his faults he's a friend we can go to for help. Especially you, with the difficulties we're going through. What do you say?

Emmanuele. Nothing, Mama.

Marcelle. I'd certainly like to know what you're thinking.

Emmanuele. I was thinking of Mademoiselle.

Marcelle. Mademoiselle has nothing to do with it. It's you . . . [EMMANUELE *goes toward stairs.*] Don't go! Monsieur Couture is coming down.

Emmanuele. Let me go, Mama. I haven't had time to get used to the idea of his being here. I don't want him to see I've been crying.

BLAISE *appears at top of stairs.*

Marcelle. It's too late. There he is. Stay here, Emmanuele. I tell you, stay! [*Forcibly restraining her.*]

Emmanuele. Mama, what have I done to you?

Blaise [*coming downstairs*]. Am I driving you away, Emmanuele?

Emmanuele. Oh, no, Monsieur Couture. But there's something I have to do upstairs.

Blaise. Well, go ahead. I won't keep you. We'll have plenty of time to see each other and chat. The winter evenings are long here. Night comes quickly. I'm looking forward to the pleasant hours of companionship and understanding we have ahead of us, Emmanuele. See you in a little while. [*He watches* EMMANUELE *as she goes upstairs.*] How she's grown the last two months! How

beautiful she has become! Don't you agree, Madame?
[*Looking around the room.*]

Marcelle. I'm too close to her to see it. Are you looking
for something, Monsieur Couture?

Blaise. No, no, I was looking at these walls. What
memories come back to me here!

Marcelle. Are they so sad?

Blaise. The sight of this room should delight me, I
suppose?

Marcelle. You're not going back over that unfortunate
evening again?

Blaise. I crouched on this step. Here. When you tormented me!

Marcelle. I thought I was doing the right thing. I was
simply trying to put an end to young Fanning's suspicions. He was imagining goodness knows what between
us!

Blaise. I must say you did a good job of it. "He's only
a poor boy who was expelled from the seminary," you
said. "And I only took him in because his superiors didn't
know what to do with him and begged me to." That's
what you said. That's what I heard that night on this
very spot, and I'll go on hearing it as long as I live.

Marcelle. What a memory for injuries you have, my
poor friend! With so much bitterness in your heart you
would have done better not to come back.

Blaise. And who do you think I came back for? I came
back only for your sake. Once I've taken on a job I never
give it up. But I don't matter. Some people thrive on
ingratitude—insults even. Consider me as nothing. That
won't be anything new to you. What am I to you? The
"tutor," as this English boy, this rich man's son, so scornfully referred to me. When I think of the remarks he
made that night without your driving him out . . . And
I'm even almost certain I heard you laugh!

Marcelle. Where did I get the absurd idea of bringing
you back? What was I thinking of, my God?

Blaise [*harshly*]. You brought me back because you
couldn't do anything else. And not a minute too soon
either. You know it. You must admit I warned you.

Marcelle. What's the use of going over all this again?

Help me and don't force me to account for everything.

Blaise [*observing her*]. Do you even know what you want? Could you tell me clearly what you expect of me?

Marcelle [*hesitating*]. I want things to be just as they were before.

Blaise. Before young Fanning came? Well, you'll get what you want. Isn't he leaving in a day or two?

Marcelle [*softly*]. But when he's gone he'll still be here in Emmanuele's heart.

Blaise. In Emmanuele's heart?

Marcelle. Don't pretend not to understand.

Blaise [*looking closely at her*]. Well then, you want me to talk to her?

Marcelle. That wouldn't do any good. You have no influence over Emmanuele.

Blaise. You think so? I would soon have her in hand if I wanted to. It wouldn't take long.

Marcelle. The truth of the matter is she doesn't care much for you.

Blaise. In fact she hates me.

Marcelle. I didn't say that.

Blaise. I'm only afraid of indifference. All the women I have influenced hated me at the start. Emmanuele? It would take me only three days to make her see everything through my eyes. She wouldn't make a move not inspired by me. My will would take the place of hers and dominate even the beating of her heart!

Marcelle [*horrified*]. No, no! Forget what I said! Leave Emmanuele alone!

Blaise. We'd better not talk any more about this now. We must not act hastily. Trust me as you used to do when you were happy. Just rest. Close your eyes.

Marcelle [*very weary*]. I have such need of rest! You've no idea.

Blaise [*taking her hand*]. We'll straighten things out. You'll see!

Marcelle [*about to cry*]. I believe it. Yes, I believe it!

Blaise [*drawing her to the fireplace*]. Your hands are icy! Come to the fire.

Marcelle. You did leave me, though! I never would have believed you'd leave me!

Blaise. Don't you see? I just couldn't stand it any longer . . .

As BLAISE *and* MARCELLE *chat quietly* EMMANUELE *and* HARRY *appear at top of stairs and lean over balustrade.*

Harry. He's here?

Emmanuele. Yes, he's here. I'm afraid to go down.

Harry. I'll stay with you. Don't be afraid! [*He takes her in his arms and tenderly kisses her hair.*]

Emmanuele [*her head on Harry's shoulder*]. My love, even if you leave tomorrow you will have kissed me!

Harry. Yes, I will have kissed you!

Emmanuele. I know now it isn't wrong.

Harry. No, it certainly isn't wrong!

Emmanuele. Tell me again it isn't wrong and I was crazy to think so!

Harry. You were crazy, my little one!

Emmanuele. I was crazy! I was crazy! Harry, we must go down now.

Harry. You're not afraid any more?

Emmanuele. Not if you hold my hand!

They stop at bottom of stairs, hand in hand, as BLAISE *and* MARCELLE *turn round.* BLAISE *gets up and half holds out his arms.*

Blaise. Ah! Here's our little Emmanuele!

CURTAIN

SCENE II—*Two days later. Cold moonlight on the terrace. The stage is dimly lighted.* MARCELLE *sits lost in thought beside the fire.* BLAISE *pretends to read but watches her.* EMMANUELE *interrupts her sewing often to look at her watch. She gets up and goes to stairs.*

MARCELLE. Going to bed so soon, Emmanuele?

Emmanuele. No, Mama. I'm going to help Harry finish packing.

Marcelle. Please stay in the drawing room.

Emmanuele. But he's leaving tomorrow and I promised . . .

Marcelle. No, you mustn't go to his room.

Blaise. Mademoiselle can go with her.

Marcelle. A girl must never go to a young man's room. That was the rule when I was a girl.

Blaise. If Mademoiselle is with them . . . I must say you're unnecessarily strict.

Marcelle. Well, if you think I'm overdoing it . . . Go ahead, my child, go ahead.

Emmanuele. Oh, no, Mama, if you don't think it's right.

Marcelle [*sarcastically*]. We can rely on Monsieur Couture's judgment. I give you half an hour. Not a minute more.

Emmanuele [*kissing her*]. Oh, thanks, Mama! [*She goes toward stairs but is stopped by* BLAISE.]

Blaise [*aside to* EMMANUELE]. I was nice, wasn't I?

Emmanuele [*aside to* BLAISE]. Oh, yes, Monsieur Couture. Try to talk to Mama.

BLAISE *nods in agreement*. EMMANUELE *goes upstairs*.

Marcelle [*she has seen their byplay and approaches* BLAISE]. What sort of game are you playing now?

Blaise. I never play, Madame.

Marcelle. This pretending to side with Emmanuele all the time . . .

Blaise. I don't side with anyone here.

Marcelle. Not even with me? To think I was foolish enough to believe your promises!

Blaise. I didn't promise anything, except to do all I could to make everything just as it was before.

Marcelle. You're going about it in a funny way.

Blaise. I'm acting according to my conscience.

Marcelle [*scornfully*]. Your conscience!

Blaise. . . . And after long inner debate, I assure you.

Marcelle. Really? And what have you concluded from this long debate?

Blaise [*looking into her eyes*]. That you must accept Emmanuele's happiness!

Marcelle [*losing her temper*]. Your insinuation is hor-

rible—horrible and absurd! I don't oppose Emmanuele's
happiness. I'm not her enemy, I'm her mother, do you
hear? The mother of a little girl who has dreamed up an
impossible marriage.

Blaise. Why impossible? The very idea of such a marriage terrifies you!

Marcelle. I'm not in the least terrified! It's simply that
Emmanuele isn't yet eighteen and she has always been
frail. Only yesterday she thought of nothing but going
into a convent. Now, because the first boy that comes
along makes love to her—a foreigner, and what's more,
a Protestant—you expect me to throw caution to the
wind—the most elementary caution?

Blaise. No! When Emmanuele wanted to enter a convent you were as frightened as if she were going to die.
As for her health, everybody knows how it is with these
frail-looking little girls. You'll see how she'll bloom when
she's happy in love. On top of it all you pretend not to
know about the Fannings, although we investigated the
family thoroughly before entrusting Bertrand to them.
And since then it has all been confirmed by your son's
enthusiastic letters. Come now! This match fulfills your
fondest hopes. As they say in your set, it has everything—
that is, what society calls everything. First of all, money
of course; then breeding and social position—as I say,
everything! Yes, I know there's the delicate question of
the children's religion. But that still isn't what makes you
dislike this really ideal match. Can you look at me and
tell me you don't know the name of the passion which
has been tearing you to pieces for two months when you
think of your daughter?

Marcelle [*going to fireplace and leaning on mantel*].
That's enough, Monsieur Couture! Please understand I
can listen to no more of this. Will you be kind enough
to get out?

Blaise [*gradually drawing nearer to* MARCELLE *as he
speaks*]. My God, what have I done? I'm out of my
mind! I've blundered! You feel the hideous temptation
to punish me by driving me away? Yes? Is that what
you want? You're thinking of driving me away? Listen

to me! It just isn't possible! During these two months away from you I hardly had the strength to live. I would have killed myself if I could have left a world in which you breathe, in which you live! The slightest remarks you and that . . . that fellow exchanged on that frightful evening—I couldn't stop hearing them! They woke me up at night . . . "I'm touching your arm." He dared say that to you here on the terrace! It is true you told him: "Take your hand away." But with such tenderness in your voice! You put his scarf around your neck. You said: "Your scarf smells good." Yes, yes, you said that. And yet there is nothing I don't forgive. There's nothing I'm not determined to forget—even the suffering that comes to you from him and has so altered your face that the night I returned it took me a few moments even to recognize you when you came into my room . . . For God's sake say something! Your silence frightens me! [*Drawing ever closer to her.*] At least you must know that I worship you. Forget all my suspicions. The truth is you're the most reasonable of women, the most sensible. No, no, in spite of all I've said, I know you're not a monster. And that's why—I admit it—I hope Emmanuele goes through with this marriage. As soon as this boy is her husband everything will fall into place. You'll see. He won't exist any more for you, I'm sure of it! You, the wisest woman I've ever known—it's not because just once a boy has stirred your heart . . . It doesn't hurt you for me to speak of him? Furthermore, he plans to be a diplomat, doesn't he? He'll go all over the world. He'll live somewhere in the Balkans, in America, Japan. No one here will separate us any more. The children will go away one after another and we'll be left alone—you and I in this house . . . alone until I die. And we'll enjoy that perfect union of both our souls which has always been the only hope of my poor life! Will you listen to me, Marcelle? Have you forgiven me? You won't drive me out?

  Marcelle [*turning slowly around*]. It's strange. Perhaps I didn't hear right. It seemed to me you called me by my first name!

  Blaise. Please excuse me, Madame. It was a slip.

Marcelle. I'm touched, Monsieur Couture, by the interest you take in me and the attention you're kind enough to devote to my soul, as you say. But you have a more urgent job here. For Bertrand it's the year to try for his bachelor's degree.

Blaise. I haven't forgotten that, Madame.

Marcelle. I have been weak enough to consider some of your remarks important. Above all I made the mistake of not stopping you before you began. I alone am responsible for a ridiculous scene that you will be gracious enough to forget. You have in this house a place of trust with my son. It's my fault, I realize, if you haven't confined yourself to it. From now on I beg you to do so. Now let us discuss serious matters. Do you have the list of books Bertrand will need?

Blaise. Yes, Madame, I've ordered them already.

Marcelle. Have you done anything about finding him a science teacher?

Blaise. I have several in mind. The best would be to get a high school teacher. But Bertrand will have to go to Bordeaux twice a week.

Marcelle. It only takes a couple of hours by car. You won't have to go with him either. That is all for now. I'll not keep you any longer. Good night, Monsieur Couture.

She goes out through the dining room door. BLAISE *sits down beside the fire. He leans over slightly toward the hearth.* EMMANUELE *comes downstairs.* BLAISE *turns around and sees her.*

Blaise. Emmanuele!

Emmanuele [*surprised*]. Oh, Mama is not here?

Blaise. She'll be back. Did I frighten you?

EMMANUELE *turns back upstairs.* BLAISE *calls her back.*

Wait a minute! I have something important to tell you. I talked to your mother as I promised.

Emmanuele [*coming down again*]. Did she speak about Harry?

Blaise. Come sit down beside me, little Emmanuele. You don't still think I'm an ogre, do you?

Emmanuele [*approaching him*]. Of course not, Monsieur Couture.

Blaise. If it hadn't been for me a while ago you couldn't have gone to help him pack, could you?

Emmanuele. Since you've come back you've been very, very nice to us. So Mama spoke to you about Harry?

Blaise. Yes, she spoke to me about him—about him and you. She's very worried.

Emmanuele. I hate to think that I make her unhappy.

Blaise. It's not only you.

Emmanuele. Alas, who could it be but me?

Blaise. You first of all, yes. But also young Fanning a little.

Emmanuele. Oh, but he's an outsider. That doesn't matter so much.

Blaise. An outsider, yes. But one you've all adopted. From the first day he's been a part of the family.

Emmanuele. That's true, Monsieur Couture. And knowing Harry as well as she does, I'm surprised that Mama could misjudge him like this.

Blaise. You're wrong. I don't think she does misjudge him. Far from it.

Emmanuele. If you think it's not misjudging him to call him fickle, changeable, unable to keep a promise . . . I know it's because she loves *me* too much, poor Mama. She's always afraid I'll be unhappy. She doesn't know Harry's goodness. Perhaps you only know the people you love.

Blaise. Believe me, your mother knows Harry Fanning.

Emmanuele. If she knows him, I don't understand. No, I can't understand how she can distrust someone so noble, so brave, so pure. Especially since she's very fond of him.

Blaise. Yes, very fond!

Emmanuele. That's the strangest part of it, don't you think?

Blaise. You see, little Emmanuele, a girl of seventeen who has everything, as you do, should be indulgent and take pity on a woman who is beginning to age.

Emmanuele. I don't see what you mean, Monsieur Couture.

Blaise. Your mother was left all alone in the world before she was thirty.

Emmanuele. I know . . . Poor darling! It's true that we are selfish and never think how much she has suffered—and still does!

Blaise. She had a heart, too.

Emmanuele. She still does, Monsieur Couture.

Blaise. Yes, she still does.

Emmanuele. Then tell me, why doesn't she want a new child to come into the family? Another one to love and who'd love her. Because Harry has real affection for Mama.

Blaise. Yes, but that kind of affection, you see, doesn't amount to much.

Emmanuele. What do you mean?

Blaise. I don't mean anything that need alarm you. Listen, Emmanuele, as soon as you become Mrs. Fanning, everything will fall into place. Above all you mustn't take this period of tension your mother's going through too seriously. I know her. She's not really frivolous or romantic.

Emmanuele. Mama frivolous, romantic? Even to imagine such a thing is perfectly absurd.

Blaise. I don't imagine it. You see, my child—you create here an atmosphere that's—I won't say disturbing—no, the word's too strong . . .

Emmanuele. Goodness! What have I done that could disturb anyone?

Blaise. Nothing wrong, of course. However without your knowing it the fragrance of your young love fills the house. A fragrance that goes to the head. As soon as you two have gone away, young Fanning and you, your mother will still be restless perhaps. But I'll take care of her, trust me. You can go with an easy mind.

Emmanuele. Oh, no. I won't go with an easy mind, if I ever do go. I'll never have an easy mind again. [*Hides her face in her hands.*]

Blaise. What's the matter, Emmanuele? Can I have hurt you without meaning to?

Emmanuele. Without meaning to, I'm sure. Oh, I must

get rid of the thoughts that come over me all of a sudden! Mama—like Mademoiselle!

Blaise. I don't know what these thoughts are. Anyway you won't accuse me of putting them into your head, will you?

Emmanuele. No, no, I just didn't understand till now.

Blaise. What didn't you understand, my little Emmanuele?

Emmanuele. God is punishing me. I had forsaken Him. I wanted to be happy without Him and now I'll have to live with these doubts. [*Hides her face in her arms.*]

Blaise. What doubts? It's not my fault. You said yourself it's not my fault. But I want to hear you say it again. Come, Emmanuele. Say: "No, Monsieur Couture, it's not your fault if I misinterpreted what you said." Come, say it: "No, Monsieur Couture . . ."

Emmanuele [*crying*]. No, Monsieur Couture . . .

Blaise. It's not your fault . . .

Emmanuele. It's not your fault . . .

Blaise. If I misinterpreted what you said.

EMMANUELE *cries too hard to be able to speak.*

Come, get on with it, Emmanuele!

MARCELLE *enters abruptly from dining room.*

Marcelle. Emmanuele! What's the trouble, my little child? What have you done to her?

Blaise. You surely don't think . . .

Marcelle. He didn't hurt you?

Emmanuele. No, he hasn't touched me.

Marcelle. Well then?

Emmanuele. He only talked to me. He said things that I misunderstood. It's my fault of course.

Blaise. Madame, Emmanuele will tell you that I didn't say a single word to be ashamed of. Yes or no, Emmanuele, did I say the slightest thing you could object to?

Emmanuele. No, no, it's all my fault!

Blaise. Do you hear, Madame? Are you satisfied?

Marcelle. Quite satisfied. But be good enough to leave us alone a moment, will you?

Blaise [starting upstairs]. You still don't think it's my
fault?

Marcelle. No, no. Go away!

Blaise [still going upstairs]. I may have blundered.

Marcelle. Yes, you can blunder like anyone else when
you want to.

BLAISE *exits.* MARCELLE *sits and pulls* EMMANUELE *close
to her.*

Come, dearest . . . No, nearer . . . On my lap. Was he
talking about me?

Emmanuele. Mama, I beg you, don't ask me anything.

Marcelle. Hush, dear. Tell me only what you want to.
Put your little face on my shoulder—there, the place you
used to like. Don't try to keep from crying. [*Lulls her a
moment in silence.*] Listen, Emmanuele, do you think
I'm the enemy of your happiness?

Emmanuele. Oh, no, Mama!

Marcelle. Don't you know you're my beloved child?

Emmanuele. Yes, Mama, I know.

Marcelle. I may have been mistaken. I'm not infallible.
A woman alone always has a hard time. If only your
father had been alive! But I would give the rest of my
life for you to be happy. Do you believe me?

Emmanuele [snuggling closer to her]. Yes, Mama.

Marcelle. My little girl! Let's not say anything yet.
You're seventeen. You must let happiness be born little
by little. If there are difficulties and obstacles, trust me.
You'll see . . .

Emmanuele [getting up abruptly]. Mama, I wonder if
you mean what I think you do.

Marcelle. Has Harry finished packing? Go see if you
can help him again. And then bring him back here. I'll
be waiting for you.

HARRY *appears on stairs.*

Oh, Harry!

HARRY *comes down. They go to meet him.*

There's moonlight, Harry, like the night you came.

Harry. It's almost winter moonlight. Perhaps we could go for a walk if we wrap up warmly. It isn't ten yet.

Marcelle. Yes, you have my permission. Because it's the last night.

Harry [*kissing her hand*]. Oh, the last night! I'm not really leaving, you know. You'll see me again soon. Before three weeks perhaps. Until then I'll write you all I don't dare tell you, Madame. All I have in my heart for you.

Marcelle [*putting her hand on his head*]. You're my big son, Harry. Take this coat, Emmanuele. It's warmer than yours.

HARRY *goes to terrace.* MARCELLE *aside to* EMMANUELE.

I don't want us to part tonight without my telling you something very close to my heart. [*Drawing her to her.*] You've found your way, my dearest. You're not making any mistake, you may be sure. Be calm, confident, happy.

Emmanuele. Oh, Mama, how were you able to know?

Marcelle. Harry came from far away into this lost country without knowing it was you he came to seek. But God who loves you knew.

Emmanuele. Mama, how did you know I was waiting for you to say this—that I needed so much to have you say it?

Marcelle [*pushing her toward terrace*]. There is a special grace for mothers . . . sudden inspirations. Don't keep him waiting. Go, little daughter.

Emmanuele [*from terrace*]. The night is beautiful!

Harry. Do you hear the brook? What a pity the children aren't here to sing "Resplendent Night!" Dearest, are you happy?

Emmanuele. So this is happiness?

Harry. Not even the beginning of happiness. This is what comes before happiness.

Emmanuele [*with an ardor in which you feel all her future suffering*]. Will there be a time when we'll say: "Here it is; we have it at last; this is happiness?"

Marcelle [*joining them*]. I'll probably be in bed when you come in. Don't forget to lock the door.

Emmanuele. Oh, I won't forget. I'm too afraid of robbers! Good night, darling Mama. Don't stay there. You'll get chilled.

Harry. See you in the morning, Madame.

Marcelle. Good-by, Harry.

She stands leaning against the door as EMMANUELE'S *and* HARRY'S *footsteps and voices recede. Then she says softly in an entirely different tone:*

Good-by, Harry!

She goes to fireplace and sits. She doesn't hear BLAISE, *who comes downstairs cautiously and approaches on tiptoes. She starts.*

Oh! You frightened me!

Blaise. Forgive me. I thought you were sleeping. I was trying to be quiet.

Marcelle. As quiet as a murderer!

Blaise [*heatedly*]. Think what you're saying! That's frightful!

Marcelle. I didn't mean anything. It was only words. Don't worry.

Blaise. How you're going to hate me now!

Marcelle. Why should I hate you? You do me good even without intending to. You did it again today!

Blaise. Don't make fun of me.

Marcelle. I'm not making fun of you. God knows I don't feel like laughing! It's very true that but for you I would still be blind. I wouldn't have seen the torment on the face of my little girl. Such horror, such fear! Be blessed for opening my eyes!

Blaise. Come now. You'll never forgive me!

Marcelle [*tremendously weary*]. It's late, Monsieur Couture. Why hurt each other with words? It seems to me I have the right to rest now, the right to demand your silence. Don't you agree? I want to draw my curtains, make everything dark around me, stretch out and close my eyes.

Blaise. You know very well there's no hope of sleep for either of us. Each in his own room, separated by a wall, we'll lie awake till dawn. [*Goes and bolts the door.*]

Marcelle. Why are you locking the door?

Blaise. I'm locking up as I do every night. Do you know what time it is?

Marcelle. No, don't lock up. The children are taking one last walk before going to sleep.

Blaise. The children? What children?

Marcelle. Emmanuele and Harry.

Blaise. You gave them permission to go walking alone at night?

Marcelle [*exasperated, and, rising, walks about*]. Surely you're not going to reproach me for that now!

Blaise [*also exasperated*]. You're suffering! I can't bear to see you suffer!

Marcelle. It doesn't bother you much as a rule.

Blaise. What I can't stand is to see you suffer because of that wretched boy, that nonentity!

Marcelle. Don't worry. He's leaving tomorrow.

Blaise. He's leaving tomorrow. That's true. But he'll be back soon.

Marcelle. Yes, he'll be back. I don't know whether I dread it or long for it. It would be awful never to see him again. Perhaps it will be still worse for him to come back for someone else. Oh, what I'm saying is frightful!

Crossing to terrace door, she opens it and looks out.

Blaise. I still have at least this: I'm the only person in the world to whom you talk as if you were alone.

Marcelle. It's true. I'll have the consolation of not having to keep anything from you.

Blaise. That's right. Don't keep anything from me. I'm strong again now. I can stand hearing anything.

Marcelle [*with intensity*]. You can stand hearing anything? Then listen to me. I hate the night that covers them, this pure and empty night that enfolds them, this engagement night whose memory will outlive even their love. You're listening to me?

Blaise. Yes, yes, I'm listening.

Marcelle. Do you believe that God takes revenge? The truth is that Emmanuele was chosen, called to a higher

life. I know it, I'm sure of it. I know my daughter. The
thought of this God she has forsaken is bound to haunt
her tonight. She has a conscience. I tell you, I know her.
And conscience is a frightful poison! Deliriously happy
as she may be at this moment, when she's alone in her
room and kneels to say her prayers, her heart will be
filled with anxiety and pain. No, no, this place she has
taken beside a young man is not hers. She has usurped
it. She will be punished. She was made for a life of
solitude. This happiness wasn't meant for her.

Blaise. This happiness? You think it was meant for you,
Madame, for you? You're mad!

Marcelle. No, of course not. It wasn't meant for me.
What are you making me say? But not for her either! I
ought to have had the courage to shout it in her face. Not
for her either! I ought to have told her she was betraying
her trust. She would have given in like that! [*Snapping
her fingers.*] I'm sure of it. But I was only able to make
up poor excuses. And to think that there was no one here
to open her eyes!

Blaise. No one? Not even me? Is that what you mean?
You called me back just for that? You counted on me to
get her away from Fanning—this little girl with a conscience?

Marcelle [*hiding her face in her hands and after a moment taking them away. In an altered voice*]. Yes, it's true,
it's true! You must remind me of it forever! Yes, it was
indeed for this crime I called you back. And I'm still sorry
you didn't commit it. Yet, less than an hour ago Emmanuele was in my arms. I was overflowing with the peace I
had restored to her. And now again inside me this mud
churns up. My God!

Blaise [*with despair*]. So you wanted from me only this
ignoble help! I couldn't bring you anything else. I knew
it, of course. But to hear you say it!

Marcelle. If it's any comfort to you, I no longer need
this help. And yet you're still here after what you've done!

Blaise. Because my pain has become necessary to you.
Making me suffer gives you something to think about.

Marcelle. No, no! But your presence is like a wave that
lifts and carries me. If you go I thrash about miserably.

You irritate me. It's like a storm perpetually around me.
But as soon as it's gone I shiver. After what you've done,
who can separate us?

Blaise [*timidly*]. Marcelle!

MARCELLE *makes a gesture of denial and remains leaning
against the door looking out.*

Don't stay there. You'll catch cold. You have no coat.

Marcelle. I lent mine to Emmanuele.

Blaise [*taking her hand and drawing her to fireplace*].
Come, you can feel the dampness of the brook. Come
nearer the fire. I'll put on another log.

Marcelle [*going to fireplace and sitting*]. Don't bother.
I'm not cold.

Pause.

Blaise. Bertrand will be home day after tomorrow. Life
will begin again here, peaceful, as it used to be. You'll see.

Marcelle. Yes, life will begin again. Life . . .

Blaise [*sitting near* MARCELLE]. We should pick out a
novel to read aloud at night as we did last winter. Remember? It was Tolstoy's "War and Peace."

Marcelle. We never got to the end of it. But God knows
the winter was long!

Blaise. Because when I read you're always interrupting
me.

Marcelle. I won't interrupt you any more, Monsieur
Couture. I promise.

EMMANUELE *comes in, out of breath.*

Emmanuele! You're back!

Emmanuele. I came to get you, Mama. The night is
marvelous! You'd think it was still September. Harry's
waiting for us on the driveway. He told me to bring you
back by force.

Marcelle [*hesitating, and half rising*]. He told you to
bring me back by force?

Blaise. See here, Madame. That wouldn't be sensible.
You need rest.

Marcelle [*sitting down again*]. It's true. It wouldn't be
sensible.

Emmanuele. Oh, Mama, be sweet. Please come!

Marcelle. No, my little girl. I'm really worn out. I'm going to lie down, close my eyes and sleep . . . perhaps.

Emmanuele. I'm sure Harry will scold me if he sees me come back without you.

Marcelle. Do you think he'll scold you very much?

Emmanuele. Oh, yes! If you'd seen how distressed he was, on the last night, to leave you alone . . .

Marcelle [*bitterly*]. No, Emmanuele. You see, I'm not alone . . . I'm with Monsieur Couture!

CURTAIN

PORT-ROYAL

by

HENRY DE MONTHERLANT

Translated by

JONATHAN GRIFFIN

CHARACTERS

Sister Angélique de Saint-Jean (*Angélique Arnauld d'Andilly*), *niece of "le grand Arnauld," subprioress of the Monastery of Port-Royal de Paris, and sometime mistress of the novices, 39 years, 9 months*

Sister Marie-Françoise of the Eucharist, *22 years, 4 months*

Mother Catherine-Agnès de Saint-Paul (*Agnès Arnauld*), *sister of "le grand Arnauld," at the time Abbess of the Monastery, coadjutress of the present Abbess, 71 years*

Sister Catherine de Sainte-Flavie (*Passart*), *who is also* The Third, *55 years*

Sister Gabrielle, *25 years*

Sister Hélène, *about 30*

Mother Madeleine de Sainte-Agnès (*Madeleine de Ligny*), *the Abbess, 48 years*

Mother Marie-Dorothée de l'Incarnation (*Le Conte*), *the Prioress, 54 years*

Sister Louise, *elderly*

Sister Julie, *young*

M. De Beaumont de Péréfixe, *Archbishop of Paris, member of the Académie Française, 59 years*

The Vicar-General (*M. l'Abbé du Plessis de la Brunetière*)

The Visitor

The Civil Lieutenant

First Chaplain

Second Chaplain

The Knight of the Watch

An Officer

The Prévôt de l'Ile, Commissioners (*four*), Officers of the Watch (*twenty*), Guards, Lackeys

Nuns of Port-Royal, *dressed in white, with a black veil, and a scarlet cross on the scapulary* (*sixty*). Nuns of the Visitation Sainte-Marie, *dressed in black* (*twelve*).

The action takes place in the Monastery of Port-Royal du Saint-Sacrement, in one of the parlors of its building in Paris, *in the Faubourg Saint-Jacques in August 1664.*

The set is extremely simple. Right, a door leading to the inner precincts of the monastery. Left, not far from the front, the barred hatch between the parlor and the outside world. Beyond it, a window. Farther off still, a rather large door giving on a flight of steps to the outer courtyard. At the back, left, a small oratory; right, a fairly large door leading to the chapel. Walls a light yellowy gray. Here and there some chairs with cane seats. Through the open window the sunshine comes violently into the room.

This scene is imaginary, and corresponds to nothing that is still visible today at Port-Royal de Paris (the Hôpital de la Maternité).

PORT-ROYAL

Sister Gabrielle, *veiled, is standing close against the grill, whose curtains are drawn aside, and is talking with a visitor beyond the bars. Beside her, on her left, there is a sister, the* Third Person,[1] *whom the spectator sees only from behind. She too is veiled, and at no moment, even when she unveils, will the spectator be able to see her face; she will remain sometimes with her back turned, sometimes facing sideways.*

The Visitor. Ah yes! there is God. . . . But there are also your parents, child, in spite of everything! Don't let yourself be caught by that fierce doctrine that, once you have passed these bars, your parents have ceased to exist for you. Your mother and I are no longer young; if you cannot give us affection, you might give us peace. But our life is infected by the fact that you are at Port-Royal. Please at least help, as far as you personally can, to make your convent no longer a rebel convent, an accursed place which puts a curse on whatever touches it.

Sister Gabrielle. A blessed place which puts a blessing on whatever touches it.

The Visitor. The Assembly of Bishops, acting on bulls issued by two popes, is decreeing a formulary which every ecclesiastical person must sign, according to which he submits himself to every decision of the Holy See. Admit that an archbishop of Paris is merely doing his duty when he demands that you nuns of Port-Royal should sign this Formulary.

Sister Gabrielle. That goes deep, Father, deeper than I can go here.

The Third. Speak louder!

The Visitor. Do you mean the Archbishop is not right?

Sister Gabrielle. No, no, Father, he is not right! [*After*

---

[1] The term was used, in the seventeenth century, for the sister who took up her position—as a third party—close beside any sister talking with a male or female visitor beyond the grill, in order to keep a watch over what they said.

a glance at THE THIRD.] Well, he's right up to a
point. . . .

The Visitor. Explain what you mean.

Sister Gabrielle. I took the veil to keep silence between
me and the world, not to teach it.

The Visitor. You insolent girl! Is that how you speak
to your father? And is your father "the world" to you?
Ah! behind that veil of yours, you must have acquired
the pursed mouth and the hard eyes one always sees,
after a certain time, in those who have entered this
place, if some accident unveils them. Very well then!
I will do the explaining. You who have given yourself
to a God of suffering, it is, one might say, your destiny to
live in torment. But you have no idea what we, who
have not left ordinary life, are being made to go through
on account of you and of the gentlemen who are directing you. All has been going well, relations are all smooth
and confident. Then suddenly smiles go out, faces grow
long, voices turn icy; the door closes, the deal fails, the
case is lost, the engagement is broken off. What is it?
What has happened? Simply that someone has tacked
onto one's name the word "Jansenist." People don't
know if one is really a Jansenist, and indeed they're not
very sure what that is. But that's enough; the word has
been said, and there one is, one of the pariahs, with
barely the right to a scrap of room, and to the bones that
are thrown under the table—brushed aside, thrown on
the heap, cringing, creeping close to the wall, like one of
the conquered in an occupied country. . . .

Sister Gabrielle. As for us daughters of Port-Royal, it
can truly be said we have been given royal measure: we
are at one and the same time misunderstood, in fashion,
and detested.

The Visitor. Sign, daughter, sign the Formulary which
will set us all at rest. Obey your archbishop. How one
breathes again, when one simply obeys! How life suddenly becomes easy! Take it from me as an old soldier.
Come! will you promise?

Sister Gabrielle. I should be breaking myself in God's
eyes, and in my own, if I promised you that. [*After a
glance at* THE THIRD.] All the same, I'll try. . . . What

I do promise is. . . . [*She speaks a few words in a lower voice, which cannot be heard.*]

The Third. Now then! what are you whispering there? Don't you know that at the grill you must talk so that the third can hear? and must not talk in riddles? I couldn't hear. . . .

Sister Gabrielle. I said . . . I said—— [*She stops short, and supports herself with both hands against the bars of the grill.*]

The Third. Well, speak! Who's stopping you from speaking?

Sister Gabrielle. Father, please go. I don't feel well. We'll go on with the conversation another time. [*She turns to* THE THIRD, *and suddenly stoops and leans her forehead upon the hands of* THE THIRD, *who keeps them inside her sleeves.*]

The Visitor. Look what they turn them into, look how they torment them. Isn't it pitiful?

The Third. Excuse me, sir, but I think it would be better . . .

She draws the curtain of the hatch. SISTER GABRIELLE *raises her head and unveils.* THE THIRD *unveils.*

Sister Gabrielle. I pray God, as is customary, that He may purify me of all I have heard that comes from the outer world, and that I may forget it. I pray God that He may purify me of y . . . ——Why did you force me to promise? Why did you force me to lie to my father?—— What have I been doing? I have been resting my head on the bosom of my enemy!

The Third. I forced you to promise? And I am your enemy? What are these extravagances? I never said a word, other than to beg you to speak more loudly so that I could hear. You know very well that that's why I am here, that our rules command it.

Sister Gabrielle. It was your presence made me speak against what I think. Because of you, a daughter of Port-Royal, one of our seniors, I have spoken against Port-Royal. No, I will not sign a formulary that condemns all the ideas on which our monastery was reformed—that is, in a way, founded. Mother Agnès, who is the revered

survivor from Monsieur de Saint-Cyran's time, does not
wish us to sign it, nor does Monsieur Arnauld, whom we
follow in everything, nor does Sister Angélique de Saint-
Jean, who is not so much his niece as his daughter in the
spirit. Mother Angélique, the reformer, and Monsieur de
Saint-Cyran, our spiritual director in eternity, would not
wish it, were they still alive. How much we understand
or don't understand in the utterances of Jansenius, condemned by the formulary, matters little. Whether they
do or do not really occur in Jansenius (since this is dis-
puted), matters little. The Formulary is aimed against
everything we love and against all whom we love. I will
never sign it.

The Third. When the Pope——

Sister Gabrielle. The Pope can perfectly well be wrong.
He is human like the others.

The Third. I will not listen to that! I will not listen to
that!

Sister Gabrielle. A House which is the glory of Christendom and of France, and is hated by them! But that is
right, it's because our House is the glory of Christendom
and of France that it is hated. That is right, that is how
it *ought* to be.

The Third. Our House, "the glory of Christendom and
of France"! Very fine, Sister, but those are things it
would be better not to say and perhaps even——

Sister Gabrielle. Why not say it since it is true? Does
not Saint Paul lay down that you have the right to praise
yourself, when accusation against you is pushed too far?

The Third. There is always a secret judgment which
God passes upon things, and which you ought to fear.

*At this moment, behind the door at the back, which is
that of the chapel, violent voices arise.* THE THIRD *goes
over to set the door ajar. Cries of:* "Heretics! Calvinists!
Hypocrites who act the devout to be able to hide!" *can
be distinguished, dominated by an urchin's shrill cry of:*
"To hell with them, the she-devils!" *and by his horrible
little laugh.* THE THIRD *is on the point of shutting the
door again when three sisters, opening it, emerge from
the chapel into the parlor, in agitation:* SISTER HÉLÈNE,

SISTER MARIE-FRANÇOISE, *and* SISTER LOUISE. *At the same time four sisters, coming from the inner precincts, cross the parlor and go out through the door giving on the courtyard. In the midst of this movement the spectator has lost sight of* THE THIRD—*among all these moving forms that are very much alike—and will certainly not realize that the* SISTER FLAVIE *who is to take part in the following scene is the one whom he has viewed only from behind during the first scene.*

Sister Hélène. Oh, Sister! what a nightmare! Those men, those women, those children—children!—coming into the chapel, shouting insults at us and banging on the screen while we were finishing the Adoration. . . . It is they who are in Hell. O God! I can now say I have seen Hell.

Sister Flavie. The Saint-Jacques quarter never was safe.

Sister Françoise. And those are perhaps the same children who, after Mother Angélique died, pushed little pieces of paper through the bars of the very same screen, to have them placed in contact with her body, because they had nothing else to give. See how times have hardened.

Sister Louise. Better those who shout insults at us through the screen than those who come here full of unction—and really to tell tales. Those good ecclesiastics, Monsieur Bail and Monsieur Chamillard, whom they've given us as directors after driving our own away—who come and interrogate us, each one separately, with the same questions for all, to find out if we think as we should. . . .

Sister Gabrielle. Yes, they have taken away from us our counselors for everyday matters, and our counselors for matters of conscience, and by a dreadful mockery have imposed on us, as counselors, our enemies.

Sister Françoise. And this morning's carriage—has anyone spoken to the commissary about it?

Sister Flavie. No. Because it was thought that the gentlemen who came in the carriage were perhaps gentlemen from the police.

Sister Gabrielle. For shame! The first time the Civil Lieutenant and the King's Procurator came—three years ago, at half-past six in the morning—they took care to leave their carriage a good way off in the quarter, and to come on foot, to gain surprise.

Sister Louise. These persons have been content to call the porter out, and to say to him: "Come on, Monsieur Jansenist. We shall soon have you all out of this place. Not one of you will be left."

Sister Françoise. I envy those who can act on the advice Our Lord gives us: "When they persecute you in one town, flee to another." Alas, that is what we cannot do. [*From this line down to that on page 90,* SISTER FRANÇOISE *will appear to take no interest in the conversation, and even once or twice to show some impatience with it.*]

Sister Flavie. Ah, yes, at the first alarm our Directors scatter, take shelter, and from there write some extremely sharp pamphlets. And we, inert and defenseless, have merely to wait for the blows which they have provoked. Our barefoot processions and holy water: those are our only weapons.

Sister Hélène. Sister Flavie is right. But I wonder what the Archbishop's attitude will be. Since he was appointed four months ago, the Legate's visit and then his own illness have given us some respite. He came in person to supervise our interrogation—I believe we have been forgotten ever since.

Sister Louise. To me it's a bad sign when things drag on. It means that the other side is giving them a great deal of thought.

Sister Hélène. The Formulary is merely a pretext. Twenty-six years ago, Cardinal de Richelieu had Monsieur de Saint-Cyran arrested. There was no question of a formulary then.

Sister Gabrielle. Already then there was a government that wanted only slaves. To denigrate us, accuse us, calumniate us, and put us in prison; to take away from us our novices, our postulants, our pupils, the children in our schools, and to forbid us to receive others; all this with frightful noise and scandal. And what is taken from us is not lost to everyone. Which schools have received the children removed from us? Which convents the novices removed from us? But here, not a word! Those who are the cause of everything are the ones whose names must not be mentioned.

Sister Hélène. The Archbishop is not wicked; they call him "good old Péréfixe." But that merely makes it more horrible, if what they whisper is true.

Sister Louise. What do they whisper?

Sister Gabrielle. That he only obtained the archbishopric in return for his promise to overthrow Port-Royal.

Sister Flavie. Sister, you know what is said about us, and how much truth there is in it. Then don't blindly believe what is said about those whom you don't like.

Sister Hélène [*In a low voice, to* SISTER GABRIELLE]. Did you notice how, when he came to question us, neither at the beginning nor at the end of his exhortation did he make the sign of the cross?

Sister Gabrielle [*In the same way*]. I don't know what he understands about religion, or whether he learned it when he was the King's tutor.

Sister Hélène. They say he has ideas about Christianity when he's——[*She checks herself.*]

Sister Gabrielle. When he's—what?

Sister Hélène. When he's [*She discreetly makes the gesture of one drinking.*] refreshed himself a little. Sister de Brégy says that some of his actions would be more suitable to a soldier than to an Archbishop of Paris, and an Academician into the bargain. . . .

Sister Gabrielle. Or to a house steward, since his father was house steward——

Sister Hélène. At Cardinal de Richelieu's.[2] His mother too was in the Cardinal's household.

Sister Louise [*Naively*]. And he's like the Cardinal! The very image of him! You'd think they were of the same family.

Sister Hélène. And he follows the Cardinal's policy. What's bred in the bone comes out in the flesh.

Sister Gabrielle. On the day of the interrogation, he

---

[2] Cécile Gazier (*Histoire de Port-Royal*, p. 190) is not afraid to insinuate that the Cardinal had got rid of this house steward, and that the future archbishop was a bastard son of Richelieu. But there is little foundation for this.

half jumped up from his throne and raised his arm, so that I thought he meant to beat me; he did give me a blow on the arm, as he said to me: "There's no denying you're as obstinate as they make 'em."

Sister Louise. Oh, Sister! the Archbishop!

Sister Gabrielle. And the way his nose bled, that same day! Because he'd got too excited—fancy his bleeding at the nose so much that five napkins were soaked with blood!

Sister Louise. That's true, Sister. The poor Archbishop!

Sister Hélène. But what I wish I had seen was at the assembly in the Sorbonne, when he made for the door in a fury—and so impetuously that he sent the Bishop of Chartres flying, not to mention his own miter. . . .

Sister Louise. Well, Sister! in an Archbishop!

Sister Flavie. At the King's council, in April, things would have gone against us to the last extreme if the Archbishop had not opposed it so strongly. He said to Monsieur Hermant: "I have a father's feelings towards those poor young women. I would gladly shed my own blood to get them out of this fix."

Sister Hélène. That's good! why, it was his blood he shed—from his nose.

Sister Flavie. Sister, that is an unseemly remark, a matter for confession and penance.

Sister Hélène. He also told Monsieur Champagne: "They have powerful enemies. I myself would be called a Jansenist if I spoke about them to the King."

Sister Gabrielle. Which confirms the saying Monsieur de Saint-Cyran used often to repeat, that "the weak are more to be feared than the wicked."

Sister Hélène. When I utter the words "Rome" and "the Louvre," it is as if I said "the Bastille": it gives me the same thrill of horror. Rome and the Louvre exist at the same time as we do, and God remains silent. And there are churchmen who live in the Louvre or in its dependencies and do not mind: there they are, like fishes in water. God remains silent about all that.

Sister Gabrielle. One day He will weigh it, and will divide it to His right hand and to His left.

Sister Hélène. There ought to be a monastery where they do nothing but pray for the weaknesses of monks and priests.

Sister Louise. They threaten us, they reassure us, they raise us up, they throw us down; one day one thing, one day another; sometimes the one and then the other in the same conversation, and almost in the same sentence. That was what Cardinal de Richelieu did, sending emissaries to his prisoners to shine on them the idea that they were to be freed, simply in order to give them false hopes.

Sister Flavie. Come, the Archbishop will do you no harm. On the day of the interrogation, he promised that to me personally, out of his own most grave and sacred mouth. Please God that nasty fever he has caught will soon be gone. Today is the last day of our novena for his recovery.

Sister Gabrielle. Yes, we pray for the Archbishop, just as formerly we prayed for the Cardinal when he was keeping Monsieur de Saint-Cyran in prison.

Sister Louise. Has he at least been told that we were observing a novena for him to get well? I think, when he is better, we ought to send him a basketful of our fine peaches, the ones Monsieur d'Andilly looks after so well.

Sister Hélène. Mother Agnès would approve, I'm sure. But would Sister Angélique de Saint-Jean?

Sister Flavie. Sister Angélique may, of course, sometimes have an unguarded impulse, and if her expression does not make her look as humble as she is, to those who don't know her——

Sister Françoise. Oh, Sister! I can see you are one of them.

Sister Flavie. There was a time—you were not yet at the Monastery—when no one was closer to Sister Angélique de Saint-Jean than the late Sister Pascal and I. So I know her very well. It sometimes seems to me that the bitter blood that is peculiar to Monsieur Arnauld has been handed on to his niece, Angélique, more than to his sister, Agnès, or to his brother, d'Andilly. Monsieur d'Andilly is worldly and devout: he flits from the Court to the alleys, and from the alleys

here. Taking snuff and taking the veil is a mixture that
does not appeal to me. Mother Agnès is all sugar—with
little trickles of vinegar. If she were the only one, there
would not be so much obstinacy over the Formulary.
She would take good care not to try to dominate our
faith. But it's Sister Angélique de Saint-Jean who is the
obstacle to everything.

Sister Gabrielle. Who is the obstacle! . . . Who
keeps us in the straight path.

Sister Flavie. Yes, yes, Sister, say once more what
you said to us the other day: "Attack Sister Angélique de
Saint-Jean! Just let me see someone try!"—putting your
arms akimbo. . . .

Sister Gabrielle. I, Sister? put my arms akimbo? Do
you think I was brought up in the market?

Sister Flavie. Yes, you did, Sister, you put them as I
am doing now. [*She puts her hands on her hips.*] And
you stood on tiptoe.

Sister Gabrielle. I stood on tiptoe! And you, Sister,
when you were asking me to give in a little to the Archbishop—you were so urgent that you had placed your
hands on mine, which were inside my sleeves.

Sister Flavie. I, Sister? placed my hands inside your
sleeves? Did you hear that? That's how she speaks to me,
me, her senior as a nun by seven years! But here, towards
me, it's always the same thing: always this lack of con-
sideration. . . . I know perfectly well I'm on the black
list.

Sister Gabrielle. There, my poor Sister, don't be so
touchy. . . .

Sister Hélène. Sh! . . . Sister Angélique de Saint-
Jean. . . .

Enter SISTER ANGÉLIQUE DE SAINT-JEAN.

Sister Hélène. And what do you, Sister, think of this
morning's carriage, and of the people in it?

Sister Angélique de Saint-Jean. I think that, if grave
things are looming ahead for us, as we are in God, we
should only be glad of it: we are not afraid of persecution, we hope for it and expect it. And as we are in na-

ture, one may tremble without being uprooted, just as one may suffer without being troubled. When there is a high wind, the tree shudders in all its foliage, but the trunk does not falter.

Sister Françoise. May I express an opinion, Sister? Our relations with God are easy and gentle. Our relations with our brothers in religion ought to be easy and gentle too, but they are infected with a certain pedantic spirit which, to gain free play, creates everywhere difficulties where there are none. There are, lastly, our relations with the police. What I say is that our relations with our brothers, the disputants, and with the police, take up a great deal of our time which would be better employed in serving God.

Sister Louise. Every time we have had a visit from the police, there has been a storm during the two preceding days. The clouds go from Paris to Rome, and from Rome to Paris, but it is always over Paris that they burst. Today, a clear sky. And what sunshine!

Sister Gabrielle. Do you remember, Sister? It was on Ash Wednesday, 1661, that that meeting of the King's Council was held which was the beginning, or rather a fresh start, of our misfortunes. Well, the night after, without knowing anything about it, without in any way knowing that we were threatened, Sister Marie-Claire saw in a dream a very dark cloud, and in that cloud an awe-inspiring beast, extraordinarily black, bearing down upon our Monastery and roaring horribly. After roaring above our Monastery, the monster rushed on again with all its force in the direction of the Louvre, and there redoubled its roaring. And from there it bore down once more upon the Monastery, and our Sister woke up, paralyzed with terror. The story of Port-Royal is an episode in the age-long strife of the Holy Spirit against the Beast.

Sister Angélique. Well! has any of you lately had such dreams? [*The sisters shake their heads.*] No storms, no dreams of clouds. So men are quiet. But if there were storms or clouds, remember they are made of rain. And rain destroys dryness. And it is dryness that is our worst enemy. Anything, rather than dryness. Never forget that.

*The sisters go out or make to go out, towards the inner
precincts.* SISTER LOUISE *lingers behind, then comes back
towards* SISTER ANGÉLIQUE.

Sister Louise [*In a low voice*]. Sister, I have something
to say to you about Sister Flavie. You don't know
everything.

Sister Angélique. About Sister Flavie? [*To* SISTER
FRANÇOISE, *who has not yet gone.*] Please wait a moment
in the corridor. [*To* SISTER LOUISE.] What is it? [SISTER
LOUISE *makes a sign towards the door to the inner pre-
cincts.*] Speak. Unlike what is usual in all communities,
Sister Françoise does not listen at doors.

Sister Louise. Well! Sister Flavie. . . . No, Sister,
I don't think I should say it. Denouncing is ugly.

Sister Angélique. Say it, Sister. It may be important.

Sister Louise. This morning Sister Marguerite, who
was in charge of the fruit-picking, assured me that in
the garden Sister Flavie had eaten at least half a
hundred big plums—Imperials and other kinds. She told
me, too, that it was pure charity that made her say only
"half a hundred," for she reckons she ate a good hundred, or nearly. I must say I think there has never been
such an irregularity in our Monastery before.

Sister Angélique. Go in peace, Sister. Sister Flavie
must have wanted to take medicine without any cost
to our pharmacy.

SISTER LOUISE *withdraws.* SISTER ANGÉLIQUE *calls
towards the door to the inner precincts:* "Sister Françoise . . ." SISTER FRANÇOISE *comes in again.*

Sister Angélique. What a noise you make walking,
Sister, in those creaking shoes of yours! It's a small thing,
but everything matters in a community.

Sister Françoise. I'll give them to Sister Jeanne to see
to. That will be sounder than doing like Sister
Flavie. . . .

Sister Angélique. Meaning?

Sister Françoise. Yesterday Sister Flavie came unexpectedly into the vesting-room, where we were, and
asked for some altar bread . . . to stop a hole in the sole
of her shoe!

Sister Angélique. It is indeed strange to repair a shoe with altar bread, and strange to look for that in the vesting-room.

Sister Françoise. Sister, I've been wanting. . . . Yesterday, during service, when my voice failed in the singing, at that place where I always stumble, you covered it up with yours, to save me from confusion. It was only, I know, a small act of charity . . .

Sister Angélique. Not charity. Simply good order. [SISTER FRANÇOISE *lowers her head.*] And good order in accessory things. Monastic life was not established for us to sing well, but for us to die well to ourselves.—We have just been talking of something strange. There's another thing that's strange, and that is a phrase you uttered not long ago.

Sister Françoise. What phrase?

Sister Angélique. About "certain pedantic spirits . . ."

Sister Françoise. Ah, yes!

Sister Angélique. What did you mean? [SISTER FRANÇOISE *makes a vague gesture.*] Who are these pedantic spirits who create difficulties where there are none, for the fun of it?

Sister Françoise. Oh, Sister, there has never been any lack of those spirits in France.

Sister Angélique. Speak out all you have in mind.

Sister Françoise. I'm afraid of giving you pain.

Sister Angélique. I'm used to it.

Sister Françoise. To my giving you pain? Me?

Sister Angélique. Everything gives me pain. Please tell me all you have in mind.

Sister Françoise. Well, Sister, it's this: I am rather tired of hearing the same arguments chewed over and over for the last three years, about Port-Royal's differences with the authorities, and I assure you I cannot understand how it is that there are people who have thought of nothing but these things and talked of nothing but these things, all day long, for more than three years.

Sister Angélique. As it is merely beginning, you had better tell yourself that those people have their minds made differently from yours.

Sister Françoise. There are quarrels in which people go at it, go at it, get heated, maybe exchange blows—and there comes a moment when they notice that they have no longer the least remembrance of the matter of the quarrel, or even that, when the matter is looked at coolly, your adversary and yourself are of the same opinion. In Saint Matthew you can read: "Agree with thine adversary." I should like to read there: "Thou agreest with thine adversary."

Sister Angélique. "Thou agreest with thine adversary." . . . Mother Agnès finds that I lack simplicity of spirit. You are twenty-two and a few months. . . .

Sister Françoise. How many months, do you know?

Sister Angélique. As if I could care. You're twenty-two, and I find that, for a girl of your age, you too lack simplicity of spirit.

Sister Françoise. Does that seem to you so disagreeable?

Sister Angélique. Everyone knows that, in every community, one finds barely one in ten who is really capable. You are educated and capable, and I make no complaint of that; but you lack simplicity of spirit, and you speak too boldly.

Sister Françoise. Don't make me subtle by preaching simplicity to me too much.

Sister Angélique. What do you mean?

Sister Françoise. Sometimes, when we need to be subtle, we make use of all we learned from those who exhorted us not to be so when we weren't.

Sister Angélique. Tell me about the disputants, and tell me simply.

Sister Françoise. There are disputants who create for themselves monsters which are nonexistent, and it's because I am simple that I can see they are nonexistent. Our directors are known as "the Solitaries," but there is no community in France that is more of a vassal to men, and to the monsters they create for themselves, than ours. And yet you remember that sentence which Mother Angélique used to repeat so often: "Men? What's that? They're flies." And she would go through the motion of driving away flies.

Sister Angélique. She was driving away flies; therefore she had her mind on them. We are harassed by flies. We have to chase them away.

Sister Françoise. She used also to say: "Never talk about the matters of the day. The Angels would be as surprised as if they saw a dead man talking." But what else do we do except talk about the matters of the day? There is only one thing necessary, and from its point of view the Archbishop, the papal Bulls, the Formulary, the lampoons, pamphlets, and censures appear very distant and, well, frivolous things. When Monseigneur, or Monsieur Chamillard, or Monsieur Bail comes to question us, I answer more to be one with the community than out of conviction, because it seems to me that all that is unimportant and that the only thing is to give no matter what answer, provided he leaves me in peace. For all he does is to give me a headache, which advances neither God's affairs nor ours. I am only happy at Service, and in the evening, when I have drawn the curtain of my bed: in the tomb of the cell, and the tomb of bed. I should like to be a lay sister, so as no longer to have to do with these famous matters of the day, and so that everything I did, in this humble condition, would be effaced as I did it. To be like a lost ship, of which nobody thinks. . . .

³ [*Sister Angélique.* So your disposition is to be neither on one side or on the other. In the eyes of the Archbishop, to be neither within nor outside the Church. Let me tell you, you are not free not to take sides. Either you are with the Archbishop, or you are with your conscience.

Sister Françoise. Let them go and ask Sister Fabienne, who is barely up to making dishcloths out of the old sheets, her opinion about grace! Of the five propositions which are or are not heretical, and which are or are not in Jansenius, there are three they never mention to us, no doubt because they find them too difficult for us. They keep to the more simple propositions, and in the interrogations they ask us if we are capable of resisting grace, and if Christ died for all men. I was one of the first to be questioned at the first interrogation, and when I came

---

³ The passages between square brackets may be cut in a stage performance.—Author's note.

out from Monsieur Bail's presence I asked Sister Eulalie, who was awaiting her turn: "Sister, tell me, can you resist grace?" "Oh, no!" she answered me. "A poor woman like me resist grace, just imagine it!" "Oh, well," I told her, "you're a bad woman and a heretic. You can resist grace: that's what one has to say." And other Sisters, with better wits than Sister Eulalie, gave me much the same answer. Sister Eulalie wrote down on a piece of paper: "I can resist grace. Alas, poor woman that I am, I do so only too much." "I'm going to learn it by heart," she told me. "Otherwise I would be quite capable of giving just the wrong answer."]

Sister Angélique. I have let you run on. We never cease repeating to you that the right way to answer at the interrogations is: "Those are matters which I do not understand. I have never been told about them. That does not concern my sex." Which is perfectly true. And what else was it you have to say to me?

Sister Françoise. If all that doesn't concern us, why make the fate of our Monastery depend on a signature which will alter nothing in any way, except that it will set our minds free enough for us to be able to devote ourselves to what is our only task on earth: contemplation, prayer, charity, and penitence?

Sister Angélique. The point at issue, the subject of so much tumult, does not touch the faith and has no importance in itself. That makes it all the more horrible a crime to place simple souls, that desire only to act according to their conscience, in a position where they must take sides on these points, of which they are ignorant and which matter so little, and, if they do not sign, to cast them out from God and from the Church; a horrible crime to wish to give innocent souls the belief that they are guilty in the extreme. Well, to sign is to subscribe to this crime, and that is why we are unwilling to sign.

Sister Françoise. And this leads to our life, which is supposed to be wholly turned towards Heaven, being spent not merely in drafting memoirs and accounts with an eye to the men of the future, but also in drawing up minutes, making petitions, and submitting appeals for the men of the present. Since we love and desire to be

misunderstood, why should we worry about the opinion
of future ages? And since we love and wish for suffering,
why resist our being persecuted?

Sister Angélique. We must resist injustice, as far as the
laws permit, because it is one of our obligations to main-
tain the rights of our community, and because not to
resist it would be, in a way, to consent to injustice. Put
shortly, this is our rule: when our rights are not at issue,
to suffer gladly; when justice and our rights are at issue,
to defend ourselves. And let me add that our moments of
resistance and our desire to suffer are very easily reconciled, since these moments of resistance have never
served any purpose but to make us be treated worse and
suffer more.

Sister Françoise. Ah! Sister, let me be frank: one would
think you like all that! You and all the Port-Royal people.
Look for them in Heaven, and at that moment they are
on earth. Look for them on earth, and at that moment
they've gone up again to Heaven. If I dared use so vulgar
an expression, Sister, I would say that with Port-Royal
one never knows where one is.

Sister Angélique. Is it you, speaking like that? Our
enemies would not speak differently.

Sister Françoise. I am thinking of another rule Mother
Angélique used to repeat to us: "Let us go straight to the
source, which is God." I . . . I am a small drop which
dries if it is detached from the source.

Sister Angélique. Sister Pascal was certainly one of those
who did not receive their soul in vain. And yet she believed—to the point of giving her life for it—in that
struggle you don't believe in, even though she was, like
me, Mistress of the novices and hidden from the world
among our young ones. . . .

Sister Françoise. I know that souls belong to God, and
that it is He who gives them the feelings they must have.

Enter SISTER FLAVIE *and* SISTER JULIE.

Sister Flavie [*To* SISTER JULIE]. Lean on me, Sister,
lean hard. Look out! can't you see you're going to fall?

Sister Julie. But I don't need you, Sister! I'm not going
to fall. I'm as solid as the Pont-Neuf.

Sister Angélique. What's this, Sister? when you've been in bed in the sickroom for four days with a high fever, what are you doing here?

Sister Flavie. I met her on the stairs, all swaying, on her way downstairs to show you how she'd got well.

Sister Julie. I'm not ill any longer, Sister. Yes, it's true, four days ago I had a high temperature, and it would not go down. But yesterday evening I felt an impulse to ask the good God to grant me, through the intercession of Monsieur de Saint-Cyran, now in Heaven, the grace of being well again this morning. And this morning my temperature has gone down, my strength has come back, I can walk; here I am.

Sister Flavie. You're dreaming; Monsieur de Saint-Cyran has other things to do in Heaven than to look after you. Always miracles in this house, always miracles! And they always come very pat. Every time we're rather frightened and need to have opinion on our side. Come, my child, go upstairs and get into bed. You can scarcely stand; we'll bleed you again.

Sister Julie. Bleed me again? No, thank you!

Sister Flavie. What! are you afraid of a little bleeding, when Jesus Christ has given so much of His blood for you?

Sister Julie. Bleeding's no good to me. Give me a bowl of soup instead.

Sister Angélique. Go up to the sickroom again, Sister. After dinner today will be time enough to see if the temperature has gone down properly, and if you are well again.

Sister Flavie. Well again! Look at her. She's flushed with fever.

Sister Julie. Flushed with fever! I look well because I am well.

Sister Flavie. Go back upstairs, Sister; those are Sister Angélique's orders. We shall put you on a very strict diet. And this evening, after Nones, I shall come and bleed you myself. In your present state of weakness, four bleedings—nothing less will do. [*She moves to support her.*] There, I told you! shivering now!

Sister Julie. I shiver because you touch me. Don't touch

me! I can go upstairs at a run if I want to. God has made
me well, and what I want is a hot drink.

Sister Flavie. You want bleeding!

Sister Julie. A hot drink!

They go out, SISTER FLAVIE *trying to support* SISTER
JULIE, *who resists.*

Sister Angélique. That was a rather silly scene, and it's
a good thing it had no witnesses but us. Of course, we
ought to be careful before claiming a miracle. But that
does not mean we should disparage, in principle, the
power possessed by those of our friends who have returned
to God.

Sister Françoise. You see, Sister, how much we are
slaves to the world. One of our girls can no longer have
an improvement in her temperature without it taking on
a political twist, without our putting her to bed or getting
her up in accordance with whether we are for or against
Monsieur de Saint-Cyran.

Sister Angélique. Your peace is indeed in danger, is
it not? For you said just now: "if only they leave me in
peace." That would be crude if one didn't know who you
are, and if one didn't presume what is contained in your
peace.

Sister Françoise. What is contained in my peace is the
one thing necessary.

Sister Angélique. You think all the rest has no connec-
tion with your salvation?

Sister Françoise. My salvation is not the issue.

Sister Angélique. But still?

Sister Françoise [*In a half-whisper, lowering her eyes*].
I am made for worship, nothing else. When I am not
before God, I live in a sort of bewilderment. . . .

[*Sister Angélique.* At least you are a soul marked out
for prayer, but your fault is that you know it. If you did
not know it, your prayer would be unceasing, and it
would be worth more. It would exist just as much in the
distractions which we impose on you, and which God
imposes on you through us. How often have I had to
forbid you to retire alone to your cell or to the chapel,
at times when our Sisters are assembled? Even when we

are coming in from recreation, you arrange for something or other to delay you, and you come in a few steps behind the others; I notice it nearly every day. And yet you are in a community, and if you wish to isolate yourself within yourself, silence should be enough. When one really belongs to God, one is solitary everywhere. But one would think this community was a burden to you. . . .

Sister Françoise. We have removed from our altars the flowers and the pleated linen and all sorts of trinkets that encumber the other monasteries, but that isn't enough. I would like to be blind, and deaf, and dumb, and no longer to smell things with my nose, and no longer to touch with my fingers. Sometimes, indeed, that seems to be happening to me. Sometimes I look at our buildings, the trees, the lawns, our Sisters or the housekeepers who come and go, and my eyes are opened and I say to myself: "None of all that exists. Nothing in the world exists but God and me."]

Sister Angélique. That is not the spirit of our Institute. That is from elsewhere. You are not altogether a daughter of Port-Royal.

Sister Françoise. I am a daughter of the Holy Sacrament, before Port-Royal. My name is Sister Françoise of the Eucharist, because, in the Eucharist, Our Lord is separate and alone. That is how I want to be in Him.

Sister Angélique. You are seeking approbation.

Sister Françoise. I am not seeking approbation. . . .

Sister Angélique. Well! you are right not to be too greatly attached to our House. One attaches oneself to certain things under the pretext of devotion, whereas devotion consists in a stripping bare of everything: God fills us only in so far as we are empty. There are other Orders. If your gaze is set on God alone, you will value the good where it is, and you will praise God for the favors He does to those other Orders, as well as for those He does to our own.

Sister Françoise. What do you mean?

Sister Angélique. Thinking as you do, is your place really among us? It has occurred to me several times already to doubt it.

Sister Françoise [*With emotion*]. You reject me like

that, Sister! You who have already refused me so firmly the small trifle of attention and charity I at one time asked of you, over and above what the others have. . . .

Sister Angélique. There is no rule we have prized more than the one against ever appropriating souls. I quoted to you the Gospel saying: "Take that which is thine, and go thy way." What did it matter to you whether it was given more or less to the others?

Sister Françoise. What did I do? I only gave a slight tug to your robe, to make you turn. . . .

Sister Angélique. Creatures are contagious in themselves. There is nothing like a human affection for casting a shadow over the sunshine of God. By parting from us, you would perhaps be withdrawing from one of those shadows, as a true daughter of light should do. And you might also perhaps find in another House a spirit that would help you to sustain better the name you have chosen for yourself. What we see makes us inclined to believe that religious orders devour one another like tigers. But not always, and in your case it might be that the Carmel . . .

Sister Françoise. To learn all of a sudden that one counts for so little. . . . Forgive me if I am dazed.

Sister Angélique. You are not a privileged person; you have no function or mission. Let us say that, if anything, you are a foreigner—one more foreigner among so much that is foreign to us. Christendom envelops us, and part of Christendom is against us. There are sixty-nine of us here, nuns, and I could name to you the ones who are foreigners, and who will show it at the first occasion.

Sister Françoise. Because I have spoken to you as I have, you now believe that I shall sign.

Sister Angélique. You will not sign, or you will sign last of all.

Sister Françoise. No, I'll never betray our Mothers!

Sister Angélique. Some of us will sign because they cannot bear this suspense any longer, because they tired of suffering before we have yet suffered; one can read it on their faces: like open books, if only they knew! I catch them weeping: they are weeping over themselves. Others would like to take the place of those who would be dispersed as rebels: they report everything to Monsieur

Bail and Monsieur Chamillard, who pour it out afresh to the Archbishop. The Church is a house of ambition and envy. I know one who would so like to be Abbess . . .

Sister Françoise. Who? Sister, tell me who!

[*Sister Angélique.* Yesterday your uncle asked for you, to come and speak with him. Did he talk to you about signing?

Sister Françoise. We talked of nothing else.

Sister Angélique. What did he say?

Sister Françoise. He urges me to do what is not base in itself, but becomes so when he urges me to do it. He considers that we are in the right, but that we must yield because the powerful are against us. My uncle is the true honest man according to the lights of the world.

Sister Angélique. Most of our sisters who have relatives receive the same sort of help from them. Every time they come to the parlor they return from it soiled. And is it surprising? We know what we have left, and why we left it. Our profession cuts us off as much from the common run of Christians as Christians are cut off from infidels.

Sister Françoise. He told me also that, if my grandfather were alive, he would urge me to sign.

Sister Angélique. I should have been amazed if the dead had had no voice in the matter.

Sister Françoise. I am indifferent about signing, but I would struggle against it till my strength gave out simply in order not to be on the same side as those people.]

Sister Angélique. The person I am thinking of is betraying, and knows she is betraying, although she does not believe it is betrayal: she believes it is we who are betraying. You, who said to me: "I shall not betray our Mothers"—you betray them every day by what is best in you. You will not sign, and this will not be in order to sever yourself from your family, it will not be on a point of honor, it will not even be in order not to betray our Mothers. It will be merely in order not to give them pain. In that case I say to myself: what is the good? We must never believe that God has extraordinary designs for us. It would be an extraordinary design of God for you to make you suffer for a Port-Royal in which you do not believe. Martyrdom without faith? Leave that to pro-

founder spirits than yours. You said our disputes were of
no importance to you. I should like to point out to you
that your opinion on those disputes is also of little importance. You doubt if our fight has any sense. That
doubt of yours is a petty doubt. You used the word "worship." At the time when the girls were here, when I was
Mistress of the novices and the threats to take them away
from us were beginning, there was one of them who was
terrified of going back into the world, and who no longer
prayed except to ask God to preserve her from that. She
considered, quite rightly, that it was an offense to God
no longer to pray except to ask for something, and she
told me that she sometimes even cried: "O God; take away
from me the prayers of fear, and give me those of worship." So her dread stopped her from praying purely.
Perhaps there is a kind of dread that stops one from praying altogether. That makes a different doubt from yours.

MOTHER AGNÈS *enters, coming from the inner precincts,
to which* SISTER FRANÇOISE *withdraws.*

Sister Angélique. I have just been rather harsh with that
little sister. Wrongly, no doubt. One should not treat
others harshly at times when one is afraid they may treat
oneself harshly; when one would like, on the contrary,
to be reconciled with someone. . . . I was kind to my
novices; why wasn't I more so?

Mother Agnès. You are the salt of this House; don't
let yourself be dissolved.

Sister Angélique. There's no salt in this sad and tender
mood of mine, which—yes, it reminds me of how I felt
last winter, at night, when from the sickroom I used to
hear the singing of Matins. . . . But still sadder than
then, and above all less firm. Always concealing within
oneself a wound of pain and dread. . . . [*Laying her
head on the scarlet cross of her scapulary.*] How right it
is that we should wear this cross of blood! It is the heart
that has sweated through.

Mother Agnès. To me it is enough to bend my head:
I see it and I feel strengthened. What is troubling you,
good Sister? Sister Françoise?

Sister Angélique. Sister Françoise? Oh! petty difficulties. Huge with the hugeness of a grain of millet.

Mother Agnès. And yet you kept her talking a good while. Take care lest you've caused her scandal by useless words. Let us never forget what is thought of them here: that they may be considered as sins.

Sister Angélique. I believe I was glad not to be alone. You know well, Mother, how every year I dread this middle of the summer, those August days when there is no longer anyone there. One feels so little protected, so open to attack. . . . I don't know why our friends have this passion for moving about. And one all the time saying to oneself that they will not be there at the moment when they are needed. That paper which we sent the other day to the Duchess of Liancourt, for her to convey it urgently to Monsieur Chamillard, and which she had not time to have copied because she was leaving that day for the country, so that it was not conveyed. . . .

Mother Agnès. I am fully determined not to let myself be affected any more by such accidents, from the experience I have that a quarter of an hour spent before God effaces many things which seemed great things, and in fact are nothing.

Sister Angélique. What we have on our minds is nothing: I have already heard that language. But after all, is it I who introduced a principle of agitation and alarm into this House? Always hiding everything—and what has to be hidden is virtue and truth; always keeping on one's guard on behalf of the others and on one's own; always false names, always papers in code, always papers one has written dispersed outside in this or that person's house—and often one cannot even remember whose; always the threat that everything around one may be unexpectedly seized, placed under seal and lost forever, after being pawed, scraped, squeezed, distorted; always men prowling and spying, always at the mercy of everyone—and of bitter or stupid people; always defending oneself, always making statements, always having to give explanations about walls, about doors, about things that are simple and clear—and in an instant become criminal; always coming and going between what is most grave, delicate, and tender in this world and that machinery of inquiries, sequestrations, and police. If we were guilty, or even rash people, we would say: "So be it. I'll pay." But being what we are! Our Lord said that the truth sets free. Alas! the truth imprisons. And innocence imprisons. [*Taking her hands.*] Tell me what you really think, Mother. Shall we be dispersed? Shall we go to prison? Stop trying to reassure me. The people who reassure me frighten me. We have been deceived too often.

Mother Agnès. But if, on the other hand, I alarm you . . .

Sister Angélique [*In a low voice*]. Don't alarm me either.

Mother Agnès. Everything good we do is done with a mind at peace. Anxiety is a great proof of the little profit we derive from the Holy Communion, and whoever does not consider herself happy in this world cannot be so in the next. You believe in God and are afraid of something?

Sister Angélique. I'm afraid of myself. I'm afraid of all the rest as well. You remember little Sombreuil, when she used to say: "I'm frightened of the trees. I'm frightened of water. I'm frightened of the wind. I'm frightened of everything." I too am frightened of everything.

Mother Agnès. There are some who carry their fear. Others who drag it after them.

Sister Angélique. It is my soul I seem to be carrying, and rocking to sleep, that it may forget its pain, like the child a woman weans and then rocks in her arms to make it forget its nurse.

Mother Agnès. You are my niece, my dear daughter, and I would like to give you, more than anyone else, a word of relief. But a creature has no power to give relief in an affliction; that is an office God has reserved for Himself alone. And what need is there of relief? You are suffering and you have the love of God. You have everything.

Sister Angélique. I have not everything.

Mother Agnès. Why torment yourself? In our religion, everything is so simple. Are you happy? You give thanks for it. Are you unhappy? You give thanks for it. You have only to let yourself be led, to wait for the moments of God, to adore all that He sends you. For seventy-one years tribulations have encircled me with their din, without making me feel anything but a deepening of the divine mystery, which I would not have felt without them. And I am going to death as one goes to Mass. All time is nothing; and all that happens in it. There is nothing real except eternity. [SISTER ANGÉLIQUE *goes and closes the shutters over the window. The parlor grows dark.*] You are right to push the shutters to. I have often told you how much better I prayed in the Church of our Convent in the Fields than in the one here, which is too bright.

Sister Angélique. Today, August the twenty-sixth. . . . The middle of the year, and the middle of the day. The hour of the midday demons. I don't know which is the worse; the middle of the day, or waking in the morning, with the day that will have to be given its load. This great silence of August. There is a silence and a desertion in August that make, for me, a terrifying image of the silence and desertion of God. When the force and heat of the day are past, around five o'clock, I shall be better. And then, at five o'clock, one is untroubled till next morning: nothing happens at night. The menace rises with the sun.

Mother Agnès. You're tired, dear child. I had noticed it already, because your singing at service is less strong. You're hardly eating at all.

Sister Angélique. Humiliations don't demand strength.

Mother Agnès. You lie awake every night after Matins, you said. That means you get too little sleep. Many things are not in order in the souls here, simply because people don't sleep enough.

Sister Angélique. I thank God for waking me up at night—it enables me to give one thought the more to Him. The other night, when I was really exhausted, I was caught up with delight as I watched the stars. I gazed at the sky above the dormitory, and I imagined how it was more serene there than in any place in the world.

Mother Agnès. You are keeping watch before God,

even when you are obediently asleep. But what is it that
wakes you up in the night like this?

Sister Angélique. I don't know. Perhaps something that
has hurt me the day before. It seems that girls who live
in the world sleep when they are happy.

Mother Agnès. Who told you that?

Sister Angélique. One of ours, who came late. I don't
remember who.

Mother Agnès. Your eyes are ringed and tormented.
One would think every sorrow that comes your way had
piled up in your eyes.

Sister Angélique. Our directors would learn a great deal,
if they would merely make us lift our veils. Do you never
notice those poor girls of ours, with their eyes dug deep
like graves?

Mother Agnès. And that little spot, on you lip. . . .
Is it a fever spot?

Sister Angélique. I have a fairly high fever every evening.

Mother Agnès. Are you ill?

Sister Angélique. Not in the least.

Mother Agnès. A fever of anxiety and grief. All our sisters, turn and turn about, have that fever.

Sister Angélique. At Port-Royal, many die of that fever
of anxiety and grief. Sister Pascal died of it, Sister Ger-
trude died of it, Mother du Fargis was at death's door
with it. . . . Not to mention those who die of some
more definite illness: to think that we have had seven
nuns die in three years!

Mother Agnès. We give to God His ripened fruits
every year.

Sister Angélique. There are some days when the meteors
approach the earth, and brush against it—then they move
away, and one breathes again. Meteors, or the chariot of
fire when it grazed the earth between Elisha and Elijah.
How I long for that first of September! Still five days to
go! Then, at the far end of our gardens, we shall once
more begin to smell the fragrance of the fields. September
relaxes. But August is all hard and on fire. [*Slipping her
fingers under the band of her coif.*] How tight this band
is! I long for the chariot of fire to pass, and I am alone

in my longing. Who knows what anguish is, and has ever done anything to calm it in his neighbor?

Mother Agnès. Ah! Sister, how human you are!

Sister Angélique. And it's not enough to shudder, I must also reassure the others. Look cheerful in the refectory, and eat! Two hard tasks. Human? Even Monsieur de Saint-Cyran was human when he found himself under lock and key in the dungeon of Vincennes. He had at least that volume of Saint Augustine which my father slipped into his hands, having met him by chance just as he was being taken away. That is why nowadays I tell our gentlemen, when they go out, always to have some book of devotion about them. Let each one prepare after his fashion for what he will do when he is arrested. I do my preparing by keeping in touch with Monsieur de Saint-Cyran's prison cell.

Mother Agnès. Well, don't prepare so much! We have drawn up a statement of what our community must do if we are dispersed. There it is in black on white, and well considered, and in detail, so don't think about it any more. One day we shall be questioned not by the Civil Lieutenant, but by Jesus Christ: that is what we must prepare for.—But look! since you are so apprehensive, shall we question Holy Scripture? It is seldom we do not receive from it advice adapted to the circumstances— or even an indication about the future. [*At a venture she opens the Bible which she is holding in her hand, and lays her finger on a page.*] Read the verse where my finger is resting:—my sight is so weak that the shortest reading hurts it. In a few months I shall be blind, and that small suffering will fit me to see the invisible with joyful eyes.

Sister Angélique [*Reading*]. Saint Paul, Epistle to the Philippians: "Rejoice in the Lord always; again I say, rejoice. . . . Have no anxiety." So be it, let us rejoice, then. But we have always observed, in all the temporal misfortunes that have befallen us, that it was said beforehand that they would not befall.

Mother Agnès. For thirty years I have seen you deficient in hope. And besides, you have just said something which smacks of mockery. I beg you to stamp out that spirit in you.

Sister Angélique. I am not mocking. But lots drawn from the Holy Scriptures must be taken with discretion, just as much as dreams—although I confess I had one of them, the other night, that torments me.

Mother Agnès. What was it?

Sister Angélique. I was trying to reach Port-Royal in the Fields, alone, on foot, at night, unable to see the paths. I arrived there, I climbed in through a ground-floor window, and there I found several of our Paris Sisters, Sister Sinclètique especially, who was very sad. I turned back towards the window, and I saw the air all on fire, and a cloud that was at one and the same time dark and aglow, like those you see during these dreadful summer months when there is going to be a storm. Sister Sinclètique, gazing at it, said with a great sigh: "Ah! what a night we shall have, yet again!" I did not know what she meant, but she frightened me. And after I had gone out, because I wanted to pray before the Holy Sacrament, it was again so black that I could no longer recognize the paths, and I woke up without finishing my dream.

Mother Agnès. Do you often dream like that?

Sister Angélique. Yes, nowadays. Not nightmares. But always dreams in which I am mortified.

Mother Agnès. In our rule, remember, the young ones were forbidden ever to tell the dreams they had had during the night, however beautiful or holy these might be. It was Monsieur de Saint-Cyran who had that put in.

[*Sister Angélique.* When he was in prison he used to write. He was always being interrupted by the guards who were constantly about him, and he would hide the paper on which he was writing in a book he was supposed to be reading, whenever he heard any noise at the door, as schoolchildren do who want to outwit their master. Monsieur Vincent de Paul warned him to take care and reread any statements he had dictated to the commissioner, for fear their sense might have been altered. And Monsieur Molé wrote to him that he should even draw lines from top to bottom of each page of these statements, for fear the police might add in the margin words purporting to be his. That went on for five years.

Mother Agnès. Everything he had said and written took

on a new force from his imprisonment. Monsieur de Saint-Cyran will thank God during all eternity for that prison cell, for he did the business of God there as a good minister, in his office, does the business of his King. Let us therefore take care not to diminish his glory by a shortsighted sadness. Let us not mix up the natural feelings with the feelings of faith. The Church has maintained its truths by its sufferings, more than by those truths themselves. And for people, too, suffering is fruitful.]

Sister Angélique. There is a suffering that is not fruitful, a dead suffering, which drags with it, into its death, everything it finds in the soul surrounding it. You speak of the truths of the Church. But suppose there were a suffering that could even obscure those truths for you? I know some of our Sisters who are reduced by a certain excess of torments to so strange a condition that it then seems to them they no longer believe in God.

Mother Agnès. Is it possible?

Sister Angélique. That seems to you frightful?

Mother Agnès. Beyond anything I could say.

Sister Angélique. And yet Monsieur de Saint-Cyran himself, in his prison cell . . . When these Sisters come to me, they call up in me the picture of a soul that, in the shuddering and abandon and anguish of its body, feels it is drowning like Saint Peter, or rather acts out in reality the words of the Psalm: "My soul melteth for heaviness"—a soul truly *melted* by peril and fear. I imagine it, in this state, carried adrift to within sight of those Gates of Darkness of which God spoke to Job. . . .

Mother Agnès. Your dream is still going on. You repeat, more or less, the words of Sister Sinclètique in that dream: "Ah! what a night we are going to have!"

Sister Angélique. The phantoms that walk in the darkness, the arrows that fly by day, and the demons of the midday hour—those phantoms, arrows, and demons which we evoke at Compline—I can truly say I have had my fill of their menaces, and I have had my fill of feeling fear. I am worn out with feeling fear; I am worn out by their hatred. People talk of my pride, but it would be more to the point, often, if someone would remind me of who I am. Now is the time when one must not lower one's eyes, once they have been lifted up to the mountains. If one lowered one's eyes, one would crumble altogether.

Mother Agnès. One ought never to lower one's eyes, except before God.

Sister Angélique. A hundred times, over many years, I have pictured the situation in which I shall surely find myself sooner or later. Imagine that I am confined, like Monsieur de Saint-Cyran, in a convent or in a prison, alone and under lock and key in some hole where the darkness is the same as that of the dead; deprived of the sacraments, excommunicated perhaps, defenseless in enemy country as if I were in the midst of the Turks, an object of final contempt to everyone, in no relation with anyone at all except those who came to persecute me to make me go back on myself and go back on us; incapable of making myself heard by anyone if I feel I am about to perish—as happened to me once already here, that night when I felt ill and came out to look for a candle, and fell in a faint in the blackness on the threshold of my cell; excluded from all aid and from all news, ignorant of where all of you are, told (truly or falsely) that this one or that one has betrayed, told that you have signed—you, Mother!

Mother Agnès. I shall never sign, my child. And I even mean to draw up a paper where I shall write that, if I have been caught at a moment when I am no longer really myself—alas! three attacks in two years—my signature will be worth nothing.

Sister Angélique. Sister Gabrielle was just now recalling the dream dreamt by one of our seniors in 1661, about the Beast that came and went between the Louvre and here, roaring. She did not recall what Mother Angélique said when this dream was told her: "We shall slay the Beast, but the Beast will slay us." We are at the bottom of a pit where everything is destroyed. A period in which, as the proverb says, it is the horses that ride in a carriage and the men who draw the carriage. So one should not be astonished at seeing, in this period, the most criminal projects currently reconciled with zeal for the service of God. And yet the indifference and harshness of these

Christians who are oppressing us are still, to me, something inconceivable. If it should happen that the two greatest forces in this world, the ecclesiastic power which has come from the highest, and the secular power which has come from the highest, should close in like pincers and crush this poor House of ours; if that conspiracy of all Hell, of all the demons of the midday hour, some in the priestly tunicle, others in the kingly mantle, should succeed in ruining this House where the only aim has been to find once more the faith, earnestness and fervor of early Christianity—ought not heaven and earth to rise up and cry out that that is terrible? But no, not a leaf will stir. We have signs of this today already: people are sorry for us, but would not lift their little finger for us. And you, Mother, if this crime took place, what would you say of God, and what would you say to Him?

Mother Agnès. I would adore, from the bottom of my heart, that order from His Providence, and I would let it have its way, for it is our will that spoils everything. And since I always carry on me the letter from the blessed Françoise de Sales, written with his own hand, in which he commends by name each of the members of our family, I would ask that blessed one for his intercession. . . .

Sister Angélique. Ah! Mother. [*Aside.*] How far away it all is from me!

Mother Agnès. Well?

Sister Angélique. When the words of Scripture, which have so often given you so much strength, no longer give you anything; when, holding this in one's fingers [*She holds up the rosary on her girdle.*], one no longer has any desire to put it to one's lips; when there come to you ideas so appalling that you learn from them what despair is, and how one comes to it, and what temptation it is that may be born from that despair . . .

Mother Agnès. And what about courage, Sister, in default of grace? Are you an Arnauld? People say the Arnaulds have no esteem except for themselves, and that they admire one another excessively. There is nothing very much to admire you for, at this moment.

Sister Angélique. When the police were visiting the house, three years ago, Mother Angélique was in the sickroom, at the point of death. She was in such pain that it was impossible to move her without her crying out. She kept repeating that she wanted to die. And when we said to her: "What? leave us in the affliction we are in?" she answered that God would help us, and that we should have pity on her and let her go willingly. So, at that hour, she felt more pity for herself than for us. And yet she was the great Angélique, the reformer and the saint of Port-Royal, and an Arnauld.

Mother Agnès. You feel too much pity for yourself, in a much kindlier trial, and one that still exists only in your mind. No, don't expect me to overflow with gentleness. That causes irreparable evils, far greater ones than those that arise from a too great severity. I accuse you in God's name of putting nature before grace and, within nature, not even finding courage. You are shutting out courage and shutting out grace. What have you left?

Sister Angélique. Forgive me, Mother, but here I am, close in front of the Gates of Darkness, and I think I have indeed nothing left. If I went forward one step further . . . Already the wind that comes out from the Gates is making my lamp's flame gutter; suppose it should put it out? Already I can't speak any more, my tongue cleaves to my palate, and the prayers I would like to say would not be prayers but cries.

Mother Agnès. I am going to pray to God for you, Sister, for I have never seen you in such need. But do you yourself try to pray for yourself a little, for the saints and angels might pray for you and, if you did not do so yourself, the prayers of others would serve only for your condemnation.

Sister Angélique. Pray? Pray to God? But if God . . . ? I am lost when I think of that.

Mother Agnès. What? Go to God at once, even if only with your body. Throw yourself at the feet of the Crucified, and say to Him the words with which He Himself inspires you in the Psalm: "Lord, break my chains," for you are in chains beside which those of your prison are nothing. And if you cannot say this except in cries, say it in cries, and in groans. Do this three times, and rise

to your feet three times, in honor of the Holy Trinity.
And perhaps God will look upon you.

Sister Angélique. Is this an obedience?

Mother Agnès. It is.

The bell is heard ringing from the tower. SISTER AN-
GÉLIQUE *pulls herself bolt upright, shuddering, then does
not move. Various sounds are heard from the courtyard—
a sound of voices, then the rumbling of a carriage, the
clatter of hooves and the clink of harness.* SISTER AN-
GÉLIQUE *says, or rather breathes:* "The chariot of fire.
. . . ." MOTHER AGNÈS, *who is close to the window,
stands up, looks out and utters a cry:* "The Archbishop!"

Sister Angélique [*In a blenched voice*]. Mother, you
can see the clock in the courtyard. What time does it say?

Mother Agnès. Midday.

Two young Sisters burst into the parlor excitedly.

First Sister. Mother, the Archbishop! Just on the ninth
day of our novena. Well again, walking!

Second Sister. It's a miracle, like that of the Holy
Thorn! [4]

First Sister [*Half opening the shutter—the sunshine
comes into the room and lights it only in part—and looking out of the window*]. He's going into the chapel.

Second Sister. He has lots of people with him. The
Vicar-General, the Official, his chaplains.

Mother Agnès. Have the Reverend Mother and the
Mother Prioress fetched. [*The two Sisters go out. To*
SISTER ANGÉLIQUE.] If this were a normal visit, he would
have announced it. I can't understand. . . . Did he know
of our prayers? Has God touched him? Might he be coming . . . There are clouds that all of a sudden disperse.
There are crises that come untied, no one knows why,
just as they began no one knows why. In half an hour
perhaps we shall be innocent. Perhaps we are already.

[4] In May, 1656, a girl called Marguerite Périer was cured of
a fistula lacrymalis, and this was officially recognized as a miracle
due to the Holy Thorn, or fragment of the Crown of Christ,
preserved at Port-Royal. The Jesuits were greatly mortified, and
Pascal and his friends overjoyed, at this Jansenist miracle which
could not be openly contested.—TRANSLATOR'S note.

Sister Angélique. What! Are they going to deprive us of persecution?

Mother Agnès. Would that vex you? But if there is honor in suffering, there is as much honor in acceptance of not suffering.

Sister Angélique. It's no good, one always suffers. Whether the misfortune comes or not, fear has come, and the furrow it has plowed is never filled in.

The Abbess *and the* Prioress *enter. The clock strikes the twelve strokes of noon.*

The Abbess. In God's name, Mother, what do you think of this? What does Monseigneur want with us?

Mother Agnès. I don't know. But you are Abbess, go quickly and welcome him. We have been all too slow. *The* Abbess *and the* Prioress *move rapidly towards the door of the chapel.* Mother Agnès *keeps a little way behind.* Sister Angélique *goes back into the inner precincts. But from inside the chapel some of the* Archbishop's *lackeys open the door, and through it come the* Archbishop, *the* Vicar-General, *the* Official, *and the two* Chaplains. *The five church dignitaries stop on the threshold of the room; they are caught in the ray of sun coming from the window as though by a floodlight. With their golds, their reds, and their blacks, they look like an assembly of magnificent and slightly monstrous insects.*

The three nuns go down on their knees, and the prelate gives them his blessing.

During part of the following scene the Archbishop's *lackeys will be visible, pressing close up to the open door of the chapel, to listen. When the* Archbishop *turns his gaze in that direction, they efface themselves, only to return when he looks elsewhere.*

The Abbess. Monseigneur, we give thanks to God for your unexpected recovery. Here you are, on your feet, on the ninth day, exactly, of the novena we were observing for you!

The Archbishop. Thank you, Mother; I am sure that your prayers have helped towards this recovery. It was a heavy fever, and I had five or six bouts of it. My first

was on Wednesday, and came from Monsignor the
Nuncio's Mass, which greatly tired me. My second was
on Thursday, and came from the service of the Holy
Spirit, which also greatly tired me. And the others were
on Friday and Saturday, and came from I don't know
what. The first bouts were violent; the last ones not very
serious. I had six basinfuls of blood drained from me—
which is rare. But yesterday evening the fever fell, and I
can truly say that, despite an appreciable difficulty in
going to sleep—only think! I had to take as many as five
small grains—I have spent a beneficial night.

Mother Agnès. Being confined to bed, Monseigneur,
will at least have gained you some rest.

The Archbishop. Yes, but during this time affairs have
been piling up. And the affairs of Port-Royal! . . . I
have, in my study, a dossier on them, so high. You are
essentially a place of silence and withdrawal—this garden,
this park rather, reminds me of my grandmother's garden,
that's such a long time ago. . . . What was I saying?
you are essentially a place of silence and withdrawal, but
one hears tell of nothing but you! Four months I have
been Archbishop, and in these four months, thanks to
Port-Royal, I can truly say I have grown twenty-five years
older.

The Abbess. It seems to me it would be entirely in
your power, Monseigneur——

The Official. Entirely in Monseigneur's power! . . .
Well!

Mother Agnès. We hope, Monseigneur, that your visit
may be good and not evil.

The Archbishop. It will be good. This visit will re-
dound to the glory of God and to that of your House.
I love your House. I can swear to you upon this cross
[*He raises up his pectoral cross.*] that I wish you nothing
but good.

Mother Agnès. I can bear witness to the joy of our
Sisters at seeing you arrive, as well as to their fervor when
they prayed for you.

The Archbishop. I am their very humble and obedient
servant. Yes, I must beg you to consent to my asking
you for a few moments of—to others I would say: of your

leisure; to you I say: of your holy occupations. I could
spend whole days in conversation with you, and to me
they would last a mere hour, seeing that you are willing
to listen to me. Only, listening is not everything. One
must also allow oneself to be convinced, and one must
also obey. [A *pause*.] Monsieur Bail and Monsieur Chamillard, ten days ago, found you in an intractable state of
mind. Has nothing changed since then?

The Abbess. No, Monseigneur, nothing.

The Archbishop. I shall procede nonetheless to ask all
of you one by one for your decision, and after that I shall
act as God and my judgment may prompt me to do.

The Abbess. The consultation is superfluous. I know
how our daughters are disposed, and can answer for them
all.

The Archbishop. Is that your last word?

The Abbess. It is our last word.

The Archbishop [*Turning to* MOTHER AGNÈS.] Mother?

Mother Agnès. We think that if you would——

The Archbishop [*Harshly*]. Obey. Everything will come
after that. But obey first. [*Wheedlingly.*] Good Mother,
do it for love of me!

Mother Agnès. Nonetheless, if——

The Archbishop [*Harshly*]. Don't argue. Obey. You will
argue afterwards.

The Abbess. We refuse to sign.

The Archbishop. The Pope condemns five heretical
propositions in Jansenius's book. I, who am your lawful
Superior, assure you that they are in it. And yet you will
not believe. You prefer the lights of your Advisers, and
you burn in them like moths in a candleflame. Those
whom you believe are those who tell you that the propositions are not in Jansenius; that the Pope has condemned
him without knowing what he was doing; that he has let
himself be led by the nose; that he has been bought by
the Jesuits; that it has cost them a great deal. That is the
nonsense they retail to you, and you believe those people,
who have neither esteem nor power in the Church, nor
authority over you; you opt for their judgment against
that of the Pope and the whole Church. And why? There
is no reason, unless it be that you must play at being

martyrs: oh! how fine it is to be oppressed a little! And what I tell you is that all this is pitiful, and that you are a lot of poor young women with minds astray, vain and stubborn. [A *pause*.] You make no answer?

The Abbess. We cannot sign, Monseigneur, against our conscience.

The Archbishop. "I respect you, Monseigneur, I respect you as far as I can, but, Monseigneur, when it comes to my conscience, when it comes to my conscience, after that point I kiss your hands, Monseigneur, my inclination is more precious to me than yours." That's the language that has been held out to me, these four months. Well! the evil being without remedy, I now beg you and order you to have the community assemble immediately.

The PRIORESS *goes out.*

The Vicar-General. Monseigneur, would you like someone to fetch your chair?

The Archbishop. I shall not sit down. I need no chair.

The Abbess. And so, Monseigneur, we are heretics?

The Archbishop. I do not say you are heretics, and, if all we had to judge by was what we have seen at Port-Royal, I would even say that that is not so. But all over France everyone believes so and says so. And you know the proverb, that there is no smoke without fire.

The Abbess. Alas, Monseigneur, the proverb is as false as can be. There is smoke without fire; it is enough for a few malicious people to will it. When the scribes, the priests, the Pharisees and the whole people said to Our Lord that He was a Samaritan, that is to say a heretic, was it right to believe them, even though everybody was saying so and it was the voice of the people?

The Archbishop. And what is there comparable between Our Lord and you? Is not that an exorbitant pride?

The Official. As between private persons, proofs are needed for a condemnation. But a king condemns upon mere suspicion. When Our Lord comes to judge the world, He will not judge on what He sees, but on what His Father tells Him. *Sic audio, sic judico:* "It is on what I hear that I judge."

The community has gradually assembled in the parlor.

The Archbishop. My Sisters, since all I have done up
to this day has been useless, I shall now use other language to you. I command you, on pain of disobedience,
to subscribe to my Ordinance and to the Formulary which
follows it.

Sister Angélique de Saint-Jean. We cannot by any
means.

The Archbishop. Your Mother has told me that your
agreement on this point was complete, and that individual
consultations were superfluous. Do you support your
Mother?

Voices. Yes! Yes!

The Archbishop. Then you will by no means subscribe to
the Ordinance or to the Formulary?

Sister Angélique de Saint-Jean. No, Monseigneur, with
God's grace.

The Vicar-General. A fine use of God's grace!

The Archbishop. In that case . . . [*He signs to one of
his* CHAPLAINS, *and whispers something to him. The*
CHAPLAIN *goes out.*] If ever a man had reason to be
grieved beyond bearing, to the heart, I can truly say that
I have, for I find all of you obstinate and rebellious,
proudly putting your feelings above those of your superiors, and unwilling to surrender to their warnings and
their remonstrances. For this reason I declare you today
rebels and disobedient to the Church and to your Archbishop, and as such [*A pause.*] incapable of participation
in the sacraments. I forbid you to approach them, as
being unworthy of them, and as having deserved to be
punished and cut off from all sacred things. No directors,
no confessors, no Eucharist, no Viaticum, no Extreme
Unction, no burial in consecrated ground. I add to my
decision a ban upon seeing anyone, no matter whom,
from outside, until further order.

A Sister. We, the daughters of the Holy Sacrament,
deprived of the sacraments!

A Sister. So all we do and all we are is counted for
nothing, ever!

A Sister. Today is the day of man. Tomorrow will come God's day.

The Archbishop [To MOTHER AGNÈS]. I am sorry to make you suffer, Mother.

Mother Agnès. To tell the truth, I am hardly suffering at all, Monseigneur. But if it should befall me to suffer, I believe I would not distinguish the persons who are the instrument of that suffering.

The Official [*Under his breath*]. A tired serenity is not unbecoming to our good Mother.

The Prioress [*Who has glanced out of the window*]. What! That God should judge us worthy of this! Guards in the courtyard, a company of guards in battle order, with musket and arbalest. Like the legionaries surrounding Christ in the pretorium. Ah! it is too much glory for us! We are not to go to communion any more? But Saint Bernard affirms that to share in His sufferings is to have communion with the body and blood of Jesus Christ. [*Pointing at the guards.*] There is our communion.

The Archbishop. You admit that you snap your fingers at participation in the sacraments. That also shall be noted.

The Abbess. The Author of the sacraments matters more to us than the sacraments.

A Sister. But where do these men come from?

A Sister. They must have marched through the side streets of the quarter, with the police carriages which are coming in.

Enter the CIVIL LIEUTENANT, *the* KNIGHT OF THE WATCH, *the* PRÉVÔT DE L'ILE, *four commissioners, twenty* OFFICERS OF THE WATCH, *and a few* OFFICERS *and* SERGEANTS OF THE GUARD. *Added to the church dignitaries, they make dappled groups with more and more resemblance to a swarm of coruscating and terrifying insects—enormous insects of the virgin forest—hypnotizing a troop of frightened birds. The sacerdotal power and the civil power, holding in their hands all the instruments of their operations,—the* ARCHBISHOP *his black list, a* COMMISSIONER *the pen and paper for the reports, the* OFFICERS OF THE WATCH *their cudgels, the* KNIGHT OF THE WATCH *his sword: it is easy—*

if for a moment one puts oneself in the position of the nuns—to see in them those "demons of midday" mentioned in a letter by SISTER ELISABETH AGNÈS *("all those carriages and all that appalling train"), or mentioned just now in this room by* SISTER ANGÉLIQUE, *and really mentioned by her in her* Relation of Captivity, *when she speaks, as she does there, of "this miracle which God has performed in sustaining by an invisible strength a poor community denuded of all help, without support and without guidance, against a conspiracy of all Hell."*

There is a long silence, during which the ARCHBISHOP *examines some papers that have been passed to him by the* VICAR-GENERAL. *In the end he signs one. He gives others to the* CIVIL LIEUTENANT.

The Archbishop. I was waiting for these gentlemen's arrival in order to say to you something more. There are twelve among you—the most rebellious—whom I am going to remove at once from this monastery. They will be confined, each one in a different convent. Here are their names [*He reads his list:*] Mother Madeleine de Sainte-Agnès, Abbess; Mother Catherine-Agnès de Saint-Paul, Assistant; Mother Marie-Dorothée de l'Incarnation, Prioress; Sister Angélique-Thérèse; Sister Marguerite-Gertrude; Sister Marie-Charlotte de Sainte-Claire; Sister Françoise-Louise de Sainte-Claire; Sister Angélique de Saint-Jean; Sister Agnès de la Mère de Dieu; Sister Madeleine de Sainte-Candide; Sister Anne de Sainte-Eugénie; Sister Hélène de Sainte-Agnès.

Effects various. Some of the Sisters clasp their hands together; others kiss the cross of their rosary; others veil their faces; others, in tears, pull a handkerchief from their pocket. As she pulls out hers, SISTER FLAVIE *lets fall from her pocket a folded paper, which* SISTER ANGÉLIQUE DE SAINT-JEAN *picks up. In the background—rather fleetingly —one sister is seen to faint and be carried out.*

A Sister. God of the Christians, forgive your Church!

At this point there can be a lowering of the lights for a moment, or even, if it is thought absolutely indispensable, an interval.

The Abbess. Monseigneur, we believe ourselves in all conscience obliged to appeal against this violence and to protest the invalidity of all that is being done to us and all that may be done to us.

The Archbishop. Appeal, protest—all that makes me laugh. I know my business, I think. And is not this unseemly? Always, in this monastery, jargon about procedure!

Lackeys bring the ARCHBISHOP's *chair.*

First Chaplain. Monseigneur, your chair. . . .

The Archbishop. And did I not say that I had no need of a chair? Can you not see I've as much as I can do to keep calm?

The Prioress. If we answer, we are accused of being wranglers. If we keep silence, we are accused of pride.

The Abbess. We are forced into procedure by ceaseless injustice, and then we are reproached for knowing some of the terms of procedure.

The Archbishop. Always complaining! Always bitterness and an injured air!

The Abbess. We are trampled down, and then we are reproached for being bitter and injured!

An especial murmur has arisen among the Sisters. A sentence is passed from mouth to mouth and so reaches the ARCHBISHOP.

The Archbishop. What's this? In my list I named Sister Françoise-Louise de Sainte-Claire. Is there no one among you who answers to that name?

Various Voices. No, Monseigneur.—No! No!—But we have Sister Françoise-Claire. . . .

The Abbess. Oh, that's it; it must be her. Let her come forward.

The Prioress. Sister Françoise-Claire is our cellaress and cannot leave immediately, without having put the business and accounts in order. She is also, I think, altogether devoted to Monseigneur, and is certainly not one of those he would wish to expel.

The Archbishop [*To* SISTER FRANÇOISE-CLAIRE]. I recognize you, my daughter. I know you are a sensible girl; I can vouch for you.—Yes, yes, just look at her: she's as meek as a lamb. No, she's not the one that was meant. And how the devil can this mistake have arisen? But I've everything ready for twelve young women. I must have my twelve! When I've said a thing, it must happen. I won't be disappointed. I'm going to put another in her place. . . .

Embarrassed silence.

The Prioress. Monseigneur, perhaps Sister Anne-Cécile, who looks after our Mother, and who would be a great help to her. . . .

The Archbishop. Good, out with Sister Anne-Cécile, and that's enough of that. [*To the* OFFICERS OF THE WATCH.] And now, gentlemen, you know what you have to do.

The Knight of the Watch. I have orders to break in the doors in case of refusal to obey.

The Archbishop. Marshal these young women through there. They're to leave at once. Let them go and fetch the things they need; the rest will be brought to them tomorrow.

A Sister. God is against us!

The Abbess. Who said: "God is against us"?

The Civil Lieutenant. And be thankful we have been content with this, and have not sought to lay hands on the secrets.

The Abbess. Who said: "God is against us"?

First Chaplain [*To the other*]. Come. I can't watch this.

Second Chaplain. No, let us stay. Our presence may moderate things.

First Chaplain. I confess, the sight of such steadfast-ness . . .

The Archbishop [*Who has heard*]. It would be strange if every idiocy became good and sublime simply because people were steadfast in it. Was Balaam's she-ass spiritual because beating her was no use, there was no way of making her move on?

The Abbess. Have these men withdrawn, Monseigneur. We protest and we appeal. But we shall obey without there being any need of recourse to violence.

The Prioress. We are in your hands, and all we can do is to hope that you will not abuse your advantage.

Mother Agnès. No, Sister, we are in God's hands. And even in dread there is pleasure, at seeing oneself dependent upon His mercy.

Sister Flavie. Poor Sister de Sainte-Flavie, ah! you are indeed to be pitied. Alas, how wretched I am! I cannot see where I stand.

The Prévôt de l'Ile [*To one of the sisters, who is weeping*]. What, Sister? are you not willing to be afflicted? All the great saints were.

The Civil Lieutenant [*To* THE PRIORESS]. You have certainly more spirit than any of our men, Sister, but the King wants no more Insurrectionists here. The time of the Insurrection is over!

The Prioress. And what have we in common with the Insurrection? People brand us with a word: just the one that is needed to ruin us.

The Abbess. We write "white," and they say indignantly that we have written "black." They say that in the Monastery we will not have images: our cells are full of them. That we do not take communion often enough: we take communion at least twice a week. That we have no rosaries: look here. [*She points to the rosary at her girdle.*] It is enough to see, but they do not want to see; what they want is to see the opposite of what is there. Scarcely is one calumny destroyed, they invent another.

The OFFICERS *force the nuns gently back towards the inner precincts.* SISTER FRANÇOISE *remains in prayer in the oratory, kneeling with her back to the public, without anyone paying attention to her.*

The Prioress. Sir, as Civil Lieutenant, in 1661, you searched our House as many as seven times in four months. You went so far as to shake the mattresses, to see if there were not someone hidden inside them. This time it would be kind if you would spare the mattress on which one of our Sisters lies dying. For there is always one of us here who is dying while the police are down below.

The Civil Lieutenant. Mother, if I did have the mattresses shaken, that was because it was my duty to do so.

And this time also I shall do whatever I consider it right to do. And you will be forcing me to it all the more if you take up that tone with me.

The Abbess. When our Sister is dead, we shall place in her hands a petition to Our Lord, appealing to Him against your violence, and we shall bury her with it.

The Archbishop. Always petitions! Always papers! This is the pen-and-ink monastery. Ah! if only you and your Directors could exist for six months without writing! That would produce peace.

The First Chaplain [*Under his breath, to* THE ABBESS]. Hold out, Mother. There are those here who admire you.

The Abbess. Energy I find in my body. Courage I find in prayer. Neither my body nor God are me. So don't admire me.

Sister Angélique. Whatever treatment we may have to suffer at the hands of the secular power, it will be a consolation to us, Monseigneur, if our blood does not fall upon you.

The Archbishop. What's that? What do you say?

Sister Angélique. I say that we shall be consoled for all this, Monseigneur, if our blood does not fall upon you. I shall not say more, Monseigneur. Let us relapse into the silence of Jesus Christ during His Passion. We have justified ourselves enough on earth.

From now on she is silent, but tears can be seen flowing, almost unquenchably, over her face, without her face changing.

The Vicar-General. There is also an evil silence, Sister.

A Sister [*An elderly one, to one of the* OFFICERS, *who is motioning her back*]. Ah! Officer, so it's always you who come to arrest us!

The Officer. No, Sister, there are others.

The Sister. It's certainly the third time we've seen you here.

The Officer. No, Sister, it's the fifth.

The Sister. And the fat one who was always with you, with the wart on his nose? He was your brother, I think.

The Officer. No, Sister, he was my cousin. He's now in the Provost's office, Quai Saint Michel.

The Sister. Ah! that's it.

The Officer. There, Sister, till next time.

The Sister. Ah, yes, Officer, till next time.

The Archbishop. Twelve daughters of the Visitation Sainte-Marie will replace those of you who are leaving: they will be arriving at any moment. One of them will be Mother Eugénie, a person of high virtue, who will govern you as our commissioner.

The Abbess. We reject her.

The Prioress. They will destroy in six months what it has taken sixty years to build up. You don't know how easy it is, to destroy.

A Sister. You are taking from us what we left everything to obtain.

Mother Agnès. We can be robbed of the branches, which depend on men, but we cannot be robbed of the root, which depends only on God.

The Archbishop [To Sister Agnès de Sainte-Thècle]. Sister, among these sorrows, I have a piece of news for you, of which you will certainly be glad. This very day[5]— this morning—His Majesty has signed the grant of a gratuity of six hundred livres to your nephew, Monsieur Racine, for his tragedy *La Thébaïde* or *Les Frères ennemis*. It is the first gift to be received by your nephew from the King for a tragedy. Let us hope it is the prelude to others.

Sister Agnès de Sainte-Thècle. Oh! Monseigneur, I don't wish to hear of Jean Racine. There's someone of whom I am not proud!

The Archbishop [To the Civil Lieutenant]. There's a noise in the street. What is it? Is there a crowd gathering?

The Civil Lieutenant. There are five thousand people round about the Monastery. The whole quarter, and from well beyond.

The Archbishop. For them? Or for us?

The Civil Lieutenant. They seem mainly indifferent. But it's at the mercy of a false step.

The Archbishop [To The Knight of the Watch]. The nuns may have armed men in their gardens. Place a party of your men in the gardens.

[5] A historic fact.

The Knight of the Watch. Monseigneur, when in future you call upon me for an operation like this, please let me be told in advance what I am being sent to do. For what you are asking is not at all to my liking.

The Archbishop. Don't worry: I know what I am doing. If there is sin, it is on my head.

The Civil Lieutenant. See, Sisters, how by your obstinacy you are making us all suffer!

The Official. And see how many of your pupils have had to be taken away from you, because of that obstinacy, how many might have been given to you, who might perhaps have become nuns. If all these souls are damned, it is you who will answer for it before God.

Sister Angélique. Ah! that is horrible!

During these last two lines, SISTER FRANÇOISE *has left the oratory and advanced toward the front.*

The Archbishop. Why haven't you gone out, you? Are you one of those who are leaving?

Sister Françoise. I am not worthy, Monseigneur.

The Archbishop. Always impertinences from these girls! They are pure as angels, and proud as devils.

The Vicar-General. Yes, the devil who said: "I shall not obey!" But that is well known: people are all the stauncher over morals, the more suspect they are over doctrine.

Sister Françoise. Religion has its Mysteries. Evil also has its. One of them is the Mystery of injustice.

The Archbishop. What's that? Theology? And what are you? A philosopheress? A dogmatizeress? At Port-Royal there always comes a moment when one has in front of one a person of that sort. How long have you been here?

Sister Françoise. Five years. Three professing, two as a novice. But the first year doesn't count. I was a child then, and the only thought given to me was to send me away.

The Archbishop. It seems to me now that I recognize you. Your father is Président Clouart, is he not?

Sister Françoise. Yes, Monseigneur.

The Archbishop. You're a pretty girl, a very pretty girl. But you're an arguer: it's in the blood. What is this Mystery of injustice? Where did you find that?

Sister Françoise [*Pointing to the church dignitaries and* OFFICERS OF THE WATCH]. There. They submit us to interrogations at the end of which they tell us that we are perfect young women. Then they condemn us. Next they try to make us guilty to justify our condemnation. What is the good of the interrogations if the case is judged in advance? If we are among those of whom the Scripture says that "they are condemned already"? We are condemned from all sides.

The Civil Lieutenant. Do not say that the King's justice is judged in advance, Sister. Those are words that would do you no good if they were taken down.

The Archbishop. Listen to me. There is the Pope—or rather two popes, for two popes have spoken—then there is the King, then the bishops, then the faculties, the doctors, the communities, and everyone is agreed except a handful of girls, some of whom, like you, are very young, who want to lay down the law to the men of learning and to the authorities. That is an intolerable rebelliousness. Where should we arrive, in all the Orders, if each person set about thinking for himself? There is a creed, there is a canon, there are superiors and inferiors. And why should God have placed men over them unless it is that they should be obeyed? We live, thank god, in a realm in which the subaltern remains always in his place. As far as my share in it goes, it shall not be said that this natural order can be reversed. I shall never allow it.— And to think that so little was asked of you! You were asked to be like the others, do you hear? simply *like the others*!

Sister Françoise. We are different, and that is, in fact, the only complaint they have against us. We are different, but Christianity is different, Monseigneur. In my turn I will say to you, Monseigneur: listen to me, listen to this. In a village there was a priest who spent his time reading his breviary. Then the village people began calling him "Jansenist." In a convent there were some young pupils who always went about with their eyes lowered: then people started treating them as Jansenists. In every place where Christianity is taken a little more seriously than elsewhere, those who take it so are called Jansenists and treated as accursed and plague-stricken. It is the love we bear towards God that draws upon us the world's hatred. The world hates us as it hated Jesus Christ.

The Archbishop. Yes, of course, you are saints! Sainthood! Sainthood! You live with your eyes raised or lowered; I am obliged to look out at a man's height. I have to handle men. I have to make use of them. I have to fit in with them. All that in as Christian a way as possible. The art of living with one's neighbor is not learned in the clouds, nor in prayers.

Sister Françoise. We know that, Monseigneur. We are a community. [*To* Sister Angélique de Saint-Jean.] Sister! say something. Support me!

Sister Angélique. God saw to it, of His grace, that we were trained and far better grounded in the true principles of religion and piety than many, many religious persons are. God has so unified our cause with that of the Church that it seems as if they are two inseparable things, and that no one can oppress her or defend her without oppressing or defending us with her.

The Archbishop. The Church is you and you alone! Are not those, once again, words without any parallel? This is the greatest pride in a girl that I have ever known. But did not Monsieur de Saint-Cyran say: "For the last six hundred years there has been no Church"? [*To the* Vicar-General.] That's aimed at us. [*To* Sister Françoise.] There is the source of that unbendingness which puffs up presumption, nourishes disdain, keeps alive a proud gloom and a spirit of ostentatious singularity, and makes the world feel that virtue is too burdensome, the Gospel excessive, Christianity impossible. The world is already so close to finding Christianity too austere—and you add to it! What will become of us when everyone turns away from a religion that has been rendered impracticable?

Sister Françoise. You want numbers, we want purity. We do not like half-Christians.

The Archbishop. We do not want numbers. We merely want to continue to exist.

Sister Françoise. Those in power want to continue to exist, and at the cost of no matter what compromises;

perish principles, rather than their power. That is why they are against us, and that is why we are condemned.

The Archbishop. If there were not churchmen who are politicians—and you count them among those in power, do you not?—there would never have been a Church, or she would not have lasted long. And you, young women of Port-Royal—you would not even exist, any more than your Directors. After all, it was a bishop of Paris who founded you!

Sister Françoise. And please Heaven we shall not exist, rather than pay for it at this price!

The Archbishop. This evil of the world which has to be treated with and lived with, and which sometimes in passing smirches us—it is we who take it upon us, in order that you may remain unspotted in your precincts. And you reproach us for it!

Sister Françoise. You are, Monseigneur, a member of the Académie Française. Monsieur Arnauld d'Andilly, Sister Angélique's father, refused to be a member, and not without causing some stir. It all holds together, and all along the line.

The Archbishop. You are a mad, impertinent girl, and don't know what you're saying. To refuse the Academy is a vanity like any other: it forms part of the false honor with which you so easily fall in. Because these girls' morals are good, they think they may do anything; but it is nothing for morals to be good when the spirit is astray. All your works are lost, and you with them, if you deviate on a single point. To have the conduct and the sentiments that the Church desires is not everything: one must also speak as the Church speaks today.

Sister Françoise. Today?

The Archbishop [*Sharply*]. Today, and always.

Sister Françoise. But first you said "today," Monseigneur.

The Archbishop. What are you trying to make me say? What a joy, is it not, to think that a word may have slipped from me! You wish me to have said that there is a Christianity that changes, that turns to every wind of doctrine, that adjusts itself to the tone of the day, and a Christianity that is one and immutable, the true one, which is yours. "The Archbishop has come: the world has come in with him. We—we are eternity."

Sister Françoise. Christianity was a perfect work from the beginning, because divine. We do not understand how people can be forever retouching it. It is heresy that is always innovating.

The Archbishop. So it is I, it is we, who are heretics! . . . And is there not something devilish in this, something of woman too, that makes you succeed in turning the thing upside down in this way? It is by such words, I tell you, that you do the worst injury to your House.

Sister Françoise. Me, do an injury to my House, when I believe it is only today that I understand it!

The Archbishop [Pointblank]. What do you think about grace? Have they not spoken to you of its efficacy? What is it right to believe about that?

Sister Françoise. Heigh, Monseigneur, I was never taught about that. Those questions don't belong to our sex. I beg you to tell me what it is right to believe.

The Archbishop. Yes, yes, just look at that. . . . [*To the* VICAR-GENERAL.] She's afraid of giving herself away. [*To the Sister.*] We claim to know better than anyone, we argue and we cavil, but, when we are asked a question, we play the simpleton. "That doesn't belong to my sex."—There will be a second batch, I tell you, and that time we shall not let you slip. You too will be cut off.

Sister Françoise. I shall not be cut off from Him Who is within me.

The Archbishop. You are cut off from Him already more than you think.

Sister Françoise. Monseigneur! Do you say that to me? Our Lord spoke to the Devil more gently than you speak to your daughters. Till today there was only Monsieur Bail who was ready to threaten us with hell-fire and compare us to witches, to the possessed women of Auxonne! That, though, was bearable. But our pastor has only to speak to us to make us weep! If you were a Calvinist, yes, or a foreigner—how should I know? an Englishman, a Spaniard. . . . But you, our Father! And he, our King! [*She sobs.*]

The Archbishop. Silence! Don't weep. You have no cause.

Sister Françoise. I'm weeping for grief at being right.

The Archbishop. I too am right, and I don't weep.

Mother Agnès. True piety does not check tears; it makes them flow where they should.

Sister Françoise. There is another God than the gods of the world, who have set themselves up to judge, and to be judged of no one. There is another judge in Heaven, who will render us more justice. There is another world, where we shall be preserved from you.

The Archbishop. Come, come, you'll not die before you see me again. I promise you it will be soon. Later, when we're in Heaven, we'll see how things go! [SISTER FRANÇOISE *in a fury leaves the room.*] There's a dangerous little girl. And mad! mad! They're all mad. But mind! There is, in all they say, especially the ones who have some experience, such a twisting of reasons that it would not take much to make one feel guilty, at a certain point in their talk, if common sense did not come back to me. I have my common sense, 'sdeath! and I want only one thing: for you to obey. Well then? Can I not be terrible? Shall I not have the last word as against you? No! it shall never be said that a few little nuns held out against an archbishop, and an archbishop of *Paris*, as I am. I'll never endure it, I will not be balked. We shall see if you will get the better of me.—A little nun! A slip of a girl!— Well! are they coming, the ones who are leaving? There's been enough gentleness used. If they don't come willingly, they shall be seized by the feet and by the head and dragged out by force. [*He tests his pulse, surreptitiously. To the* VICAR-GENERAL.] My fever's on me again. It was bound to happen, with all this trouble. Ah! religion's a difficult business. [*To a nun who has her veil lowered, because she is about to pass through the door leading to the courtyard.*] There's Madeleine-Christine, hola! that's Madelon Briquet. [*To the* OFFICIAL.] I call her Madelon because I knew her father well. It was Monsieur Briquet, the Advocate-General. [*To* THE SISTER.] Why are *we* off to the carriages? We aren't being taken away, as far as

I know. But there's no holding 'em,[6] we must disobey in
all things. Your turn will come soon, Madelon Briquet.
[THE SISTER *unveils*.] Oh! good God! It's not she.
Another mistake.

SISTER FRANÇOISE, *who has come in again, kneels down
before the* ARCHBISHOP.

Sister Françoise. Monseigneur, I left your presence in
such anger that I did not think of asking you for your
blessing. I ask you for it very humbly, Monseigneur.

The Archbishop [*After giving her the blessing*]. But
take care: we have our eyes on you. That's what spoils
everything—having such ranging minds. You don't like
half-Christians. We don't like the half-informed. In well-
regulated communities they never give responsible positions to women with intelligence. They leave *them* to
their cells, for they know well that intelligent people
always make a mess of something in a community. Withdraw now to your room and listen to what God has to
say. There's such a beautiful saying in the Scripture: wait
while I remember—how does it go, now?

The Vicar-General [*Prompting him*]. Ducam eam in
solitudinem . . .

The Archbishop. Yes, that's it! that's exactly it! *Ducam
eam in solitudinem et loquar ad cor ejus.* How did that
escape me? Ah! my poor Sister Clouart, one has too many
things in one's head. You see, I haven't only you; I've
my diocese to govern. . . .

The Civil Lieutenant. Monseigneur, the carriages are
drawn up. [*To the* ABBESS.] Mother . . .

The Abbess. Monseigneur, I ask you for your blessing.
[*She kneels down. He gives her the blessing.*] May I know
where you are sending me?

The Archbishop [*Taking her roughly by the shoulder*].
Come, come, out with you. It's enough that I know where
you are being sent.

The ABBESS *goes out.* MOTHER AGNÈS *and* PRIORESS *kneel
in their turn in front of the* ARCHBISHOP. *To one, then*

---

[6] "Mais il n'y a pas moyen"—the actual words used. The
whole of this small scene is historic.—AUTHOR'S note.

to the other, after blessing them, he says: "I commend myself to your prayers." *They rise to their feet.*

Mother Agnès [*To one of the young* SISTERS]. I ask your forgiveness, Sister, if I have ever offended you. Because of my infirmities, allow me not to kneel down a second time, and to ask you for it simply with my hands clasped.

They embrace. Then MOTHER AGNÈS *withdraws to the back, where she is embraced by all the* SISTERS, *who also kiss her hands.*

The Archbishop [*To* SISTER ANGÉLIQUE]. You will suffer: your prayers will be good. Do not forget me in them.

Sister Angélique. The men who persecute us must be the special object of our tenderness and our prayers.

The Archbishop [*Leaning forward, and taking the* SISTER'S *two clasped hands, which he encloses and holds in his*]. Me, persecute you! I protest to you that there is only I and one other person at Court who are preventing you from being persecuted in another fashion. Why are you afraid of me? They have made a habit, here, of trembling. . . . I want you to love me. You will be only the better for everything that has happened.

Sister Angélique. Alas!

The Archbishop. Who, after all, knows better than you that one finds the Cross only at the foot of the Cross? And on that I can indeed give you an assurance: those who love to suffer will be satisfied. But mind! If you thought that to suffer is all that is needed in order to be saved, you were greatly mistaken. It is no good suffering— if one is outside the Church, it serves no purpose. How many heretics have there been who have exposed themselves to the torture—who indeed longed for it—and now are burning in the fire? The Devil also has his martyrs.

Sister Angélique. I see that I shall be spared nothing.

The Archbishop. You have not even a notion of what I am sparing you. And besides, are you one of those who spare others much? [*Softly.*] And I—am I a man who is spared much? Always crossed, flouted, calumniated. You don't know what my life is like.

Sister Angélique. Monseigneur, where am I being taken?
Am I allowed to know?

The Archbishop. To the Annonciades, on the Boule-
vard.

Sister Angélique. How shall I be treated there?

The Archbishop. I will be frank with you: severely.
You will be under lock and key, I fear; you will see nobody from within or without, you will not be able to
communicate with anyone, except those who will come
to see if you are still persisting. That is severe, but it is
necessary.

Sister Angélique. Are we excommunicated? Forgive me;
in my bewilderment, I no longer remember everything
you said to me.

The Archbishop. You are not excommunicated, for the
time being.

Sister Angélique. Who directs the Annonciades?

The Archbishop. I will be frank with you: the Jesuits.
[SISTER ANGÉLIQUE *clasps her hands together, and her
body shudders from head to foot.*] It was the Jesuits
who drew up their constitutions,[7] and they are practi-
cally their founders.

Sister Angélique. And no doubt it has not been laid
down how long this confinement will last.

The Archbishop. As long as you do not change.

Sister Angélique. Nor how long I shall be deprived
of the sacraments.

The Archbishop. As long as you do not change.

Sister Angélique. Shall I be shut up with others of
our sisters? Shall we be at least two to a cell?

The Archbishop. You will be alone.

Sister Angélique. Monseigneur, do not place us in this
void. There are some of us whom God would desert,
and who would desert themselves: they would crumble
to dust. You don't know what you are risking.

The Archbishop. At least there is no temptation for
Sister Angélique de Saint-Jean.

Sister Angélique. Don't ask of her more than her
strength can bear.

---

[7] This is untrue. But Sister Angélique, in her *Relation de
Captivité,* bears witness that it was said to her.—AUTHOR's note.

The Archbishop. Obey, and you will be asked for nothing more. But remember this: I am telling it to you for the last time. You at one and the same moment, deny to religion free will and insinuate into it a spirit of liberty: liberty from the yoke of the pope, liberty from the yoke of the Jesuits, liberty for man in his examination of the word of God. You hate everything that smacks of authority and, above all, the authority of one man alone. Liberty, verity, purity: that is your war cry! Well, purity—it is I, and those whom I represent, who defend it, and it is you people who tend to corrupt it. As for verity, there is only one: that which is given by the pope and on which all the faithful are agreed. That young person said that Christianity was *different.* Certainly, and it is its glory to be so. But there can be no being different *inside* Christianity; if one is, there's a name for that, and it is precisely that name that is being thrown at the people of this place. I know very well how your friends speak and write about me—that I am published abroad as a madman and a figure of fun, and this and that: there are always frogs who croak in the marshes of Port-Royal. I am, in point of fact, only a humble servant of God, very feeble, very deficient maybe in the lights I ought to have, very unworthy maybe. But the service I perform, I perform according to my conscience, and I perform it with unshakable firmness, because the one and only verity is what I serve. Not to mention the service of the King, which I perform at the same time. "Everything that causes disturbance in religion causes as much in the state": those are the very words Cardinal de Richelieu used to me when he had Monsieur de Saint-Cyran arrested. And the King himself has repeated them to me many times. That is why I am very firm, since I serve both verity and the state, and that is why I give you my assurance that all will be restored to order, either by me or, if not, by those who come after me. We have begun; we shall finish.—You are about to leave, Sister. I give you my blessing, and I bless in you the motion which will lead you to understand me, and to sign.

He blesses the Sister, *who has knelt down. When he has blessed her, she raises her right hand, hesitantly, as though from a kind of mimicry, and says, as the* Arch-bishop *and his train depart:*

Sister Angélique. May this hand remain pure from what is expected of it!

Mother Agnès [*Softly to* Sister Angélique]. You dread a condition in which the sayings of Scripture would have lost their force for you. Since this is imminent for you, I give you one which you will draw from within yourself, yet based upon Scripture. The Prophet Job said: "Although he should kill me, I will trust in him." You—you will say: "Though I have killed Him, yet will I trust in Him."

Sister Angélique. Yes, Mother, I will say that.

They embrace. Then Mother Agnès *goes and kneels at the oratory, and departs.*

The expelled Sisters, *carrying bags or parcels, begin to move through and out, kneeling in the oratory on their way. One of them, halfway, points to her bag, cries: "Oh! I've forgotten what I most need!" and turns back.* Sister Angélique de Saint-Jean *has remained in front.* Sister Flavie *enters and approaches her, followed by* Sister Françoise *and* Sister Gabrielle, *who keep slightly to one side.*

Sister Flavie. I hope, my very dear Sister, that you may soon come back to us. Oh! what a day! Never have I seen the like. And poor Mother Agnès, whom I love so much, alas! O God! that she should leave like that!

Sister Angélique. You are on good terms with Monseigneur. Beg him to give her back to us quickly.

Sister Flavie. Me, on good terms with Monseigneur? I have only seen him once, at the interrogation. And you know that I never meddle in anything, and that here I'm nobody.

Sister Angélique. All the same, I once saw you whisper in his ear.

Sister Flavie. What! in his ear? As if I had even noticed that Monseigneur has ears!

Sister Angélique. You very often talk with Monsieur Bail and Monsieur Chamillard, who are his tools.

Sister Flavie. You've never seen me with either of them for more than a quarter of an hour. And what should I say to him? I can only tell him my sins, and that only at confession. Lord Jesus! what else should I say to him? On the other hand, I have sometimes come across people who were telling tales, and I trod on their toes to warn them that they must tell nothing against their neighbor. —You distrust me. Oh! all this distrust kills me. Nobody loves me, me who live for others! Alas! if you knew what this poor heart suffers!

Sister Angélique [*Changing her tone*]. It was you who pried open the cover of my bag, in which you thought I kept secret papers.

Sister Flavie. Me, Sister! . . .

Sister Angélique. It was you who went with a lantern the other night to the water-conduit vault, to see if there was not a hole through which we might be passing letters to our Directors.

Sister Flavie [*Indicating the other* SISTERS]. Speak softly.

Sister Gabrielle. And it's she, a short while ago, who was Third at the grill, and made me promise my father that I would sign! Without saying a word. Simply by being there.

Sister Angélique [*Showing* SISTER FLAVIE *the piece of paper fallen from her pocket, which she picked up not long before*]. Do you know this? The list, written in your hand, of the twelve sisters who are being taken away. It's you who drew up that list and gave it to the Archbishop; and this is the copy you had made and were keeping about you.—Do you think I can't see you, with your face pale as death?

SISTER FLAVIE *does, in fact, go through a moment of disturbance, in which one can read, if one will, on her face "the pallor and wildness of Judas" attributed to her by Sister Geneviève Pineau in the* Relation des Persécutions.
Then she pulls herself together.

Sister Flavie. I shall not be sorry to be in a House where these twelve no longer are, so that another archbishop will be recognized there than Monsieur Arnauld.

Sister Angélique. I have no reason to blush for that name, for it is like confessing the name of God to confess ours.

Sister Flavie. The treatment you are to be made to undergo, my very dear Sister, will no doubt flatten out in you that haughtiness which is, of all things in the world, the most unseemly in this place.

Sister Angélique. You who used to be so friendly and trusting with me, as though we were not sisters by the veil, but by blood. Ah! now I know the reason for so much hate. It is there.

Sister Flavie. Were you not, Sister, warned against attachments? You have not been taken unawares! And besides! what hate? I am with my superiors. It is you others who are forever trying to escape.

Sister Angélique. And if, after the death of Monseigneur, there came another archbishop who commanded you to condemn this one, or another pope who likewise sailed on the opposite tack, would you follow them?

Sister Flavie. I would turn as they did, and follow them with all my heart.

Sister Angélique. And if there came five or six archbishops of Paris, each of whom made you undo what his predecessor had ordered you to do . . .

Sister Flavie. If fifty archbishops of Paris succeeded one another, I would always do what the one in charge commanded me. I am in the hands of my superiors: they can move me about like a corpse. Even if you obey an unjust command, God will not fail to recompense your obedience.

Sister Angélique. How you mix up what serves your ends with what you claim to serve! Intoxicated with obedience! And you are no longer capable of anything but worshiping your intoxication. Ah! it is good, is it not? to be under the wing of power. One is better there than under the wing of Jesus Christ. For there are others, perhaps, for whom blind obedience is a doctrinal attitude —open to objection, but at least religious and sincere. For you, to obey is to be, whatever happens, the protégée of power. Of power which will make you an abbess. For one wants to obey, but that's because one wants to command. Obey the great to command the small, and command them in one's own way. Our liberty—ours—is that of God's children: it leads us to prison. Yours is the liberty of the children of Belial: to be able to do anything, because you will always do it with impunity.

Sister Flavie. I sacrificed enough, by entering here, for something to be given me from here.

Sister Angélique. Sacrificed what? And to be given what? A position? But one does not seek a position: one refuses it, or one accepts it groaning. A position! When the first position is in the kitchen and at the sink. And that came to you in a day. Yes, in exactly one day: the day when the Archbishop paid a visit here. That taste for being an abbess was slipped into your head: you were changed round in an instant. This sort of childish ambition, without any warning, any preparation. . . . Forty years of purity corrupted in an instant.

Sister Flavie. I shall tell the Archbishop—that you have spoken of him as a corrupter.

Sister Angélique. You make me sorry for you, Sister! Stay, then, with your sisters of obedience, and lord it over them. You at least know why you will be signing.

Sister Flavie. Those who die without signing will have their bodies thrown on the garbage heap! But there won't by any. All of you! you'll all sign! In the end, you will see things so strange that it will be you who will ask to sign, and ask it on your knees.

Sister Angélique. I do not know what dreadful power is inspiring you. That signature is the mark of the Beast. [*She crosses herself, on her bosom.*]

Sister Flavie. We were made to understand each other, Sister, you the quite perfect one and I the very imperfect, as those who are brought together for the novitiate, to sustain one another. With so little proportion, we had at least this in common, that we were not stupid. But you have let the carriage pass by. And now it is a different carriage that is taking you away. God 'ild you, Sister, God 'ild you! May the good God take care of you!

Sister Angélique. Just listen to her, the one who was received at Port-Royal out of——[*She checks herself.*]

Sister Flavie. Say the word, do, if you dare. But you won't dare. "Out of charity." Yes, I was received at Port-Royal out of charity. And it is you, the niece of Monsieur Arnauld, who cast it in my face! And yet were we not told often enough that it was the poorest among us who were the first in God's sight? You were free to cast anything in my face, but not that. I'm ashamed for you, Sister, niece to Monsieur Arnauld.

She goes back into the inner precincts, followed, after a while, by SISTER GABRIELLE.

Sister Françoise. I am appalled.

Sister Angélique. I suspected her for a long time. Now she has given herself away; tell everyone. You saw how she kept looking at him—at the Archbishop. He can do no wrong! He has bewitched her! Strong, aren't they? both of them, but with what a sorry strength! Their master's strength.—Keep the secret of where our Directors are, more closely than ever: she would have them all put in prison.

Sister Françoise. Don't leave my soul in her hands!

Sister Angélique. I would ask God for your death, rather than see you sign!

Sister Françoise. Ask Him for that! [SISTER ANGÉLIQUE *takes a step towards the door leading to the courtyard.*] I don't want the carriage to take you away! I shall lie down across the gateway. . . .

Sister Angélique. Don't be eccentric.

Sister Françoise. And yet, this change that has just come over my soul . . .

Sister Angélique. It's no more than a natural movement. Grace has no part in it.

Sister Françoise. Even now you try to strike me down. Always striking me down!

Sister Angélique. I'm telling you the truth.

Sister Françoise. I rushed to the oratory: I had to pray, at all costs. If I had not prayed there and then, I think I would have fainted.

Sister Angélique. How did you pray? What did you say? What words could you find?

Sister Françoise. I think I simply said: "My Lord and my God!"

Sister Angélique. That and nothing more? [*A vague gesture from* SISTER FRANÇOISE.] You said everything.

Sister Françoise. I listened; I could not help listening. Sister, please answer my question: is he a man who judges us guilty, or is he a man who is merely earning the wage he has been paid in advance?

Sister Angélique. Don't try to see into these things. Certain souls have in them something of everything. And sometimes all at once.

Sister Françoise. Is he a man who believes in God, or is he, like the Bishop of——

Sister Angélique. Don't try to see into these things. If one could see who believes and who does not believe . . .

Sister Françoise. A dignitary of the Church not be what his cloth suggests!

Sister Angélique. Perhaps there are some who are like that, and who deserve above all to be pitied.

Sister Françoise. Ah! Sister, pity for that! From you!

Sister Angélique. What! no mercy for a person who, under this dress [*She touches her scapulary.*], might be troubled, feel a doubt. . . .

Sister Françoise. Doubt of what?

Sister Angélique. Doubt . . . about everything to do with religion and Providence; doubt whether the world is really so ordered as to justify us in living as we live.

Sister Françoise. No mercy for a person who, feeling such doubt, did not immediately tear off that habit—which would then be an abominable deception. For God sometimes punishes a whole community for the sin of one alone.

Sister Angélique. A whole community . . . punished . . . for the sin of one alone.

Sister Françoise. And rightly. Disease in one finger can make the whole body ill.

Sister Angélique [*Aside*]. What have I done to be so utterly deserted?

Sister Françoise. I ought not to have come back and asked Monseigneur for his blessing. I ought not to have said so much to him. The positions are taken up; discussion is useless. While I was speaking, you were praying. You were the one who was right.

Sister Angélique. Did I pray? I don't know. I was in another world; I still am. And perhaps I only prayed with my tears.

Sister Françoise. I saw them falling on the cross of your scapulary. . . .

Sister Angélique. That was their place.

Sister Françoise. Mother . . . let me call you by this name—Mother—now that you are on the verge of great suffering.

Sister Angélique. You shall call me by it when you know how I have borne the suffering.

Sister Françoise. Sister—Mother, dear Mother, where are you? Shall I ever see you again?

Sister Angélique. I have nursed you for five years, with milk that no mother . . . But I don't know what I'm thinking of, saying that to you. . . . You are grown up enough, you could stand on your own feet, even if I left you. But I'm not leaving you: one only leaves what one ceases to love.

Sister Françoise. Is it you, saying that to me? You who a little while ago were reproaching me so sternly for the small human friendship you thought I wanted to claim?

She takes SISTER ANGÉLIQUE *by the hand.* SISTER ANGÉLIQUE *gently frees her hand.*

Sister Angélique. We must not, at any price, let a human soul, by its shortcomings, discourage us from ever again having confidence in other souls. It would have succeeded too well, if it had killed in us our trust in our neighbor.

Sister Françoise. Ah! is that all?

Sister Angélique. You have understood what you never understood before. For you the Gates of Day have just opened. . . .

Sister Françoise. What day? What a tarnished one it is!

Sister Angélique. As for me, I have gone in at the Gates of Darkness, with a horror which you cannot know, and which must not be known by anybody.

Sister Françoise. What darkness? I pray God that by His grace I may one day be in Heaven at your feet.

The First Chaplain [Entering from the courtyard]. Sister, the carriage. . . . Don't linger. The Sisters of the Visitation are arriving.

Sister Angélique. The Sisters of the night: the night that is descending upon our Monastery. That night, and the other night. *[She prostrates herself.]* I kiss the ground of this house, to which I shall perhaps never come back, as we make our young ones kiss the ground as soon as they step out of bed, as the first action of their day— when they are still girls. . . . *[She kisses the ground, and rises.]*

Sister Françoise. I shall be faithful to that time when I was a girl. I shall be faithful. . . . I shall be faithful. . . .

Sister Angélique. Be faithful on behalf of all the Sisters, and of all men, who . . .

Sister Françoise. You will find God and Port-Royal everywhere. One is never alone when one has faith.

Sister Angélique. My child!—I don't know what I shall find.

Sister Françoise [Looks at her with astonishment, then asks her in a low voice]. What do you mean?

Sister Angélique [Pulling herself together]. I mean that the night which is beginning will pass like all the things of this world. And the truth of God will endure eternally, and will deliver all those who desire to be saved by it alone.

She has said this with an effort, in so strange—so mechanical—a way, and seeming so absent from what she is saying, that SISTER FRANÇOISE is left bewildered. She follows SISTER ANGÉLIQUE DE SAINT-JEAN with her eyes as she makes her way towards the door to the courtyard and disappears through it. SISTER FRANÇOISE buries her face in her hands, and returns into the inner precincts.

The scene remains empty, for rather a long time. The bell is heard ringing for Nones (the mystery evoked by this hour is that of the death of Jesus Christ). Then: the noise of carriages outside. Then a sister—anonymous—

comes out from within and stands motionless against the chapel door, gazing towards the still open door to the courtyard, with an expression of intense expectancy, which changes suddenly to an expression of horror—and then she moves back into the inner precincts, backwards, branded with horror.

A pause. From the chapel nuns' voices rise, singing Nones, recto tono (in unison), and will continue to recite the service until the curtain falls.

Finally, entering by the door from the courtyard, there appears the new MOTHER who has been appointed to govern the monastery. She kneels down at the threshold of the oratory, then moves on towards the inner precincts. Behind her, one after another, each of the twelve "Sisters of the night"—dressed wholly in black—who are replacing the twelve condemned sisters enters, kneels for a moment, then moves on and disappears slowly to the right, into the inner precincts.

TOBIAS AND SARA

(L'histoire de Tobie et de Sara)

by

PAUL CLAUDEL

Translated by

ADELE FISKE

Published by arrangement with Librairie Gallimard. Copyright
1942 by Librairie Gallimard. English translation copyright ©
1962 by Adele Fiske.

All applications to perform this play must be made to Librairie
Gallimard, 5 rue Sébastien-Bottin, Paris VII, France.

CHARACTERS

Old Tobias
Anna, *his wife*
Young Tobias
Sara
The Angel Raphael, *who is also* Azarias
Three Narrators
The Dog
The Fish
A Servant

Acts I *and* III *at* Ninive; Act II, *the road from* Ninive *to*
    Ecbatana.

*A two-level stage, the higher level upstage. A screen as back-
drop, for motion-picture projections. At stage center, a raised
platform. Thus there are three levels for action, one behind the
other. On either side of the stage stands a* Chorus, *to interpret
or comment on the action. One of the* Chorus *on each side
holds a large book.*

TOBIAS AND SARA

ACT ONE

SCENE I—*On the screen we see—or imagine—a desolate land, intersected by salt lakes, rising clouds of naphtha fumes, winding rivers, snow-covered mountains: the same land that we look down upon in a flight from Iraq to Iran today.*

CHORUS I. Where is this desolate land?

Chorus II. The desert that lies between Ninive and the land of the Medes.

Chorus I. I know it! I know it only too well!

Chorus II. Paradise has withered the green trees with their healing leaves, with their fruit of eternal life, that grew on the bank of the Tigris and the Euphrates—you will look for them in vain!

Chorus I. Over there, far away, beyond that dreadful desert . . .

Chorus II. Over there, far away, beyond that dreadful desert . . .

Chorus I. There the human soul has been driven!

Chorus II. So poor! So disinherited! So needy! So abandoned!

Chorus I. What is written in the Book?

Chorus II [*Reading with nasal accent*]. *In a desert land, a land where is no way and no water . . .*[1]

Chorus I [*Natural tone*]. *A desert land, a land where is no way and no water*—— Does that mean anything to you?

Chorus II [*Natural tone*]. *A desert land, a land where is no way and no water . . .*

Then have I lifted up my eyes to heaven . . .

Chorus I. That was the best thing you could do.

Chorus II. To the mountains! *I have raised my eyes to the mountains whence help shall come to me.*[2]

[1] Ps. 62 : 3.
[2] Ps. 120 : 1.

149

SCENE II—*Enter the three* NARRATORS; *one, a woman, who may hold a large Basque tambourine. They take their places in the tribune. They chant:*

NARRATORS [——*indicates change from one narrator to another*].

In Israel there was a man named Tobias of the tribe of Nephthali

——who had been led captive to Assyria with his tribe, by King Salmanasar.

Chorus ||ıⁱ|ıⁱ|| *indicates lowering and raising of indistinct voice*].

Who ||ıⁱ|ıⁱ|| captive to Assyria by King Salmanasar!

Narrators. He was led captive to Ninive with his tribe by King Salmanasar—and even in captivity he did not abandon the ways of truth and the holy rites of Israel!

——He fed the hungry.

——He clothed the naked, he gave honorable burial to the dead, and every day, morning and evening, he lifted up his hands to honor the Eternal!

Woman NARRATOR *raises tambourine without striking it.*

Chorus. Tobias! the man who is mindful of the dead, who honors this poor thing that was once a man.

Narrators. Now by the will of God Tobias has become—blind! By the will of God his eyes have been closed to the light of this world.

A SERVANT *goes to* TOBIAS, *who is sitting on a rug at the* NARRATOR'S *feet.*

Chorus I. Now by the will of God Tobias has become blind . . .

Chorus II. By the will of God his eyes have been closed to the light of this world.

Chorus I [*Reading in book*]. May my eyes never cease to be lifted to the Lord.

Chorus II [*Reading in book*]. To the mountains! May my eyes be raised to the mountains whence help shall come to me.

Tobias [*Swaying back and forth in the Jewish fashion*].
The Lord has given! The Lord has taken away. . . .[3]

One of each CHORUS *comes to listen to* TOBIAS.

Chorus [*Turning their back*]. Amen!

Chorus I [*One voice speaking*]. What is he saying?

Chorus II [*One voice, speaking*]. He says: Praised be
the Will of God.

Chorus I [*One voice, speaking*]. Amen!

Narrators. And Tobias who had been a rich man lost
all his fortune [*in natural tone*] except for a little flock
that you will see and this dog that will never abandon
him. —No, he will never abandon him! —the same dog
will lick the wounds of Lazarus!—[*Chanted.*] And Tobias
who had been a rich man lost all his fortune. And he
lived in Ninive with his wife and his son, who was also
called Tobias. [*Enter* ANNA, *wife of* TOBIAS, *led by* YOUNG
TOBIAS. *She holds a stick in her hand. They sit to left
and right of the old man.*] And Tobias persevered in
prayer! [ANNA *takes her husband's head in her hands and
pulls it down to her. She wipes his eyes with a corner of
her veil.*] And at the same time, far away on the other
side of the desert—in a city of the Medes called Rages—
there was another Israelite called Raguel. . . . [*On the
screen Rages and* RAGUEL *appear, somewhat indistinctly.*]
This Raguel had a daughter called Sara. [*She is seen on
the screen, or in person on the stage, at back.*]

Chorus I. Sara: she is the human soul!

Chorus II. Exiled!

Chorus I. Exiled, disinherited, dishonored, despised!
    She is there, dishonored, in a far-off land.

Chorus II. Exiled, dishonored, despised, trodden down
by a faceless enemy!
    Who will come to her aid?

Voice of Sara [*From afar*]. To you O Lord I turn my
face, to you I raise my eyes!

    You are the mountain that in my humiliation
    I climb from the foot to the very peak.

    I entreat you, Lord, deliver me from the bonds of
        this uncleanness,

[3] Job, 1 : 21.

—or take me away from the face of the earth!

Young Tobias. Father, it is strange, it seems to me I hear a voice, far away, lamenting.

Anna. I don't hear anything.

Young Tobias. The voice of a woman far away, praying and lamenting.

Old Tobias. What place is there on this earth, my son,
     what moment of time
     when there is not a voice that laments and prays?

Narrators. Far away in Rages in the land of the Medes —in the days of his prosperity Tobias had entrusted money —ten talents of pure silver—to Raguel, the father of Sara whose voice you have just heard.

ANNA *rises and hustles the* NARRATORS *off, pushing and pulling them roughly, one man to one side, one to the other; she spins the woman around, snatching her tambourine and hitting her on the head with it.*

Anna. Get out! There's nothing more for you to do, I'll explain it all to these people here. [*Mounts tribune to speak.*]

SCENE III

ANNA [*Takes her time, with arms akimbo contemplating the audience. Suddenly she shoots out a rapid stream of talk, from time to time breaking off, or raising her voice to a shrill scream*]. The good God the religion of the good God the religion of the good God religion! I hon—or God! I pr—actice religion! What does God say? What does religion say? God says for us to love our NEAREST neighbor as ourselves. Not our neighbor. Our NEAREST neighbor! Who is our NEAREST neigh—bor? Our wife, our children, they're our near—est neighbor! Do you hear that, old man? do you hear, you with your blind eyes? do you hear, you with your blind ears? THIN—K just the droppings of that swallow and he found a way for it to hit him in the eye! That's what it is to be always stargazing! That's what it is to be always looking up to heaven! Bad luck, bad luck! Serves him right, serves him right! You don't need good eyes when you prefer the

dead to the living and strangers to your own family! Right!
Left! All that money he threw away! All that money *we*
threw away! And now we——haven't even enough sheep
to keep our dog busy, he goes into the city, he works for
strangers. [*Takes a long breath.*] But never never never
will I let my son go away, my only son, to that far away
country, Rages, they call it, something or other, Suze,
Ecbat—ane, Persepolis! That money, that he threw away—
that he lent as he puts it, the old idiot—right and left,
ten talents to Gabelus, ten talents to Raguel! What
would it amount to today, ten talents, with interest, with
compou——nd interest! No, never! never will I let my
son go, Tobias, our dear child, I haven't got any other
child! A child, he's only a child! There's the desert, there
are the lions, there's the climate, there are the robbers,
there are the floods, there are the mount—tains! [*Takes
breath.*] I'd rather lose my money, ten talents, twenty
talents, ten talents of good money. Oi—ooo io ioio! ten
talents of good money with interest, with compo—nd in-
ter-est! [*Takes breath.*] I don't want to lose my son!
[*Complete change of tone.*] That's enough! He'll not take
my son away from me—look at him, wanting to send my
son God knows where, this old fool. [*Returns to former
tone.*] This old fool who can't do anything! I have to take
care of him like a baby! And who is it that keeps the house
going? Who is it that does all the work? work, work, work
the poor woman! use up her heart! use up her hands! a
yard of cloth to weave—to bring in two copper cents! And
when she comes back from work, when she does the
washing, cooks the dinner! What good is it just to pray?
What good is it just to look up to heaven when you're
blind? blind eyes—blind hands—blind ears! Blind mind!
Kha kha kha kha khakha kha! [*She comes down from
tribune.*]

SCENE IV

Enter DOG *who tugs at* YOUNG TOBIAS *and tries to pull
him away.* ANNA *drives him off with her stick but he keeps*

returning. Now he jumps up to lick the face of OLD
TOBIAS, *now he tries again, growling, to draw* YOUNG
                    TOBIAS *away.*

YOUNG TOBIAS. Down, down, old boy!

Anna. Get out! Just wait till I give you a good whack!
Can't you leave us alone, you good-for-nothing! You
worthless mutt!

Old Tobias. Don't hurt him! He's a good dog, he knows
his duty. He keeps us alive by his job.

Anna. He's like you, he's in league with you too! He's
just like you—trying to take my child away from me——

DOG *sits up and begs, his tongue hanging out.*

SCENE V

*On screen appears an immense flock of sheep with dogs,
asses, and camels. Bellowing and sound of bells, the dogs
busy on every side. If there is no projection, one of the*
NARRATORS *can describe the scene. During it the* CHORUS
                speak in low voices.

CHORUS [*Reading from books*]. He leads Jacob like a little
lamb! And Joseph! he leads Joseph like a little lamb toward
the mother ewe.[4] He knows the number of his stars and
calls each star by its own name.[5]

Old Tobias. What is this tremendous sound that comes
to my ears, the trampling of feet, confused, countless, like
a whole nation on the march?

Young Tobias. Father, don't you know? When an angel
has poured out his chalice on the sun, when in anger
against our plains the sun scorches and burns the soil,[6]
then desert folk set out for the pasture lands.

Chorus I. The meadow lands that are forever green!

[4] Ps. 79 : 2.
[5] Isa. 40 : 26.
[6] Apoc. 16 : 8.

Chorus II. I have raised my eyes to the mountains . . .

Chorus I. . . . the mountains whence help will come to me.

Old Tobias. The mountains whence help will come to us. Beyond the mountains lies the city of Rages, and the money I once left in the hands of Raguel and Gabelus.

Anna. Then the dog's right, of course, isn't he? that cursed dog that wants to snatch my son away from me, and you—instead of holding on to him, you want to give him a shove from behind!

Old Tobias. From the heart of sheep, who will take the desire for fresh grass? from the heart of an old man, the desire for God? from the heart of the young man, this other desire, the desire that is not for money?

Anna. What desire?

Young Tobias. The desire for the horizon!

Old Tobias. And for what lies beyond the horizon.

Anna. There's nothing there! You can't take my child from me! I'm afraid! I'm afraid of the horizon!

Old Tobias. The horizon is stronger than you.

Anna. The sheep can't find their way there without a shepherd.

Old Tobias. God will raise up the shepherd.

Chorus I. He who leads Israel like a shepherd!

Chorus II. —through water and fire . . .

Chorus I. He who leads Israel—

Chorus II. —like a shepherd!

Anna. I don't need any shepherd as long as I hold this little sheep in my arms.

Old Tobias. How can you hold him, when you don't even know his name?

Anna. I don't know his name? Isn't his name Tobias, son of Tobias?

Old Tobias. But he has another name, a name that no one knows, save only the maiden whom God has waiting for him in that faraway land, she alone knows it.

Anna. The girl he'll marry? She'll be chosen by *me*.

Old Tobias. God knows his sheep, each of his sheep, by the name that belongs to it alone.[7]

[7] John, 10 : 3.

Chorus [*Rising from murmur to speech*]. . . . his
sheep.

Chorus I. The shepherd knows his sheep, and his sheep
know him.

Chorus II. The shepherd knows his sheep, each of his
sheep by name, and the sheep know him: he knows his
sheep . . .

Chorus I. —and the sheep know him.

Anna. And I've got only one, and I know him, and he's
enough for me. Get up, you two-footed sheep, it's time
to go home. [*Lifts her stick against* YOUNG TOBIAS.]

Old Tobias. When God pipes the tune, no sheepfold
can—hold back the flock.

Anna. Pipes the tune? What's he talking about? What
tune? I think he's gone crazy.

Old Tobias. When God pipes the tune, no barrier—
can hold back this heart of flesh! When the Lord pipes
the tune, the mountains themselves lift up their feet and
dance! [8] [ANNA *begins a mocking dance*.] A great flock of
mountains, all white, one on top of the other: those enormous sparkling sheep! When God pipes the tune, the
mountains begin to dance!

Anna. He's crazy! He's crazy! [*She exits, dragging*
YOUNG TOBIAS, *but, before leaving the stage, turns and
makes a little defiant dance step against her husband.*]

Chorus. To thee belongs a hymn in Zion and to thee
our vows are paid in Jerusalem!—All flesh shall come to
thee[9]—Mine eyes are raised to the mountains whence
help shall come to me.—To thee our vows will be paid
in Jerusalem!—Jerusalem whose walls are of emerald and
sapphire, whose foundations are of precious stones!

SCENE VI

OLD TOBIAS [*Stands*]. When God pipes the tune, what
flesh can resist him? Not this poor old man whose sight
you have taken away, that he may hear the better. Take

[8] Ps. 113 : 4.
[9] Ps. 64 : 1–2.

for instance the bleating of that little goat that fled to me
for refuge the other day—my wife wanted us to have it for
supper. Lord, you did not have to take away my sight to
improve my hearing. I hear them all—all the little sheep
in the world, bleating, uncountable bleatings . . . those
little voices, one after another, beginning, stopping, beginning again, all the innocents on whom the oppressor has
laid his hand—I hear their voices—and it seems they are
calling me! [*He turns brusquely.*]

Voice of Sara [*From behind scenes, fading up and
down, now faint, now exaggeratedly loud, again almost
lost*].

>To you O Lord I turn my face, to you . . . I raise
>   my eyes!
>You are the mountain that in my humiliation . . .
>   [*Fading*] . . .
>I climb from foot to peak! And I entreat you . . .
>   [*Louder.*]
>Lord, deliver me from this uncleanness ‖‖ or take
>   me away. ‖‖ [*Her voice is lost.*]

Old Tobias. As long as I've been on this earth, Lord,
I've done what I could! I have not left the work of your
hands to be trampled underfoot, nor torn to pieces by the
birds, nor burned up like worthless straw! Even as paper
that has been hallowed by Writing, holy Writing, is
picked up reverently and carefully put away. So have I
reverently gathered up, so have I tenderly laid away, all
these dead bodies of Israelites, your children, all these
dead bodies of Israelites, bodies that will rise again. But
now the time has come when I am no longer any use, the
time for me to speak to you directly! There are things that
the blood of goats and of bulls and black clouds cannot
say to you. You are not the God of the dead but of the
living. You care for more than the bodies of the dead, the
cry of slaughtered innocents goes up to you with this old
man's feeble pleading, it is time I want to tell it all to you.

Voice of Sara [*In distance.*] To you, Lord, ‖‖‖‖ my
eyes! To you ‖‖

Voice of Servant Girl. Ssssssssssssssssssss!

Voice of Anna [*Quarreling, nearby*]. Kha kha kha kha
kha!

Old Tobias [*He has gone up to tribune*]. Lord, in one
of your psalms it says that the rams of the flock are
clothed [10]—the high priest, who wears the pectoral and
the ephod. And I, I am clothed with all human sorrow
from head to foot, and I stand before you, my arms outstretched: in one of my hands is all the weight of human
sorrow, and this chalice full of the blood and tears of the
innocents, and in the other there is the roll of the Scriptures, your promise, that is the counterweight. In one
hand there is this unknown sorrow whose voice I hear
from far away, and in the other there is my own sorrow,
so heavy that I can hardly hold it up and my hand trem-
bles! How long will you leave me like this, my arms
stretched out, and the left hand, instead of balancing the
weight of the right hand, only weighing it down with
heaviness? Has it not been written that where two children of men pray at the same time, I, I am in the midst
of them? [11]

Voice of Sara [*Growing faint in the distance*]. To you,
O Lord.

Voice of Servant Girl. Sssssssssssssss!

Voice of Anna [*Nearby*]. Kha kha kha kha kha!

A servant comes to take TOBIAS *away.*

SCENE VII

*Enormous swirling masses of black mist moving obliquely,
left to right, across the backdrop; luminous spots gleam
out occasionally, or the darkness opens to reveal below in
a sparkling line of light the waters of the ocean.*

CHORUS I. Sorrow, sorrow in the East!

Chorus II. Sorrow, sorrow in the West!

Chorus I. Sorrow, sorrow in the East!

Chorus II. And sorrow, sorrow for its counterweight in
the West!

[10] Ps. 64 : 14.
[11] Matt. 18 : 20.

Chorus I. The one sorrow does not know the other.

Chorus II. But the weight of one is not unknown to the weight of the other.

Chorus I. The young girl in the East who weeps . . .

Chorus II. The old man in the West who prays . . .

Chorus I. They are together in the eyes of God.

Chorus II. Their hearts and their voices mingle and merge.

High in the heavens a scales, dark at first, then luminous, growing into a cross.

Chorus. It is written:

Chorus I. When two souls weep together . . .

Chorus II. When two bodies suffer together . . .

Chorus I. One sorrow springs from the two souls and two bodies . . .

Chorus II. A common sorrow, a consummated prayer. . . .

Chorus I. It is written, I myself am in the midst of them.

Chorus II. To weigh a soul, He uses another soul.

Chorus I. To weigh a sorrow, He uses another sorrow.

Chorus II. By the stars and by music, he brings them to one another.

Chorus I. Raise your eyes, O created being! You who are near, and you who are far off, and I will grant you to invoke the same stars.

Seven lights appear in the heaven, the censers of the seven mediator spirits.[12]

Chorus I. What are these whirlwinds of black smoke?

Chorus II. His strong hands draw the bow as an archer in the clouds.[13]

Chorus I. And his arrow flies from the Rising Sun to the Setting, from West to East.

Chorus II. His chariot cuts a bright furrow in the sea[14]—

Chorus I. But what are these whirlwinds of black smoke?

Chorus II. The dark cloud that rises from the depths

[12] Apoc. 8 : 3.
[13] Gen. 9 : 13.
[14] Ps. 103 : 3.

of the Abyss, from the depths of human sorrow, to the nostrils of the Eternal.

Chorus I. From the depths of the Abyss, from human sorrow, the bitter clouds of blasphemy and prayer rise to the nostrils of the Eternal.

Chorus II. The same fire that burns in the depths of human hearts—

Chorus I. —burns in the eternal censers!

Chorus II. Now the hour has come!

Chorus I. Send thine angel!

Chorus II. O thou who dost aim the arrow . . .

Chorus I. —thou who on the winged wheels of the chariot cleavest the Abyss with blinding rays . . .

Chorus II. Send thine angel! send thine angel before thee to prepare the way, to level the road, to straighten the twisting paths.[15]

A long ray is projected from the top of the stage, revealing on the tribune a dazzling figure, the ANGEL RAPHAEL.

SCENE VIII

ANGEL RAPHAEL [*Mime—extremely slow*].

1. The angel descends from heaven, his hands joined above his head, his arms framing his face. On tips of toes. Vertical.

2. Arms folded in front, united by finger tips, he establishes a sense of the horizontal.

3. Arms extended, he gives sense of instability, as of a diver who has difficulty getting his balance in a denser medium.

4. Arms extended, sign of balancing. Vibration of finger tips, when balance is achieved. [*Twice.*] Hands palm down.

5. Left arm rises, right hand turns palm up.

6. Right arm rises, left hand turns palm up.

[15] Isa. 40 : 3–4, Matt. 3 : 3.

7. Right hand seeks something in left hand. Balance as in 4, but palms up.
8. Repetition of 2.
9. Repetition of 1.
10. Disappears.

ACT TWO

SCENE I—SARA's *dream.*

This scene, and the three following are purely musical. Night, SARA *lying on her couch, on platform. On backdrop appears the Tree of Jesse, growing and putting out branches, at first very misty, but little by little growing clearer in detail. The final flower at the top, however, remains faint, a hint only.*

The Tree of Jesse is garlanded with a phylactery on which we read:

Et egredietur virga de radice Jesse et flos de radice ejus ascendet.[16] *extolletur super Libanum fructus ejus.*

SCENE II—*The Road and the River.*

Little by little the Tree fades away, leaving visible only the phylactery, which changes into a road along which we see an image of the YOUNG TOBIAS *painfully making his way,* THE DOG *running ahead—now he is seen far away, now near, now retracing his own steps.*

---

[16] Isa. 11 : 1 "And a rod shall go forth from the root of Jesse and a flower shall rise up from his root." Ps. 71 : 16 "His fruit shall be exalted above Lebanon."

He himself appears with THE DOG, *and sits down, over-*
come with weariness, on one of the steps at the foot
of the tribune.

On the backdrop an enormous urn appears; from it an
immense river flows in great waves.

THE DOG *looks, then runs behind the backdrop, barking.*

SCENE III—SARA's *Battle with the Seven Phantoms.*

The YOUNG TOBIAS *remains there, his head on his elbow.*
On backdrop swarm and pullulate—now distinct, now
vague—dreadful fossil skeleton forms.

From behind scene the SERVANT GIRL's *voice, hissing and*
syllabizing:

SERVANT GIRL. SSSS! Are you going to kill me too, you
witch, with a curse on you, you serpent—the way your
evil eye murdered those seven men one after the other,
who came to marry you? Whoever touches you, dies. May
nothing alive, neither son or daughter, come from your
womb, accursed, poison, root of poison, serpent, mandra-
gore, husband-killer! Don't you hope for any salvation!
You took their life away, those seven men, one after the
other—and here they are now around you to tear it away
from you again.

SARA *descends from the couch and tribune as though*
fascinated, hypnotized; she moves to stage right, as though
driving back a ghost that recoils before her, then in terror
she backs swiftly to the other end of the stage. There she
turns brusquely as if faced with another terrible phantom!
again retreats step by step, hiding her head in her arms.
Then she turns slowly around, raising and lowering her
arms in a ritual gesture of exorcism, as if all encircled by
menacing forms. Large sweeping gestures with her arms.
Then again slowly from end to end of stage, head turning

*first right, then left as if pursuing a retreating monster.
As she slowly returns she knocks against* TOBIAS; *pausing,
she moves her hands over him as if she were blind. She
disappears behind the tribune.*

SCENE IV—*The Battle against the Fish.*

The river of SCENE I *reappears on screen.* THE DOG *returns and pulls at* TOBIAS *by his garment. Both disappear
behind screen, and at same moment their images appear on
the screen fighting against* THE FISH *in great whirlpools of
muddy water—now plunging down, now surfacing.* TOBIAS,
THE FISH *and* THE DOG, *all dripping with water, then
reappear on the stage where the struggle continues. At
the end, we see the phantom—*TOBIAS *drawn by* THE FISH
across the river. On the stage, TOBIAS *lies exhausted
beside* THE DOG, THE FISH *lying dead at his feet. Night
has come. We see only a line of distant snow-covered
mountains. The stars come out.*

SCENE V

The CHORUS *murmurs the following passage from the
Psalms:*

Save me from the mire of the deep
Save me from the mire in which I stick fast
from the whirlpool that would swallow me up
from the deep, open to absorb me
from the abyss that closes its jaws upon me.[17]

Enter AZARIAS, *who sits down beside* TOBIAS *and wipes
his face with his sleeve.*

TOBIAS. Azarias, my guide, my brother, why did you
abandon me?

[17] Ps. 68 : 3, 15–16.

Azarias. Who was always beside you? whose hand was in yours? My young brother took my hand and held it in his own.

Tobias. Ah, that time, that time, I certainly thought it was all over! The fish, that powerful fish had dragged me down to the bottom of the great river, down into the very entrails of the Tigris, where you cannot tell whether you are drowning in water or in mud. I was dying, dying——

Azarias. Yet my young brother did not let go of the fish.

Tobias. How could I let it go, when you had told me to hold onto it?

Azarias. And now the fish itself has brought you across the river—for see, you are on the other side! And tell me, how else could you have gotten across?

Tobias. It's true, I have crossed the river! That great swift river—it's true, I've crossed it!

Azarias. And this fish here at your feet, that you thought wanted to devour you, this great fish at your feet, full of mysteries and sacraments, he is yours for you to do what you want with.

Tobias. Azarias! I remember! This fish—why it's the very fish you told me about in Ninive when I met you at the market. But this one here now at my feet is much larger—I never could have dreamed it was so terrible to be a fisher of fish!

Azarias. Have you fished for him, or did he fish for you?

Tobias. Did I come to look for Azarias or did Azarias come to look for his brother Tobias?

On the screen is a faint outline of the market scene mentioned. An Eastern bazaar with swarming buyers and sellers. The orchestra and choir describe it all—the cries, the confused sound of voices, the tinkle of metal and of money—like a whispering memory. AZARIAS is standing behind a large scales on which lies a fish like the one now on the stage. TOBIAS approaches, greets him, talks to him, then takes him by the hand.

Azarias. Your mother, your mother, you told me, had sent you to market to buy a fish.

Tobias. A tiny little fish, very cheap—we're poor! Not

that enormous fish that you were offering for sale with his splendid purple scales! An enormous fish!—but, even so not as big nor as beautiful as the one here at my feet!

Azarias. And didn't I explain to you how you should grapple with that enormous fish, when he leaped to devour you? By the gills, without fear! by the entrance of life, by the very breath of these underwater beings, that is where you seize the nightmare, the monster with his huge gullet open to swallow! Just to hold on was enough.

Tobias [*With a mischievous smile, counting on* AZARIAS's *hand*]. Yes, yes, but one denarius, one denarius and a half a day, Azarias, don't you know that that is a lot of money for poor people like us? It would take a long time, it would take a lot of work for my old mother to save up so much money. And everyone says I'm good for nothing. One denarius, one denarius and a half a day, that's what we promised you! And who knows how long this journey will take?

Azarias. But, young miser, don't you admit that I've earned the salary you promised me? . . . Why don't you answer?

Tobias. I'm holding onto you, holding your hand tight. Isn't that enough—that I'm holding onto your hand?

Azarias. "That Azarias," you say, "with all his promises! For two days, three days, he was with me, and then after three days when I looked for him—he was no longer there."

Tobias. Yes, but now I have you again, fine sir, and I won't let you go this time. I've got hold of it, I've got tight hold of it again—this strong hand of yours.

Azarias. This poor child is trying to ask me—without saying the words— "Where were you? Why did you abandon me like that?"

Tobias. Where were you and why did you abandon me like that? My father had said that you would go before me and all I'd have to do was to follow you.

Azarias. You looked in front of you and perhaps I was behind you.

Tobias. My father did not hire an invisible guide.

Azarias. My place is behind you. All dangers come to

pilgrims from behind. The desire to return home, for example.

Tobias. I don't want to go back. Listen!

Raises finger. We hear again very faintly SARA's *lament.*

Azarias. What should I listen to?

Tobias. A call!

Azarias. What call?

Tobias. A voice from over there, far away, a human voice. The same voice I heard before in Ninive.

Azarias. And since then have you heard it again?

Tobias. Every morning without any sound it wakes me up! And every evening before I fall asleep, it is there still reproaching me. Every step I take forward, I hear it more clearly.

Azarias. And you say I left you without a guide! Haven't I brought you to this point where now you no longer hear the voices of your parents behind you, but begin to hear far ahead the voice of the woman?

Tobias. What woman?

Azarias. Far away, beyond the desert, beyond the mountains, there is one who needs you, and you alone.

Tobias. But beyond the mountains there is the bread I need, that my parents sent me to find, that will keep them from dying!

Azarias. Little brother, have I left you in need of anything on this long, hard journey?

Tobias. No. Whenever my knapsack was empty, there was someone to fill it, whenever I was thirsty, there was someone to give me a cup of water, or milk! Every night when the day's journey ended, there was a roof to shelter me, even if only a tree or a cave, an unexpected spring, ointment for my sore feet.

Azarias. Then, has not Azarias earned his pay?

Tobias. But if you went before me, why do you say you were behind me?

Azarias. Behind! Before! Didn't I keep you from taking the wrong turns? Didn't I bar the road to the left when the route lay to the right? Wasn't I there even to lead you astray when necessary?

Tobias. Yes, you and I were like the left foot that never quite catches up with the right foot—first it's ahead, then it's behind—and without each other, we couldn't take a step.

Azarias. And when your brother Azarias was not there, the fish was there, and there was nothing to do but hang on to him! A tiger crossing the river they call the Tigris! The Lord Tigris, one of the four rivers that, so they say, flow straight out of paradise! [18]

Tobias. That monster—he wanted to devour me! and now instead we are going to eat him for our dinner.

Azarias. Give the entrails to the dog. But the liver, the liver—be sure to keep that. Keep the gall. And salt the flesh—it will be food for the journey.

Tobias. Why keep the gall? and the liver? What are they for?

AZARIAS *shades his eyes with his hand.*

Tobias. What are you looking at over there?

Azarias. It is strange. . . . I see coals on a hearth, glowing in the night, and two poor little children kneeling at the foot of a bed, holding each other by the hand, full of fear. . . . No, they are not afraid! They must not be afraid, little brother. The whole room is full of something foul and hideous that is called Asmodeus.

Tobias. What is Asmodeus?

Azarias. Just as a ray of sunlight slanting through a shutter lights up a world of moving, gleaming motes, so this from hell draws swarming black shadows out of the night.

Tobias. I am not afraid of Asmodeus.

Azarias. Take care! He is your enemy, your rival in the night, lying in wait for you! You will have to meet him! He is that jealous love of the human soul, the enemy hungry for the human soul, the one that gnaws within! A guardian that stands over it, a demon, like a dog maddened with hunger—that is the way he hungers for the human soul. The odor of original sin like the smell of meat draws him to every man and every woman.

[18] Gen. 2 : 14.

Tobias. Tell me . . . you were just now speaking of a woman . . .

Azarias. She is called Sara, daughter of Raguel. You are bound to each other by kinship. The daughter of that very Raguel to whom your father is sending you to ask the return of the ten talents that once he lent to him.

Tobias. It is her voice I hear?

Azarias. It is her voice that your father and your father's father heard before you, the arrow that has pierced you too. Have you not heard that when the Lord draws his bow like an archer in the clouds of heaven, his arrow cleaves through time and space, in an instant springing from the drawn bow, hurtling to its goal?

Tobias. Sara! Yes, I can say her name! Sara! A sweet name! But I've never had a sister, I won't know how to act with this sister you tell me of.

Azarias. If you say *Sara*, that is enough.

Tobias. Sara! But *Tobias*, too—it would be sweet to hear that name, if she knew it.

Azarias. Her heart knows it already, before her lips learn it.

Tobias. Sara! Tobias! Yes, these two names fit together, you'd think they were only one. The other day, while I was asleep, all tired out, I felt a hand searching for me, the shadow of a hand upon me, not touching me but speaking to me, not speaking to me but trying to speak!

Azarias. Tobias, when you hold my hand——

Tobias. No, Azarias, you hold mine!

Azarias. —all is well, there is nothing to fear. There is great peace between heaven and earth.

Tobias. I've known that hand of yours better since you took it away!

Azarias. But when that woman holds your hand, you must never again take it away.

Tobias [*Raising both hands*]. No, I will never take it away from her! My left hand swears it in the name of my right hand.

Azarias. Is it not good to know that far away in the depths of Asia there is a soul, an unknown soul, that needs you?

Tobias. No, I need her! I am coming to her with this deed my father gave me to reclaim the loan, the money.

Azarias. She will pay you more than money. Has it not been said that silver must be purified seven times? So in the name of this old contract on which you claim your rights, this soul has been tried seven times!

Tobias. Here is my right hand for her, pledged by my left!

Azarias. But what can a human hand do against the spirit that possesses her?

Tobias. What spirit?

Azarias. The dark spirit called Asmodeus who stands guard at the foot of her bed. He is darkness and even though you do not know it, all that is dark within you is in connivance with him. He is dumb, and he is deaf, yet he hears the unspoken words of all the hidden darkness within man.

Tobias. I will get by Asmodeus!

Azarias. No better than those seven other men did, one after the other, the men whom Sara accepted as husbands at her father's command. And now their seven tombs lie under the cypresses that I'll show you at Rages.

Tobias. It is not the same. She is calling me, and that means there is something within me that is able to hear her voice.

Azarias [*Takes his head in his hands, and turns him to look behind him*]. O Tobias! Look up there! Do you see it? Do you recognize that beautiful bright star in the east?

Tobias. I know it. It is the source of water, the living source, the fruit. When evening falls and I am tired, I drink of it. I open my mouth and it seems to enter me.

Azarias. It is also the sharp clear voice that wakes you up each morning saying Go! Go! Go, go Tobias! It was there, a singing bird, when God created the world.

Tobias. Can you give me that star, brother?

Azarias. I can, if you are as pure as it is pure.

Tobias. But it is the star that must make me pure!

Azarias. God has placed it in the sky.

Tobias. But I know that if you want you can take it down and put it in my hand.

Azarias. Not that star but another.

Tobias. Just as beautiful?

Azarias. Just as beautiful and more! Listen. The star that I'll give you is a star that knows, and that is known by the star within you. It is a star that sees; it is a star that loves. God has hidden it for you in a maiden.

Tobias. How can you say that I am a star?

Azarias. Two arms and two legs with hands and feet and fingers and toes, and your heart in the center—doesn't that make a star? A star that goes wherever it wants?

Tobias. Don't make fun of me! This is a star of light, not a star of flesh.

Azarias. Speak no evil of the flesh, for it can suffer.

Tobias. It suffers, and I suffer too! Have I made this long weary journey for nothing? gone through fire and water for nothing? dragged down into the abyss, into the very center of the whirlpool? That light shines now in the very depths of her being, that gleaming silver she owes me, that I come to claim, and bring back to my father.

Azarias. Do you think that it has power to heal him?

Tobias. There are things so beautiful that no blindness can resist them! This star at the tip of her fingers, fingers of beauty and wisdom and love—it is stronger than the wretched droppings of a swallow. This star in her heart! This star on her face!—why do you take your hand away?

Azarias. You don't need me any more, you are so strong, you are already using that star I gave you as if it were your own.

Tobias. Forgive me!

Azarias. Take care—draw near in a spirit of faith and humility and fear to this sacrament, this mystery of a soul in a body. The morning star is not wed to mud.

Tobias. What should I do?

Azarias. Obey me. Let me show the way. Did I not tell you of the coals I saw burning? We must put some food on them. Look at that fish you have caught, at our feet. It is full of mystery and of power. In it too there is a healing star; with the liver under its heart, with that flesh of flesh, we will purify the work of the flesh. We will put it on the fire, and drive out that destroying horde called Asmodeus. And meanwhile, little brother, put your head

on my knees and sleep. I see your eyes are heavy. Sleep,
sleep, sleep! Tomorrow and the day after tomorrow there
is a long journey ahead of us. Once, twice, three times
and once again, the left foot must follow the right foot.
Sleep. ——And while he sleeps I will be the great tree
over his head, sheltering him.

TOBIAS *puts his head on* AZARIAS'S *breast and sleeps in
his arms. Music.*

SCENE VI—AZARIAS

AZARIAS. And now, music, come to my aid. Like the
thread the spinner spins at the distaff, drawing it out,
endlessly, endlessly, left hand linking with right hand,
I draw you out, endlessly, golden thread, line of fire,
gossamer in the air, spun out and thrice plaited, unending
thread. From the left hand to the undefined, far beyond
the right hand, I draw you, melody, I spin you endlessly,
thread of the soul, saliva, line of gold, the whole length
of an angel.

The flutes, the persistent bow upon the strings,
the moment of melody draws out an unbroken thread.
And you, O soul, run on the flowing stream of the
flute, run, soul, with tiptoes of sharps on the ribbon of
notes, like a scale running up and down a harp, O maiden
clothed in linen!

Come, O face without a face, O presence, study this
mirror, study in the mirror's depths the birth of a face!

As once in a deep sleep Adam conceived Eve, brought
forth the Mother of the living, from the depth of his
flesh spun the everlasting desire of his soul, the face that
is the measure of his own soul, now it is the turn of Eve.

Look, contemplate, penetrate, impose—impregnate,
draw, entreat with all the intensity of your poverty, of
your right, of your need—entreat this man who, from the
depths of the judgments of God and in the place of God
has power to give you being like the rising sea.

SCENE VII—Azarias

Azarias. Come forth, show yourself, show yourself solemnly in the night. Bring to the man that which once you took from him. [Sara *appears, as though in her sleep.*] Paradise of creation, come forth, paradise of delights, appear, paradise of pleasure, joy of the mind, not only of the sense, image of eternity, guarded by the abyss and, in remorse, become a promise! Enclose in the holy womb of your two arms the man who waits only for you that he may be born, who waits for that kiss to meet his mouth, for that desire to meet his prayer! [*To* Sara.] Who are you?

Sara. I am the thorn bush.

Azarias. The thorn? Have I asked paradise for thorns?

Sara. I am the thorn. Paradise begins with the thorn.

The thorn that enlaces man, his garments, his flesh, until he can no longer move.

Azarias. Not only the thorn.

Sara. What do you say I am?

Azarias. Something present before it is perceived! Even before you spoke, I was listening to your fragrance.

Sara. I am the rose!

The white rose and the red! I am the rose. I am that breath that never fails once one has once breathed it in. I am the scarlet thought! I am the word in fullness of life. I am the ecstatic petal of the burning lamp! Wisdom in full sunlight that shines and smells good. But do not ask me the secret of the living sap that feeds me.

Azarias. What is the fruit of this holy plant?

Sara. I am the fruit—the vine, the grape.

I am the grape, heavy and blue, I am the fruit of azure and of darkness.

I am the fruit of sugar and gold, forbidden to ravaging wasps.

I am the wine that makes drunk.

I am the ferment in the blood.

I am the unconquerable wine.

I am the deep draught to the very heart of the cup of immortality.

Azarias. But wine is not food, drunkenness is not nourishment!

Sara. I am all nourishment, compact, profound, exquisite—

I am the bread, the fruit between the teeth, the fig, inseparable lover of the grape, ambrosia with nectar. I am the fig tree, the food of Israel, with leaves like long fingers.

He who bites into me, he will be filled with the flesh and the wheat of God. He who cuts under the dark rind, to him I am his refection and my flesh is truly his food.

Azarias. But is it not written that Israel has no taste for this precious food that comes to it from heaven? [19]

Sara. Then to cure it of that distaste, to awaken again the pang of hunger, I burn it clean with my acid juice, I sting it again with the spice of desire. . . .

Azarias. Who are you?

Sara. . . . I am the pomegranate! I am the Mystery! In me a people lies waiting, a whole unknown people, a whole people to be, in a world not yet existing, waiting only for a call, for someone through me to make that call heard.

Azarias. What name, then, Mystery, should he call you, that he may be recognized by you?

Sara. I am food!

Azarias. And when he wishes to put his teeth into that food, what will you answer him?

Sara. I am intoxication!

Azarias. A cup, you say, that will make him forget the bread.

Sara. A fragrance that will make him forget the cup—

Azarias. Perfume evaporates—

Sara. But the thorn does not evaporate, the thorn that holds him captive, that enlaces him, binds him from head to foot with its tendrils and thorns.

Azarias. So then, mystery and food, intoxication and

[19] Num. 11 : 6.

fragrance, thus armed you will tear from me this innocent who is now sleeping in my arms!

Sara. All these names—I cannot remember them all, I know only one thing, that I am called Sara and he is called Tobias.

Azarias. Have you called to him from the depths of the distance between Rages and Ninive in the name of the seven men who died at your feet?

Sara. I have called him by name and by mine.

Azarias. Daughter of Israel, do you believe that this innocent one whom I have brought to you can save you?

Sara. I believe that my Redeemer liveth! [20]

ACT THREE

PRELUDE

The music describes a caravan returning from the East, laden with wealth. This motif reappears from time to time, more or less accentuated, during the two following scenes.

SCENE I

ANNA *is sitting on a bench on the tribune (that represents a mountain peak) looking at the ground, muttering as she scratches numbers in the sand with her stick.* SARA, *dressed as a traveler, with a large hat, has just sat down beside her, though* ANNA *does not seem aware of her presence.*

[20] Job, 19 : 25.

SARA [*Looking at the numbers that* ANNA *has just written on the ground*]. . . . No, they have deceived you, it is much further: sixty parasangs at least.

Anna [*Paying no attention to her*]. . . . and from Choran to Bogisteana, one hundred and sixty parasangs. A parasang is long. On the road there is a salt lake.

Sara. And from Bogisteana to Ecbatana: eighty parasangs. That's the hardest stretch.

Anna. And from Ectabana to Rages, two hundred more parasangs. And for the return trip . . . [*She begins to calculate.*]

Sara. That's right, but count in too the time he had to stay in Rages, time to liquidate and collect the funds, and time for something else, too, perhaps?

Anna. But it's a year since he left, and not a word since!

Sara. Who knows if he is not already on the way home?

Anna. They tell me it is a dangerous road, infested with robbers.

Sara. And precipices! and tornadoes and avalanches!

Anna. And the plague and all the other diseases people get on the Yellow Road! He has to come back by the Yellow Road to get to Ecbatana. The plague and all those other diseases!

Sara. And the rivers are full of whirlpools and monsters waiting to devour him!

Anna. Ah, I was right, I ought never to have let him go! That cursed old man forced my hand.

Sara. Good mother, don't you have any other child?

Anna. I have no husband but Tobias! I have no child but Tobias!

Sara. How did you ever let him go, then?

Anna. Once in a while the old man gets what he wants!

Sara. Perhaps the money there called him?

Anna. That's true! For me, anyway, it was the money, the money due us over there, the money called me, and I couldn't stop hearing it day and night, that shining silver moving in the night like a great heap of fish! But he—he said another voice kept him from sleeping!

Sara. What voice?

Anna. How do I know? The groans of some woman,

maybe? A young woman, of course! An old woman—
who cares about her! Far away over there, this groaning,
the groan of a human soul, a silent soul.

Sara [*Claps her hands*]. And you let your only son leave
you for the sake of this unknown woman?

Anna [*Turns slowly towards her as if for the first time
she realizes this being beside her. She looks her up and
down—then down and up*]. Well, and who are you who's
come to sit beside me like this, without me even noticing
it, who are you, answering me like this so that I didn't
even realize someone else was speaking?

Sara. A traveler, old mother! Only a traveler who asks
permission to rest here in the shade.

Anna. Take your hat off. [SARA *takes off her hat.*] It's
a woman's voice. Your dress is like any traveler. But the
voice is a woman's. And the face I see, is a woman's face.

*For a few moments they stay thus, side by side. Then
very slowly,* ANNA *looks at* SARA *who is looking straight
in front of her, and slowly lifts her hand and puts it on
that of her daughter-in-law.* SARA *throws herself weeping
on the old woman's shoulder. They stay thus for a short
time clasped in each other's arms.*

Anna. Daughter, why have you abandoned your husband? Are these Persian ways? Why did he let you go?

Sara. It is not his fault! He could never have held me
back!

My horse suddenly bolted!

The moment I saw this hill here, which I know you
climbed every evening to look for us,

This hill behind which lies Ninive—I could no longer
hold back my horse, he shot away!

How can the arrow resist the bow that shoots it!

And the dog ran barking behind me! And Tobias sig-
naled to me, laughing and crying!

Anna. Tobias, you say! Tobias! Is it true, Tobias is
with you?

Sara. I am only a little ahead of him. He has the whole
enormous caravan to take care of.

Anna. Tobias, Tobias is here! [*Closes her eyes as if
about to faint.*]

Sara. He has come back! With this woman at his side, and the whole East on the march behind him as payment! All the mercy of God on the march behind him as payment! He went away, and here he is again! He is returned, and the Orient is his name! [*She holds* ANNA *up, but as the latter realizes he is approaching, she straightens herself up firmly.*]

Anna [*Looking long at* SARA]. What is your name, my daughter? I want to know it.

Sara. Sara is my name.

Anna. Sara. [*Pause.*] Kiss me Sara. [*The two women gravely kiss each other.*] Tobias must have told you that my name is Anna. Anna. The mother of Tobias is called Anna. And now I am your mother, child, for the one who bore you.

Sara. She died. I never knew her.

Anna. How long has Tobias been married to you? When he left us, protected by the great Azarias, he was still only a child.

Sara. Four months, four months, mother, have already passed since our wedding in Rages.

ANNA *looks at her and lays her open hand lightly on her body.*

Sara [*Rising up straight, hands joined*]. My soul magnifies the Lord, for he has done great things for me.

Anna [*In a low voice as if reciting a text*]. And his mercy is from generation to generation!

Sara. Tobias came to me like a prolongation of yourself, Mother, like the prolongation of the old man who had heard my voice across space, the voice of one who devoured, of one dishonored, of one accursed—yes, it seemed to me that he would not be completely mine until I came to the very source, to the blind father, to the unknown mother, to this mother who is now mine, and now here I am; nothing could hold me back, like the hart of Scripture, I have leapt over the hills.[21]

And I am not alone! There is one within me who knows his own people, who exults! [22]

[21] Cant. 2 : 8-9.
[22] Luke, 1 : 44.

Anna. Daughter of Tobias, wife of Tobias, mother of Tobias; and little grandson within you, I greet you.

Sara [Gently putting her head on ANNA'*s shoulder].* I take possession of my fatherland!

Anna. Sion is no more, Jerusalem has been destroyed! Israel no longer has a fatherland! No more Ninive than Rages!

Sara. I ask only for the fatherland of the will of God, of the covenant of Abraham!

Anna. So be it!

Sara [As if reading from an opened page]. "Abraham begot Isaac, Isaac begot Jacob, Jacob begot Joseph and his brethren." [23] That is what we read in the rolls. "Honor thy father and thy mother," it is said, "that you may have length of days on earth," [24] a life beyond your own, from God and to God in a straight line, attachment to the past and prolongation into the future. I have no fatherland but this shoulder that receives me and this womb that has borne me! I have no other fatherland than faith in God—and hope in his protecting hand.

Anna. We are the children of saints.

Sara. We are the children of saints! Those are words my beloved never ceased repeating to me during those three terrible nights that we spent together, praying at the foot of our bridal bed, with all hell raging around us, raging against us, against the strong wall of Azarias's protection.

Anna. What protection?

Sara. I'll tell you all about it later! The fish's liver! The fish's gall! The fish that tried to devour Tobias, whose entrails Azarias told him to keep! A liver, a heart, that burned on the glowing coals, that was the rampart that Hell could not break through. Thank you, thank you, O fish!

Anna. I don't understand . . .

Sara. "Are you going to kill me too, tell me, you murderer, you husband-killer?" I still hear that hissing in my ears: that servant girl's hissing! I—I went up to the housetop and begged mercy from God! Seven men, one after

[23] Matt. 1 : 2.
[24] Exod. 20 : 12; Deut. 5 : 16.

the other, had wanted to marry me, and all had perished, seven men, one after the other, the very day of the wedding, before they had touched me! A demon called Asmodeus strangled them! There was in me a dreadful attraction, an invitation to death!

Anna. And Tobias, son of Tobias, was the óne to deliver you?

Sara. He was the one to deliver me, in the sacrament of the fish! He was the one to take that shame away. Dear Tobias! He found in me the soul that was his own soul, the soul interior to my soul. This soul dwelling in darkness, in fear, in the mud! He came to me and held out his hand to me! As soon as I saw him I knew him— he was my duty, he was my vocation! How can I say it? he was my origin! the one by whom and through whom I came into the world. "We are the children of saints." We have received the heritage of the will of God and the duty to pass it on! Neither distance nor Hell were strong enough to separate us, nor those seven men whom I had unwillingly led to desire and to sin! In my own person I had to pay my father's debt. Soul crying out to soul and the will of God seeking to be fulfilled through us. Tobias, son of Tobias!

Anna. Son of Anna also.

Sara. Yes, son of Anna also; I kiss the old hands that have worked so hard, washing and serving, splitting the wood, carrying dishes to and fro, cooking the meals so many times! And praying so much, praying so long, on those ten poor fingers. And now the old hand I hold against my cheek makes the little child within me happy. And I am weeping because I have found my fatherland again!

Anna. The old woman is weeping too!

Sara. Now, mother of Tobias, I am going to tell you a mystery. Of the fish's liver burned on the coals! Around us Hell screamed in rage, all around us the night stirred with that horrible movement, full of putridity and poison,

then I saw on the wall a vision of a tree that came forth from my womb, that grew great and tall. On every branch all kinds of kings, priests, prophets and soldiers, holding swords or harps, or carrying crowns—a single tree that was a whole forest, and on the topmost branch, ah, what a flower! so beautiful, so radiant, so pure, so blinding, I closed my eyes and my heart melted away!

And my soul magnifies the Lord for he has done great things for me, And his mercy is from generation to generation, coming forth, rising up, bearing fruit, growing great, and high and long and wide!

Anna. The woman inherits the past, but she makes the future! Instrument and accomplice of God!

Sara [*Low voice*]. My soul doth magnify the Lord because he hath done great things to me.

Anna. O my daughter, you have come to me as an angel, met unexpectedly on the road. For weeks I have come here every evening, straining my eyes to the East,
   each day while I was working,
the image of that road and that horizon never left me, that desert that had taken my son from me!

And suddenly you have come from behind me, you have risen up at my side, while I was counting the stages and the parasangs—
   I looked beside me and you were there,
   like an old spider whose net suddenly vibrates with a fly—
   beside me was the salvation of my soul!

Sara. I would not be here now if I'd not had that horse—I saw you keeping your watch high on the hill,
   I knew you at once and came to sit quietly beside you.

Anna [*Pointing to something in the distance*]. Now, after all, the horizon and the road have not disappointed me! What do you see, what do you see over there, Sara, with your young eyes?

Sara. A column of dust.

Anna. It is Tobias—
it is my son Tobias coming, and the dust of his feet rises up to heaven!

He is home! He is home! The Lord has given back my son Tobias!

At this moment OLD TOBIAS *enters, upstage, uncertainly, feeling his way with a stick. He is led by* THE DOG *who leaps around him and then tugs at his garment.*

Sara. See—our comrade, the Dog, he shot ahead like lightning! Who is this poor old man whom he is playing with so roughly? Down! leave him alone, you bad beast!

Anna. That's old Tobias—your father, child! He's blind—that fool of a dog is going to knock him down! Quick! Run to him! Help him! Hold him! Lift him up, tell him the whole story, explain it all to him! There's only one thing in the whole world for me, that cloud of dust over there, only one thing in the whole world for me, my son Tobias who was dead and behold, he has returned to me, Tobias! My son Tobias! I am here, I, your mother! You, my son Tobias—and I, I, your mother! Curse these old legs! An old woman wants only one thing—her child! I belong to you, dear child! See—I'm coming to you, I'm running to you! [*She runs as best she can, her arms stretched out to the Horizon.*]

SCENE II

OLD TOBIAS, *dragged by* THE DOG, *totters, falls and lies flat, his face against the ground.* SARA *runs to help him, and raise him up.* THE DOG *goes off after* ANNA.

SARA. Father, have you hurt yourself?

Old Tobias [*Getting his breath, and touching her face with his hand*]. Who are you? what is this voice that says "Father" to me?

Sara. Father, I am your son Tobias who has returned to you.

Old Tobias. This is not the fragrance of my son Tobias that I breathe,[25] it is all the roses of Paradise! That garden enclosed at the center of the earth—it has seemed to me from time to time in my prayer that the evening wind carried me its fragrance.[26] But now the garden itself has come to me, it has raised me up, a poor old man, and taken me into its arms.

[25] Gen. 27 : 27.
[26] Cant. 4 : 12.

Sara. Father, no, what has taken hold of you is not strange to you—I am your son Tobias. I am forever inseparable from your son Tobias.

Old Tobias. Then, my daughter, you are that woman I have asked God for? Has he brought you to me from the depths of the East?

Sara. Sara is my name, daughter of Raguel, your kin. You heard my groans in my extreme need. To me you sent your son Tobias. In him you were present with me. He has saved me from Hell by the Sacrament of the Grace of God. In him now am I Tobias, one single thing now with Tobias. And by me Tobias lifts you up and now holds you in my arms. Soon I will tell you he himself is here. The moment I saw from far away the place where you live, nothing could hold me back from you.

Old Tobias [*Passing his hand over her face*]. Tobias is here?

Sara. Tobias is here. For four months I have been one with him, and within me is a living being that belongs to him, that prays: Thanks be to God!

Tobias [*Raising his hands*]. Blessed is she who comes to me in the name of the Lord!

Sara. Father, I bring back to you your own prayers, moving and loving in my womb, fruitful and multiplied.

Tobias. Not only the rose, but also the olive tree, and the vine and the pomegranate!

Sara. The rose, the olive tree, and the cedar! the fig tree and the grape and the willow and the pomegranate! and the thorn thicket forever around him to keep him from running away! . . . Paradise complete—a poor paradise, a humble paradise, his own, for his use.

Faith within you holds out its hands to that promise within me.

Old Tobias. Sara, my daughter, for a long time I have known you—and I have listened to your heart, calling me. We have shared the same anguish, the same abandonment, the same contempt. Only your name is new to me, and this fragrance of roses! New, but not unexpected! What could be unexpected to a man—who has rid himself of all things, who is only an expectation? He looks only to the rising Sun and his soul is large enough to swallow down anything that comes, for from now on nothing will come but good, or if not good, then better! You can tell me nothing, Sara. I knew all that was happening from day to day, even as at this moment I hear my son's steps growing louder and nearer on the road, coming home to me! He left me, to journey all alone, and he returns followed by a whole multitude! A man who has withdrawn from all that is passing, whose ears are no longer filled with confused sounds, that man reads clearly within himself the meaning of all things written in symbol. I thank God that from the moment I gave him my son he has never ceased to give him back to me, and with him all heaven and all earth! I thank God that this shadow of a man has found paradise again! No, he has not found it, it has come and taken him up in its arms, and lifted him up. He'll look to the rising sun; nothing can ever be unexpected! for to the unexpected his whole expectation is attuned. Paradise at a single stroke, complete with all its flowers and all its thorns!

Sara. The sun sets too, sometimes.

Old Tobias. For me there is only the rising Sun! These eyes have been taken from me that there may be no moment when I do not look at it! *Faciem tuam exquisivi, faciem tuam, Domine, requiram!* [27] The rising Sun! It is warm on a man's face! It sets, only to rise again!

Sara. How little he asks! Only a prick from a rose. But as for seeing with his own eyes the one his son loves, the one whom he has desired beyond the mountains, the one he has snatched out of Hell—no, he has no desire, nothing to ask! Old Jewish father, if all Christians had been like you, God would have been left in peace.

Old Tobias. God has blinded me by a swallow, all I can say to him is *Yes.*

Sara. Like the holy man Job!

Old Tobias. The Lord has given and the Lord has taken away. May his name——

Sara [*Puts her hand over his mouth*].—be blessed! May it be blessed, thirty million times *amen! We are the children of saints!* Of course! But after he'd said that, what

---

[27] Ps. 26 : 8: "I have sought thy face, thy face, O Lord, I will still seek."

did Job do, that good old man, blind, a leper, alone with
the dead? He cried out aloud! a great outcry, a clamor—
the scream that cannot be held back, like a woman's in
childbirth! A whole big book is full of his howls, they've
made me read it, they read it aloud on the Sabbath! It
was no use for all his friends one after the other to try
to close his mouth! He did not even seem to hear them.
Again and again he filled eternity with that enormous sob,
that dreadful cry.

Old Tobias. Let the day perish wherein I was born,
and the night in which it was said: a man-child is conceived. . . . Why did I not die in the womb? . . . Why
is light given to him that is in misery, and life to them
that are in bitterness of soul? [28]

Sara. Good! The Lord heard that and he heard the
friends of Job, too, those scandalized respectable people
who tried to shut him up. And what did the Lord say?
How did he treat the venerable Eliu?

*Old Tobias. Who is this that wrappeth up sentences in
unskillful words?* [29]

Sara. And now I hear the voice of another old man
closer to us—what does it say?

Old Tobias. It is better for me to die than to live.

Sara. Who said that?

Old Tobias. I did, the old Tobias!

Sara. Did he lament all alone?

Old Tobias. No, there was another lamentation that
accompanied his.

Sara. Is it better for her to die than to live?

Old Tobias. It is better for you to live and for me to
be with you.

Sara. But can you be wholly alive when you're blind?

Old Tobias. The child that I have given you, that you
carry within you, is blind!

Sara. You have called me and now I am here; it is not
endurable for you to refuse to look at me, to keep up this
barrier between yourself and me!

[28] Job, 31 : 2, 11–20.
[29] Job, 38 : 2.

Old Tobias. I know that my son went to the East in search of Light.

Sara. If I am light, you must not be so content with the darkness! If I am light, you must find a way to open your eyes and no longer shut out the Light from your interior world. If you love me, dear Father, you must learn that I am made to be looked at.

Old Tobias. What must I do?

Sara. You must ask! You must stir up to the very roots all within you that is capable of discontent and of prayer! You mustn't leave God a moment's peace! You must leap over the abyss that lies between yourself and him with the loud cry of Israel, with an insane hope, with the great clamor of all the generations within you whose voice you are! "Lord, that I may see!" I have eyes for you formed in the midst of this deep darkness! I am not made to be enclosed in myself! I hate this bondage that keeps me from going to meet your will!

Old Tobias. Lord, that I may see!

Here the voices of the CHORUS *begin to be heard, like a vast crowd, in confused question and answer, gradually attaining self-consciousness, with articulate letter, syllable, word—*

Sara. Listen, the river of blessings that you in your son went to seek in the East, is here, it is here, flowing back to you! You left there only a little money, now a whole river of wealth and herds, a whole unknown nation led back by your son, comes to enlarge your frontiers, to invade your poverty, to fill up your soul to the ends of the horizon! Your son brings you Light and I am the Dawn, and the Wisdom that goes before him!

The whole cortege of YOUNG TOBIAS *fills the stage. He wears reverently hanging around his neck a golden box enclosing the gall of the mystical fish wrapped in silk. His mother is with him.* AZARIAS *is hidden in the crowd.*

Sara. Listen, old man: kneel, prostrate yourself before your son, do not touch him until he has fulfilled the mission that God has given him for you and has anointed

your eyes with the sacrament that he has risked his life
to draw from the abyss.

TOBIAS *does this.*

SCENE III

During the following action, the CHORUS *has begun
to sing these antiphons from the Book of Job. Their
tone is at first plaintive, then becomes more and more
intense, fervent, violent, heart-rending. The musicians
accompany the proposed themes.*

CHORUS. *Homo natus de muliere brevi vivens tempore
repletur multis miseriis. Taedet animam meam vitae
meae! Qui quasi flos egreditur et conteritur et fugit velut
umbra et numquam in eodem statu permanet. Et dignum
ducis super huiuscemodi aperire oculos tuos . . . ?* [30]

Lord, that I may see! [*Spoken.*]

*Putasne mortuus homo rursus vivat? Cunctis diebus
quibus nunc milito exspecto donec veniat immutatio mea.
Vocabis me et ego respondebo tibi: operi manuum
tuarum porriges dexteram.*[30a]

Lord, that I may see! [*Spoken.*]

*Scio enim quod Redemptor meus vivit et in novissimo
die de terra surrecturus sum et rursum circumdabor pelle
mea et in carne mea videbo Deum salvatorem meam.*

[30] Job, 14 : 1–3: "Man born of woman, living for a short time,
is filled with many miseries.
Who cometh forth like a flower, and is destroyed, and fleeth
as a shadow, and never continueth in the same state.
And dost thou think it meet to open thy eyes upon such a
one . . ."
[30a] 14, 14–15: "Shall man that is dead, thinkest thou, live
again? all the days in which I am now in warfare, I expect until
my change come. Thou shalt call me, and I will answer thee: to
the work of thy hands thou shalt reach out thy right hand."

Quem visurus sum ego ipse et oculi mei conspecturi sunt et non alius: reposita est haec spes mea in sinu meo.[30b]

Lord, that I may see! [*Spoken.*]

The old man has knelt down, his face raised to heaven. The YOUNG TOBIAS *kisses him on his two eyes, then takes the golden box from its cover, and raises it to heaven; then he takes the gall with his thumb and anoints each of the eyelids. Then he draws back gradually, with all the others, leaving* OLD TOBIAS *in the center of the stage. Music stops suddenly. Long silence.* OLD TOBIAS *rises slowly and painfully. His face is lifted to heaven. All raise their faces like him to heaven.*

Young Tobias. Father what do you see?

Old Tobias. I see, I see

that ladder, that ladder that has been revealed,

I see, I see

that ladder that has been revealed, that has been promised to our father Jacob,

that ladder whose highest rungs are touched with the Glory of God—and the feet of angels forever ascending and descending.[31]

Young Tobias. Tell us what do you see now?

Old Tobias [*Lowers his face a little. Raises his arms over his head, gradually lowers them to the horizontal*]. I see—

all the earth that God has created and ordered,

all the earth to the mountains and beyond the mountains! [*Mime.*]

all these things that exist together!

all the expanse of this earth where men dwell and the sob

of unnumbered multitudes rises up from the inhabited land!

[30b] 19 : 25–27: "For I know that my Redeemer liveth, and in the last day I shall rise out of the earth.

And I shall be clothed again with my skin, and in my flesh I shall see my God.

Whom I myself shall see, and my eyes shall behold, and not another: this my hope is laid up in my bosom."

[31] Gen. 28 : 12–13.

My ears hear sorrow, but my eyes see only peace!

Young Tobias [*Has come up to him and stands before his father with his mother and his wife on his right and left*]. Father, what do you see now?

Old Tobias [*As his eyes were little by little focusing on the reality near him. He opens his arms*]. I see my son Tobias.

He embraces him, and, holding him in his arms, draws in one after the other his wife and his daughter-in-law.

Where is he, Azarias, son of the great Ananias, to whom we owe everything? Why is he not the first whom it is granted me to see with these eyes that he has given back to me?

Azarias, Lord Azarias, where are you?

Young Tobias. I have lost sight of him for two days and yet I know he has not left us, he is here.

SCENE IV

OLD TOBIAS. Azarias, Lord Azarias, where are you? Azarias, O son of the great Ananias!

Young Tobias. Father, he was always with me, always making the journey easy for me, carrying me in his arms lest I hurt my foot against a stone! [32] He has been on my right hand and on my left, before me and behind! He is the faithful guardian ever protecting me! He has been my brother, a strong hand in mine. He taught me about the fish—not to fear, but to throw myself upon it, seize it by the gills, take possession of it—that fish full of mysteries, of sacraments—to take its liver and gall, the gall with which I have just anointed your eyes, that has given you back your sight! He has restored the money, that money with all its immense interest that I bring back with me. He brought me to your kinsman Raguel, in the city Rages in Media, far beyond the horizon! And while I was asleep, he brought me the daughter of Raguel, the

[32] Ps. 115 : 13.

daughter of Raguel, while I was asleep, that I might learn
to know her, he united us, soul with soul, in Paradise!
He made my hands hands of salvation and healing. He
gave me authority and power over the demons, he taught
me how to cross the space that separates the soul of a
man, the soul of a man and the soul of a woman!—And
now what return shall we make to him for all these good
things? Divide all in two, and humbly pray him to accept
half of all our goods and of ourselves? And pray that he
will preserve us forever. Amen.

Old Tobias. And I too say: amen! Azarias, where are
you?

Young Tobias. Azarias, brother, where are you?

Anna. Lord Azarias, you have given me back my son,
where are you?

Sara. Azarias, you have destroyed Asmodeus and restored my honor and saved me from the servant girl and
given me to Tobias my husband—where are you?

Through you I give by Tobias to Tobias this other
Tobias whom I bear in my womb—where are you?

The ranks of the crowd slowly open and gradually AZARIAS
appears in the background still dressed as a traveler.

SCENE V

*Everybody slowly draws away from him in reverence and
terror. He goes up on the tribune and here, stripping off
his human garments, he appears in his angelic glory—no
longer* AZARIAS, *he is the* ANGEL RAPHAEL.

ANGEL RAPHAEL. Tobias!
Tobias!
Sara, Anna!
You will no longer see your brother Azarias by your
side. He has fulfilled the mission the Lord had entrusted
to him.
Now he has set your feet on the road, he will no longer
be seen walking by your side.

Old Tobias. What! the bread we ate together . . .
Young Tobias. . . . the wine we shared . . .
Old Tobias. . . . have you forgotten how it tasted?
Young Tobias. Are you tired of it, my Lord?
Chorus [*In a deep murmur, at times growing louder*].
Unde sapientia venit homini, et quis est locus intelli-
gentiae? Abscondita est ab oculis omnium viventium. Per-
ditio et mors dixerunt: Auribus nostris audivimus famam
ejus. Et timebant eum interrogare de verbo hoc.[33]
Angel Raphael. For a long time I have seemed to eat
and drink with you. But my food was another food, food
that you do not see. My food was another food, food no
words can tell.[34]
Young Tobias. Azarias, my brother Azarias! Do you
thus draw away, divide yourself from me? how can I live
from now on, separated from my brother Azarias? How
can I do without that hand in mine, that great hand on
my head? what name must I now learn to call you?
Sara. No, you no longer need that hand in yours, that
other great hand on your head. I am all that for you
now, beloved. But since he is still here, see, he is still
with us here; there must be something more he has to do
for us, something more for us to ask him, if only we know
what to ask.
Young Tobias. What do you want me to ask him?
Sara. No, Tobias, you have nothing to ask for yourself,
for I am here with you. And the old man, your father—
he has nothing to ask either, nothing more to ask for
himself, since his sight has been given back to him. What
more would he ask for? [*She looks all around.*] Where
is your mother?
Young Tobias. True—I don't see her here, any
more . . .
Sara. No, you don't see her any more. You have never

[33] Job, 28 : 20–22: "Whence then cometh wisdom? and where
is the place of understanding?
It is hid from the eyes of all living . . .
Destruction and death have said: with our ears we have
heard the fame thereof.
And they understood not the word, and they were afraid to
ask him."
[34] Mark, 9 : 31.

really seen her, Tobias! You have never really looked at
your mother, Tobias! No more than one looks at one's own
right hand, or at the heart within, that gives us life.

Tobias your father has spent his life studying the Scriptures, all his life was with the dead, with the dead Scriptures, with all those dead bodies to bury in the ground—
that was his passion!

And Tobias the son was busy playing his flute and
looking toward the mountains behind which Sara lived.

But your mother, your mother, she kept you alive,
working from morning to night with no thought save of
you,

while you never noticed her, except to swear at her
under your breath, that bothersome old woman!—

Like the heart when it gives you sudden pain.

Will you let Azarias go away like this?

She is the one for whom he is waiting! I tell you he is
waiting for her! for no one else!

Mother, Mother, where are you?

The crowd opens. The mother is there trying to hide.
Sara *goes to her and brings her to the feet of the* Angel.

SCENE VI

Sara. Azarias, Lord Angel, you are an angel; I knew it
all the time, but that does not keep you from being
Azarias still, our elder brother. Look at this old woman
whom I bring to you, she is so afraid of you, she does not
even dare to kneel. [*She makes the mother get down on
her knees.*] Look at these poor hands that have done so
much washing, so much sewing, so much cooking, so
much hoeing the ground; tell her now that all that is over,
that it is time now for us to serve her; tell her that she
will not have to do anything any more, that that is why
Tobias went to Persia to find me. Sara has gone beyond
the barrier between man and demon to come here to her,
what can resist her! Azarias, our good friend, tell all that
to God, burn it before him like rising incense, tell him

Tobias asks it of you, Tobias whom you have put in my
arms, whom I have put in my heart, under my heart!

Azarias [To ANNA]. Arise, woman, what are you doing
on your knees? Do you not see I am a servant too, like
you! [35]

Sara. Get up, Mother.

She helps her to rise and pushes her into the arms of the
ANGEL *that close around her; she disappears as though
enshrouded and swallowed up in the great flowing white
sleeves. Night falls, and when light returns* AZARIAS *has
disappeared, and the mother is there alone, tottering,
feeling her way: we realize she is blind.*

Mother. Tobias! Tobias! My Son! Sara! where are you?
I don't see you any more!

Tobias. We are here, Mother, don't you see us?

Mother. I hear you! I don't need eyes for that! The
angel told me that I shall see you always, always, but not
with my eyes! with my ears! with my heart!

Sara. Mother of Tobias, what answer will you give this
son of Tobias within me, when he questions you?

Mother [*Cries out with all her strength*]. GOD IS
LOVE!

[35] Apoc. 22 : 9.

THE LITTLE POOR MAN
(*Le Petit Pauvre*)

by

JACQUES COPEAU

Translated by

BEVERLY THURMAN

CHARACTERS

*The men whose names only are listed, without description, are
members of the Order which Saint Francis founded.*

LADY PICA, *mother of* SAINT FRANCIS
PIETRO BERNADONE, *his father, a wealthy cloth merchant*
FRANCIS BERNADONE, *the Little Poor Man of* ASSISI (SAINT
   FRANCIS)
BERNARD OF QUINTAVALLE, *one of* SAINT FRANCIS' *most beloved
   friars*
BISHOP GUIDO *of the* ASSISI *diocese*
CHORUS LEADER, *the Archangel* SAINT MICHAEL
LEO
ELIAS
ANGELO
JOHN
MASSEO
BEGGAR
GILES
RUFINO
MARTIN, *a man possessed of a devil and cured by* SAINT FRANCIS
POOR JOAN
VILLAGE PRIEST
PHILOSOPHER
SAINT CLARE, *founder of the Franciscan women's Order*
PETER CATANI
CAESAR OF SPEYER
CARDINAL UGOLINO, *protector of the Franciscan Order, later*
   POPE GREGORY IX
PETER STACIA, *a Franciscan who disagreed with the Little Poor
   Man*
ILLUMINATO
SILVESTER
SATAN, *a tall, glittering angel with black wings*
LADY GIACOMA DI SETTESOLI, *a friend of* SAINT FRANCIS'
JOHN
GRATIANO *} her sons*

In addition, there are two CHORUSES: *a four-man* SACRED CHO-
RUS *in white vestments and a six-man* DRAMATIC CHORUS *divided into two sections of three men each. These six wear*

monks' gowns of a slightly lighter shade than those worn by
SAINT FRANCIS and his brothers. The CHORUS members make
the scene changes and play the part of extra monks, villagers,
and shepherds as feasible and as required. In order to do so,
they make suitable changes in their costume, hair, dress, etc.

The stage is without scenery. In its center stands a bare platform. Changes of scene are suggested by one or more accessories
arranged as required by the CHORUS members.

Several of the characters have only a few lines and CLARE has
none. Therefore actors may double in small parts.

THE TIME: The early thirteenth century.
THE PLACE: ASSISI and its surroundings, in central ITALY.

The version of SAINT FRANCIS' Canticle of the Sun quoted in
SCENE VI is that of Matthew Arnold. The music for the play
was selected or composed by Joseph Samson, choir director of
Dijon Cathedral.

THE LITTLE POOR MAN

SCENE I

The Place: Pietro Bernadone's *house in* Assisi—Saint
Francis' *boyhood home.*

The Time: 1204. Francis *is twenty-two years old.*

The Sacred Chorus *makes a solemn entrance, chanting,
and takes seats in the orchestra. The* Dramatic Chorus
*—three men from right and three from left—comes in
shouting and gesticulating in disorderly fashion and also
goes to orchestra. All sit down as* Bernadone *enters from
right, pulling* Francis *by the arms. In a rage, he hauls
him onto platform and hurls him to floor.* Lady Pica
follows.

Pica. Please, Bernadone! Do as I say——
    Bernadone. You keep out of this, Lady Pica! It's be-
tween me and your son! [*To* Francis.] Stay here!

Bernadone *goes out to left.* Pica *stands quiet a moment,
then climbs to platform and goes to right of* Francis.

    Pica. Dear God. . . . Francis, sweet child, those rascals
didn't hurt you with their stones, did they?
    Francis. I felt nothing.
    Pica. Did your father beat you?
    Francis. He was a little rough.
    Pica. He's unhappy, don't you see? You're hurting him.
    Francis. I know!
    Pica. He blames me. I'm your mother. I try to under-
stand what you are doing, of course, but I don't approve.
    Francis. I know that too.
    Pica. Poor dear! What has changed you so? The day
you began to get well—that very morning, I opened your
window to let the air and light in. I remember the air was
so clean and the light was softer than ever. But you didn't
seem to notice. Your eyes had a far-off look. I couldn't
tell what you were thinking. [*Suddenly falling on her
knees.*] What is it, son? A disappointment? A sorrow?

196

Francis. My only sorrow is that I feel so useless and unclean.

Pica. Because you took your share of the world's pleasures like other boys of your age? Because you loved feasting, revels, and fine clothes? Why of course you did, poor boy. All young people do. You'll get over this as you grow older—just like everyone else—because you'll turn toward duty and sacrifice—just like everyone else. Don't be so hard on yourself. It's pride that causes this. Do as your father says, dear. There's no telling what he'll do if you provoke him. You can easily calm him down, because he's kind. He has worked so hard all his life. He wanted so much to have a son like himself. He has given you everything you ever wanted. He was so proud of you! . . . You see, Francis, your father is a proud man. That's his shortcoming. Your . . . unusual behavior hurts him. He loves you—you must know. But he also likes to be respected and honored. He is proud of his high place in the world. He doesn't want you to be unworthy and make yourself look foolish because it reflects on him and his position. You see, Francis? [FRANCIS *nods in agreement.*] Oh, that's wonderful! . . . I have had to be understanding about many things myself since I married Bernadone. The dreams of my girlhood—oh, I try not to think of them. I was like you. I dreamed of things that simply couldn't be. Little by little I've made myself take things as they are. In spite of it all I've managed to be so happy that many women envy me. When you were born I gave all my dreams to you. Remember how happy you were when you were a little boy in this old house? You used to say: I'm going to be a famous nobleman! And we talked about your hopes. But now that you're a man you must be more down-to-earth, less ambitious. Do you understand? I see you do.

Francis. Yes, Mother. Oh, yes, I understand.

Pica. You'll have such a good life! A sweet wife, fine children, pleasant friends—everything you need in a home where God will have His place. But don't despise the world. If the saints think only of themselves, if they withdraw from the world, what will become of poor mankind? You mustn't be selfish. . . . Don't cry, Francis. Why are you crying?

Francis. I'm crying because I thought of what my Lord Jesus suffered.

Pica. And what about us? and me? . . . What if I suffer?

Francis. Forgive me, Mother, forgive me, I pity you . . . and I want you to be happy! I love you, but I'm getting ready to leave you. I am drawn irresistibly to things eternal.

Pica. I'm sorry, son. I don't understand. [*She gets up.*]

Francis. Think of the Virgin Mary, Mother. What if you were Jesus' mother? What if you saw with your own eyes the body of your own son hanging on the cross? His two hands bleeding, his feet bleeding and torn by nails, his wounded side? . . .

Pica. I couldn't bear it, son.

Francis. I can't either, Mother. I can't bear it. The sight of it is more than I can stand. But I don't want to be consoled. If men allow themselves to be consoled they are willing to forget. They refuse to suffer. That is why Jesus is always so alone. [*A pause.*]

Pica. I was wrong, Francis. I think we should try to do a little more for Christ than we do ordinarily. I want to try with you. We'll go to church more regularly, we'll deny ourselves and show more zeal. We'll give more to the poor. And if Bernadone criticizes us we'll not let him know what we're doing. . . .

Francis. My dear, sweet mother! If you found me lying beside the road exhausted, I know you'd have the strength to carry me home in your arms. But you see I'm . . . Ah, I'm on fire! . . . My heart is melting like wax in a flame. It's dying. It tries its best to escape but the flames hem it in. I asked Christ for His love and thought I would find it gentle and enjoy peace in it on heights where pain could never reach me. But instead I feel unimaginable torment. The heat cracks my heart. I can't even make you see what I suffer. There is nothing sweet to me in heaven or earth. All is blotted out by the love of Christ. The sun's light seems dark when I see that resplendent face. The glorious cherubim, the seraphim themselves, are nothing to one who sees the Lord!

BERNADONE *enters from left bringing fine clothes.*

Bernadone. Now you're going to get up!

Pica [*Almost in a whisper*]. Get up, Francis dear.

FRANCIS *gets up.* BERNADONE *climbs to platform.*

Bernadone. Take off those disgusting rags and put these clothes on. They're yours. They're the clothes of a sensible man. That's what you were and what you're going to be again, starting now.

Francis [*His voice trembling*]. Our Lord said: If any man will follow me . . .

Bernadone. Our Lord didn't tell sons to defy their fathers. You can't teach me my catechism. I'm the father here and I give the orders. As long as you're in my house, you'll obey me or I'll take a stick and beat some sense into you. Take these clothes and go!

Pica [*In a low voice*]. Go, Francis dear.

Bernadone. I'm waiting for you!

After a moment's hesitation, FRANCIS *takes the clothes and exits to right.*

Pica. What are you going to do, Bernadone?

Bernadone. He's just acting up. It's his age. We'll get him through it somehow.

Pica. But what if he really is obeying an order from heaven?

Bernadone. Don't make me laugh, Lady Pica. These are not the days of the Apostles. If my son had wanted to be a priest or even a monk—although I wouldn't recommend that—I would be willing to talk it over with him. But a beggar! And even less than a beggar. What sort of business is that? What is he trying to prove with his rags after more than a thousand years of Christianity? Why should he want to spend days and nights in caves and risk catching his death of cold, wear rags and cover his head with ashes? And make a laughingstock of himself? Look here, Lady Pica, I'll tell you, if this son of yours doesn't give up his crazy notions, it will kill me. That's all there is to it. It will kill me, I tell you. Do you want it to kill me?

Pica. Please try hard to be kind to him, Bernadone.

Bernadone. I'm perfectly able to be kind when I know the purpose of it. But I'm not weak like you. No, sir, no weakness. Kindness, yes. But first of all, let him obey. I'll forgive him everything. Even the thievery. Bernadone's son a thief! Yes, madam, a wretched little thief. Am I supposed to work all my life, become rich, fill my shop with the finest materials in the world, and then see a little fool make off with them and strew them about? No, a thousand times! I'll have no more of this! [*Enter* FRANCIS, *wearing fine clothes.*] Ah, that's better. That's fine! . . . You see, Francis. I'm calm. I'm mindful of my love for you, my very deep love. And I've forgotten everything, everything, including your failure to measure up to my confidence in you. Including the spectacle you made of yourself this morning in the street. . . . What a frightful scandal!

Pica [*In a low voice*]. Give your father a kiss, Francis, quick!

Bernadone. Do you hear? I've forgotten it all, son. On one condition—that you stop—— Wait! on one condition —that you give your mother and me a solemn promise to stop running through the streets and the country as you have been doing, dirty, wild-eyed, and filled with some kind of madness. . . .

Francis. Father . . .

Bernadone. Well, Francis.

Francis. Forgive me for making you angry and giving you so much worry and trouble. . . .

Bernadone. Do you refuse to act as people of our family have done for generations?

Francis. Yes, because I cannot.

Bernadone. Why not, Francis?

Francis. Because I'm not free.

Bernadone. Not free to take your place in your parents' house and live according to their principles and customs?

Francis. No. Because this life is not a Christian life. . . . At least it isn't the life that the Lord requires of me.

Bernadone. So you despise us?

Francis. Forgive me, forgive me! I am nothing.

Bernadone. We might as well go, Pica. There's nothing to be done with him now.

BERNADONE *and* PICA *go out right.* FRANCIS *falls on his knees.*

Francis [Praying]. I have sinned against Thee, O God! in thought, word and deed. I have smitten Thy face and spat upon Thee. I have crucified Thee not once, not ten times, but a hundred, a thousand times. I am more cowardly than Judas, more inhuman than Pontius Pilate, meaner than a hardened thief. . . . My God and my All . . . my God and my All. . . . [BERNARD *appears at rear, stops at stairway and listens as* FRANCIS *prays.*] Lift Thy hand, O Lord! Strike down Thy useless servant. Shake the fruit from the tree, pluck off its very leaves. Remove at last from my heart all I have loved the most and fill it with Thy call, Thy strength, and Thy will. . . . My God and my All . . . my God and my All. . . . [BERNARD *quietly goes up the steps, and stands on platform behind* FRANCIS.] Lord God, I offer Thee my heart and body and with joy would I do more for love of Thee if only I knew how . . . if only I knew how! . . . my God and my All . . . my God and my All. . . .

FRANCIS *is in tears.* BERNARD *leans over him.*

Bernard. I never would have believed it.

FRANCIS *turns his head, recognizes his friend, gets up and they stand face to face.*

Francis. Ah . . . Bernard of Quintavalle. . . .
Bernard. I never, never would have believed it. . . .
Francis. What would you never have believed?
Bernard. I saw you going forth to war, Francis Bernadone. . . . [FRANCIS *smiles and nods in assent.*] The most shining, most eager of the young horsemen! [FRANCIS *smiles and nods again.*] And now I find you downhearted . . .
Francis. Yes.
Bernard. Weeping . . .
Francis. Yes.

Bernard. You were eager for battle and fame. Now you are going toward loneliness and misery.

Francis. Joy, Bernard. I have never looked for anything but joy. Joy is what I want. I have always loved it, yearned for it, imagined it. Every morning, when I awoke, I would look into my heart and try to imagine the joy the day would bring. I could not live without it. Whenever I felt discouraged it was because joy had gone from me and I didn't know where to find it.

Bernard. Surely the feasting, the races in the spring, the wine, singing, and beautiful girls . . .

Francis. No, never! . . . I was the most joyous of all, or at least I seemed to be. I was the most eager, the first of all on all the roads to joy. But often I broke away in order to dream. I wanted great things. I rushed headlong, like a fool, toward all that seemed great to me. I threw my whole being into that absurd quest. . . . Ah, my friend! since my return from Spoleto, what have I not endured? I was more uncertain than ever and torn by continual suffering. God did not help me. My friends gathered round and took me back to our old amusements. They disgusted me but I could not tear myself away. Again and again, without the slightest joy, I made the abominable pilgrimage of pleasure. Yes, for a long time, although weary of sin, I still sought entertainment in it. But today, my friend, you see, I tremble as I say it . . .

Bernard. What is it? Say it, Francis.

Francis. God has allowed me to taste the firstfruits of His joy and I believe it will soon be mine to keep forever.

Bernard. In tears?

Francis. In poverty, Bernard, in separation from everything and in humility.

A pause. They look at each other. BERNARD's *lips tremble.*

Bernard. Is that the road to joy?

Francis. It's hard to understand, isn't it, my friend? And if you take only a few timid steps on that road and keep back the least bit of yourself, you'll understand even less. You have to go all the way. That's the secret. I hope . . .

I hope I am able to go all the way. . . . If only I can prove that Our Lord Jesus did not die in vain!

Bernard. How can we help despairing? There is so much sin.

Francis. So much weakness, you mean, so much ignorance and forgetfulness. You see, Bernard, as the world grows older, people's lives become so complicated, they become so burdened with care and selfish. It isn't entirely their fault. All these poor people gradually forget that Jesus died for them. Jesus' death, His agony, His blood—O God, how terrible!—the body and blood of Jesus have ceased to be something real, true, for each and every man in his daily life.

Bernard. It's true. Religion goes out of their hearts. Theorizing drives it away and heresy gains day by day.

Francis. I wasn't thinking of heretics, schismatics, those who have been excommunicated, or of any of those that live outside the Holy Roman Church. I was thinking of those who are in the Church or think they are. Noblemen who believe in nothing but violence, scientists who believe only in their science, merchants who believe in nothing but their money—all those poor little forsaken outcasts who believe in nothing but their wretched needs and obey nothing but their instincts.

Bernard. We must pray very hard for them.

Francis. Yes, they are greatly in need of prayer. They need instruction. They especially need an example. The poor little people, they don't know what they do. Those who have received the tonsure and the habit—even they, alas!—do not always set an example. Corruption is everywhere, Bernard. The world is rotten.

A pause. They look at each other again.

Bernard. If anyone truly believed that the sacrifice of a single person or of several would help . . .

Francis. Don't talk like those of little faith, Bernard. One can always offer up and give oneself. Do you hear? We must make these poor people see the Passion of Our Lord. We must bring to their hearts the wounds of Lord Jesus. We must be one with Christ, crucify ourselves

visibly with Him, body and soul, give our blood, make of
our body a living sermon.

Again they pause and look at each other.

Bernard. Who can hope to sacrifice himself to this
extent, my friend?

Francis. I am the greatest sinner of all, the puniest, least
deserving. . . . Let me tell you, whisper to you, my
friend, what the All-Powerful, in spite of this, and . . .
yes, I believe because of this, has already done for me. I
was very far from Him, believe me, when He came to
me. I even thought I was free of all spiritual anxiety. I
drank and sang and enjoyed the wild merrymaking without
a qualm. But suddenly, Bernard, you see . . . I was shaken
to the center of my being, as if I had been paralyzed. I
couldn't drink, sing, smile, or even speak. In the twinkling
of an eye everything had left me. I held out my arms,
opened my hands, but couldn't take told of anything. You
see, Bernard? The world was no longer present, or rather
I no longer belonged to this world. God had taken me.

Bernard. I see, Francis. Yes, I do.

Francis. So, praying constantly day and night, I began
to ask the Lord what He wanted of me.

Bernard. And He answered?

Francis. Not at that time. No, not He Himself. But see
here. . . . One morning I was riding. It was one of those
perfect mornings when the air is so bright and pure that
everything in and around us is uplifted. I wondered at
the harmony of it all—the earth about to flower, the
tender green on the boughs, the misty sky and the song
of the first cuckoo. My horse was trotting along in fine
style, vibrant beneath me. But suddenly he stiffened,
snorted, and shook his mane. Twenty feet ahead on the
road I saw a leper standing in the hot sun . . . his face
swollen, blood-red, with sunken eyes and covered with
scabs, his arms only bare bones, his hands all wounds.
I couldn't see his feet for they were covered with dust.
The breeze brought his stench to me. I felt ill and turned
my head away. But at the same time I felt that if I succeeded in overcoming my revulsion at once, I would be

free forever. . . . Free! All fetters of the flesh destroyed!

Bernard. What happened?

Francis. With a prayer in my heart I got off my horse, walked straight to the leper without taking my eyes off him, handed him my purse and as he stretched out his hand to take it I kissed that hand. . . . Then I jumped on my horse and galloped away. My heart was full of joy, Bernard. This was the beginning of freedom in the Lord.

Bernard. Tell me about that joy. Show me that freedom, Francis.

Francis. I cannot, I'm sorry, my friend. He who enjoys such wealth must not hasten to spread it abroad. God commands us to be discreet. But if you are curious to know about these wonders, have no fear, brother. Sooner or later they will be revealed to you. . . . Since that day I have visited the lepers often. I have touched their wounds and cared for them. I love very much these outcasts who can reply only with love to the love that is given them. They are the incarnation of Our Lord Jesus among us— the dregs of the world and objects of loathing without any hope here below. I understand now that if we are to please Him and draw nearer to Him, we must be like them.

Bernard. I am almost afraid to speak in your presence, Francis. Your heart will never again find sweetness or contentment in this world. What will you do now?

Francis. I don't know. I don't even think about it any longer. I will do what He tells me. I could have stayed in my woods. I only came back because He ordered me to. I do nothing except when He calls and according to His will. . . . The words of the Master are written on my heart . . . his living words. He speaks to me . . .

Bernard. He speaks to you?

Francis. Promise not to tell anyone, Bernard. I must tell you to make you happy. He speaks to me. I hear Him. I have that inexplicable privilege of hearing words uttered by the Saviour, from his own lips.

Bernard. He speaks to you. . . .

Francis. He speaks to me when I am alone. I could never explain to you my feeling of freedom in solitude, the sinner's peace with the world in the heart of solitude. If

you can be silent and still and melt into the quiet expectancy of the clearings in the forest, into the softness o
the air and the boughs, you will see the animals, even the
wildest of them, come to you. You will see all creation
come to you. God led me into solitude. He spoke to me o
the soul. He showed me that the needs of the body are
nothing, and count for nothing compared to the unfold-
ing of a soul that has found its way.

Bernard. I long to hear more. But here comes the Bishop

Turning to right, FRANCIS *sees* BISHOP GUIDO, BERNADONE
PICA, *and the* BISHOP'S RETINUE *enter. They do not climb
to the platform.* FRANCIS *goes to them.* BERNARD *steps
aside to left.*

Francis. Yes, Monsignor, it's true. I stole the things
Everything my father told you is true. I stole valuable
cloth. I took a horse and went to Foligno and sold the
cloth. I sold the horse too at the market.

Guido. Why did you have such a need of money, my
son?

Francis. To rebuild the crumbling churches, fill the holy
lamps with oil, and help the poor. This is Christ's work

Guido. Did it not occur to you that a good thing obtained in an evil way cannot be devoted to the needs of
the church?

Francis. I am starting on a way of penitence which will
last as long as I live.

Guido. You acted imprudently. Your father's sorrow is
legitimate and his resentment is justified. You are guilty,
Francis.

Francis. It was God's will that my conversion should be
soiled by a vile sin at the outset, so that I may never
remember His blessing without being mindful of my
baseness.

Guido. But what will your baseness do to make amends,
my son?

Francis. I have offered my heart and body. I will also
give my life. You must make me do penance of constantly
increasing severity. You must help me destroy all inordinate
appetite, all devotion to things of the flesh.

Bernadone. Careful, Monsignor! He is riding his saintli-

ness hobby again. Break his pride, that's the vital thing.
Give him orders if you are his commander.

Guido. God's will——

Bernadone. How can I tell that it's God's will? How
do I know my son has not yielded to the temptations of
the evil spirit?

Guido. Will you please let me speak, my poor Bernadone? . . . Francis, look into your heart. I pray God not
to deceive you by the zeal he has filled you with. [*Praying
for a moment.*] My child, your father demands, if he is to
pardon your errors, that you give up the way of life you
have started upon and obey him as you used to do.

Bernadone. He must not only obey me, but accept our
loving care. His mother and I want to recover the son we
asked God for so long. We love him and have done everything for him.

Guido. What do you say?

Francis. You know my heart, Monsignor. God has revealed it to you and you have often confessed me. You
know I have no desire to revolt. On the contrary, I am
compelled to obey and cannot conceive of avoiding the
orders I have received which place me irrevocably under
the command of the Creator.

Guido. Do you hear, Pietro Bernadone?

Bernadone. I hear rising within me a father's curse. I
urge you to spare us this, both of us, Monsignor.

Francis. Father, don't ask me to do what I cannot do:
forsake Jesus!

Bernadone. Tell me, Monsignor, to build a church, a
convent, spend a large part of my wealth in almsgiving.
Ask me to make a pilgrimage to Jerusalem. I will do all
of it, I promise. But don't allow our only son to be taken
from us.

Guido. I pity your grief with all my soul, my friend.
But tell me, what do you think would become of your
fine son if he stayed with you?

Bernadone. He would be a cloth merchant like us, a
good citizen, a good parishioner, the father of a family—
a useful, honest man, wouldn't he, wife?

Pica. A happy man too. [*All look at one another silently.*] Remember, Francis, I bore you, fed you, reared

you, gave you everything. A little while ago I nursed you through your illness and pulled you back . . . with these hands you have forgotten . . . pulled you back from death.

A silence. PICA *weeps.* FRANCIS *noiselessly forms with his lips a few words that express his grief and his triumph over it.*

Guido. Don't cry, Lady Pica. God will do wonders, you'll see. . . . And as for you, Pietro Bernadone, don't try to stand between this boy and God. The world needs saints.

Chorus [Chanting]. The table is set, Francis. All the guests have arrived except you. The musicians have come and the cups are filled.

Francis. There is only one cup, filled with the blood of Christ Jesus. I thirst for it. It alone can bring me rapture.

Chorus. Put on your armor, Francis. The horses are shaking their manes, the weapons resound, fame beckons to you.

Francis. Faith is my buckler. My helmet is Salvation. I will grasp the sword of the Spirit, O Word of God!

Chorus. I am chaste, Francis, and I will be faithful. I will bring you happiness, a home, children.

Francis. The more barren I am, the more children I will have and the more beautiful they will be. The bride I have chosen is nobler and purer than any earthly woman. She is a great queen who has been treated with scorn. She is here. She draws near and gives me her hand. O Lady Poverty, O holy Poverty, lead me until I die!

Pause. GUIDO *turns to* FRANCIS.

Guido. It is certain then, my dear son, that you want to join God's service?

Francis. Yes, I want to, and immediately, Monsignor. I want it with all my heart. My heart is so filled with the love of poor Christ and the love of poor men that there is no room in it for the slightest desire, or, I hope, for the slightest weakness.

BERNADONE *and* PICA *turn away.* BERNARD *falls on his knees. The* CHORUS *and* CHORUS LEADER *rise.*

Bernadone. A father's curse upon him! . . . a father's curse!

Pica. My little Francis. My little Francis. . . .

Guido. Almighty God, You will not forget and You will make perfect in Your love the great sacrifice that a poor man and a poor woman are now making to You.

FRANCIS *starts to undress.*

Bernard. Lord, I pray You, prepare me, prepare me. . . .

Chorus Leader [*Reading the Holy Gospel*]. "If thou wilt be perfect, go, sell what thou hast, and give to the poor . . ."

Chorus [*Singing softly*]. Praise be to God, the Son, and the Holy Ghost. . . .

Guido. What are you doing, Francis?

Francis [*Undressing*]. I am going to return to my father the clothing I received from him.

GUIDO, *his back to the audience, shields* FRANCIS *from view with his cloak.*

Pica. Here we are alone, my poor husband. . . .

Bernadone. A father's curse upon him! A father's curse!

Bernard. My heart is ready, O God! My heart is ready!

Chorus Leader [*Reading*]. "If any man will to come after me, let him deny himself, and take up his cross . . ."

Chorus [*Softly*]. As it was in the beginning, is now and ever shall be. . . .

GUIDO *turns around, still covering* FRANCIS' *nakedness with his cloak.*

Francis. At last I can say: Our Father who art in heaven. . . .

Guido [*Softly*]. Give him some clothing.

The CHORUS *and* GUIDO'S *retinue pass along from hand to hand to* FRANCIS *a gown, a beggar's wallet, a staff and shoes.*

Bernadone. How hardhearted he is.

Pica. Not even a look, a last kiss for us!

Bernard. I will sing Thy praise in the midst of the peoples, O Lord! I will sing Thee a psalm amidst the nations!

Chorus Leader. "Get you no gold, nor silver, nor brass in your purse; no wallet for your journey, neither coat, nor shoes, nor staff. . . ."

Chorus [*In a muted chant*]. World without end, Amen.

FRANCIS *throws down his staff, his wallet, and his shoes, and exits singing.*

SCENE II

THE PLACE: RIVO-TORTO, *in the woods near* ASSISI, *where* SAINT FRANCIS *and his Brothers lived in a hovel in the early days of their Order. It was their training ground.*

THE TIME: *Sometime in 1210.*

FRANCIS *and* BERNARD *are sitting on platform near each other.* FRANCIS *is darning* BERNARD'S *tunic.*

FRANCIS. Many thorns were strewn along the paths of your pilgrimage, Brother Pilgrim. They have torn your tunic. Have they also injured your feet? [*He kneels to examine* BERNARD'S *bare feet and gently rubs them.*] A lot of dust, a few skinned places and a little blood. Nothing serious, beloved son. [*Sitting down again and continuing to darn the tunic, he sings softly.*] ". . . And not men only, but all beasts also, both wild and tame . . ." Oh, Bernard, it is so beautiful to find that even the animals accept our love and our loving care when they see that these are given in obedience to the Creator!

BROTHER LEO *enters from left and climbs to platform.*

Leo. So Bernard is here again. [BERNARD *rises and embraces* LEO.] Peace be with you, Brother.
Bernard. Praise the Lord.

They cross themselves.

Leo. Did your heart rejoice at great Saint James's tomb?

Bernard. Nowhere is it so full of joy as here in our little enclosure.

BROTHER ELIAS *comes in from right and goes to* BERNARD.

Elias. So you're with us again, Bernard.

Bernard. Brother Elias!

Elias. Peace be with you, Brother.

They embrace.

Bernard. Praise the Lord.

They cross themselves.

Elias. How lucky you are, Bernard! Did you enjoy the beauties of Compostela, the splendid sanctuary, the magnificent ceremonies?

Bernard. They did not make me forget holy poverty. A church can never be humble enough for me. I have always loved the humblest of them and I love the caves in the mountains even more.

Francis. I do too.

Elias. Were there many people?

Bernard. I avoided them. On the way back, the crowd of pilgrims stuck to the highway but I cut across the fields. It was a good idea as you will see. Late yesterday, not far from here, I was alone on a river bank when suddenly a young man came up. He was the most handsome fellow I ever saw. He was coming from our Portiuncula and was sad because he had not been able to speak to Francis there. He asked why I did not go ahead and cross the river. I told him I was afraid of the spring floods. "Very well, then," he said. "We'll go together and you won't be afraid." He took me by the hand, made me glide over the water, set me down on the other bank and almost before I knew what was happening, he disappeared!

Elias. I knew it! He spoke to me too. Francis was praying at the time. I refused to disturb him and threw the intruder out. That's just what I did. I threw him out! Then I was ashamed and felt that God wanted me to run back and look for him. Too late! The angel had disappeared.

Francis. So, Brother Elias, you drive away the Holy

Messengers that are good enough to visit us? Aren't you afraid you'll discourage the Lord?

Elias. Of course I am. I know only too well I discourage the Lord. I'll always be slow to reply to His loving kindness. It's pride, you see. It's my accursed tendency to become angry. A fog of pride steams up in my brain and prevents me from seeing my fellow men. I know this, I blame myself for it but I can't seem to get over it. I'll never be able to!

Francis. Don't be so violent, Elias. Violence is your weak point.

Elias. I know only too well it's my weak point. . . . Oh, if only I could be calm! Dear brothers, I envy you for being so simple and true. Ah, humility, humility!

Francis. Yes, Elias, humility. Those who don't have it are cut off from everything.

Elias. I know, I know! I'll try to do penance. . . . Dear Lord, I want to do penance. Forgive me!

He jerks his hood forcibly down over his head, sits down to right and begins to pray. BERNARD *and* LEO *look silently at* FRANCIS.

Francis. We must not let ourselves be overcome by sadness. Each of us will have his day and find his path. A tremendous number of people have already begun to follow us. . . . There was a time, Bernard, when you, my first-born, were always in my thoughts. Today I think very much of another wonderful gift the Lord is preparing for us . . . an eighteen-year-old girl. I can't describe her for I've hardly looked at her. They say she is beautiful, but her beauty has not led her into love of worldly things. She comes from a famous and powerful family. God has promised me to do great things for her and through her. I hope soon . . . probably on the night of Palm Sunday. . . . I am so happy, Bernard and Leo! We will plant this tender flower in our garden, care for it with charity. Her name is Clare.

A pause.

Leo. Clare means bright and clear like a spring of fresh water.

Bernard. Like the morning star.

Leo. She will be our star. She will walk before us. We will all look at her. We will not remember, not remember at all the time when our souls were scattered.

Bernard. Mine will gather strength, Francis, I promise. I can already imagine the last moments of my stay on earth. It will be almost too easy to put my soul into God's hands. It will rise straight into the air with joy.

A lark's song is heard.

Francis. Like the lark. [*Looking at the bird and others that fly up.*] Does the lark need more than a drop of water from the spring and a bit of grain from the field to give her strength to soar into the air and sing God's praises so joyously that men interrupt their work and gaze at the sky? Greetings, my sister the lark! Greetings to you, warbler, titmouse, nightingale! Greetings to you, swallow, and you, my sister the turtledove, so simple, innocent and pure! Greetings to all, all! [*Birds fly in from all sides. A sound of music is heard.* FRANCIS *stands erect, then stoops, then lifts his head and turns around. He stretches out his arms and birds perch upon them.*] My little brothers, the birds. . . .

Chorus. Praise the Lord, praise the Lord. . . .

Francis. For this freedom of yours to fly everywhere.

Chorus. And for the songs your Creator taught you.

Francis. My little brothers, the birds. . . .

Chorus. Praise the Lord, praise the Lord. . . .

Other friars of FRANCIS *enter one by one—*ANGELO, MASSEO, JOHN. *They embrace as they meet, walk on tiptoes, and warn one another by gestures to keep silent.*

Leo. Look, look. . . .

Angelo. On his head and hands. . . .

Francis. For you neither sow nor reap. . . .

Chorus. And God supplies you with food. . . .

Francis. He has given you springs to drink from. . . .

Chorus. And mountains, hills, and rocks for refuge. . . .

Leo. Look, look. . . .

Masseo. They flutter round his ears.

John. And nest inside his hood.

Francis. My little brothers. . . . My little brothers, the birds. . . .

Chorus. Praise the Lord, praise the Lord, praise the Lord!

Leo. Look, look. . . .

Angelo. He is completely covered with birds.

Leo. And in ecstasy. . . .

FRANCIS *stands motionless with arms outstretched, his back to audience. The friars also stand still looking at* FRANCIS. *Suddenly the birds with a great noise fly away and* FRANCIS *makes the sign of the cross after them. He turns round, sees his Brothers, and stretches out his arms to them. They all rush forward and fling themselves down before him.*

Francis. My blessed sons, beloved sons. . . . I, Brother Francis, your little servant, bless you with all my heart.

All the Monks. Our Father, who art in heaven . . .

They rise and continue the Lord's Prayer in a murmur. For a moment bird songs are still heard from a distance.

Francis. In the name of the Lord, my little brothers, each of you must tell me where he has been and what he has done this morning. Angelo, you will speak first.

Angelo. I confess I was very hungry and begged for a loaf of bread. But as soon as I got it I said to myself: "Brother Angelo, you must not keep that big loaf all for yourself and eat it alone like a glutton." So I looked around for someone to share it with and saw a poor woman who seemed about to faint. I hurried to offer her my bread. When I came to her she held out a little pebble. It was hard, shiny, and streaked with blue. It looked so pretty that I took it with joy. When she saw my joy her sad face lighted up with such a smile that I was afraid—how can I explain it, brothers? It occurred to me she was happier to have given me the little pebble than she would be if she received my bread. I was afraid of spoiling such a pure feeling by my act of charity. So I kept the pebble and hid my bread.

Francis. Good Brother Angelo, you will please give me the little poor woman's pebble. Thank you. [*Smiling.*] I want it so that I may be reminded that the pleasure of receiving is often nearer to perfect joy than that of giving. . . . Well, Brother John, what's the matter?

John. You must pardon me, holy man. Ever since I got up this morning I have tried only to please my heart.

Some swallows make a deafening chatter. Everyone looks up.

Francis. Oh, my little sisters, the swallows, will you please be quiet a moment and let us hear what Brother John has to say? You may sing as loud as you like, afterwards.

The birds make a little more noise, then fall silent.

Angelo. They are still now.

Francis. Now tell us, John.

John. I was supposed to dig in the garden. See, here's my spade. I've kept it with me but I didn't dig at all. The poor spade, more obedient than I, took me to task. She said: "Brother John, you big, fat fool, why don't you be sensible? You know our sister the earth can't produce her fruits without our help. What will happen if we don't cultivate her? She will be barren." But the poor thing was wasting her breath. Brother John just stood there and couldn't keep his eyes or his heart off Brother Francis; he saw him nearby and imitated every gesture he made!

Francis. This is bad, John!

John. I'm sure it's bad, Mary Mother of Jesus! since you say so. But by my patron saint, suppose I can't help it? God Himself commanded me to do that. Ever since the day—remember?—I met you in the little church you were sweeping in my village—remember?—and I took the broom from you and finished sweeping—remember? You were pleased. You didn't scold me that day. Then God told me: "Just you look at Francis and do as he does, exactly as he does. It's quite simple. . . ." But no, it's not at all simple and I don't understand if you, Francis, my master and benefactor, forbid me to do what God commanded me that I might enter His Paradise. . . . Please, please, Francis, have pity on me. A poor man like me without education or virtue certainly can't hope to be like you inside, with your wisdom and prayer. But the outside, Francis, your gestures at least—you can surely let me imitate them. . . .

Francis. I'll let you do penance. You must say——No, we will say together, four Paternosters and five Aves. . . . The sun is already high. Everyone must go to his work.

The monks withdraw, except for Leo *and* Elias, *who is still praying.* Masseo *returns, leading a beggar.*

Masseo. Here's a poor man. He has heard of your gifts to the poor and has come to you from far away over bad roads and with great difficulty.

Beggar. I'm hungry, Francis.

Francis. Angelo! Where are you, Angelo?

His call is relayed by three different voices.

Beggar. God cannot refuse you anything. Ask Him for bread for me.

Enter Angelo.

Leo. Brother Angelo!

Francis. Angelo, your bread!

Angelo. Lord have mercy on us. We have just eaten it.

All look at one another in silence.

Beggar. It's hard when hope is ended.

Francis. Leo, Leo, God's little lamb, all my sins rise to plague me. I am not cleansed of my iniquity. . . . Wait a minute, my poor man. . . . Rest here a while. Then, if you pity me, if you pray for me, perhaps God will provide. Leo, all my sins. . . . Let us pray together. . . . Help me.

He takes Leo *aside and they kneel side by side.*

Beggar. O God, if Thou art with us, look. . . . I am still trying. . . .

Leo [*Praying*]. Lord, if this man's prayer is not acceptable to you, what hope can we others have of your mercy?

Francis. No, Leo, that is not what you must say. You must say: Lord, you see before you the world's greatest sinner. But such as I am, I come to help him pray.

Elias. I am tempted. In spite of my prayers, temptation always returns to plague me. I see it!

Beggar. Lord, lean down to me a little. Just a little more. Give me Thy hand, O Lord!

Leo [Praying]. We are poor men. Each of us says his poor prayer.

Francis. Lord, you surely do not want the poor man's patience to go for naught.

Elias [Praying]. Break my heart and my will. Put my sins in my hand so that I may crush them. Help me destroy this cold monster that oppresses all my thoughts.

Francis. Lord, let me be accursed, take from me the sweetness of talking to Thee, but let my brother Elias find the charity he seeks.

Elias. I would like to be loved. Make me as worthy of being loved as my brother Francis.

Francis. Leo, go tell Brother Elias to come to me.

LEO *gets up and goes to* ELIAS.

Beggar. Yes, Lord, here I am, in the same place. Don't take Thy hand away from me.

Leo. Francis wants you, Elias.

Elias. Tell him I'm praying.

Francis. Elias! [ELIAS *gets up, removes his cowl, and climbs to platform.* LEO *exits to right.* FRANCIS *stands up.*] Brother Elias, I wanted to ask you to pray for me.

Elias. Am I worthy?

Francis. A man can always pray for another. It's not a question of worthiness, but love.

Elias. And you, Father, do you love me?

He throws himself at FRANCIS' *feet and* FRANCIS *leans over him.*

Francis. Of all my sons you are one of the dearest to me.

Elias. What torments me is the thought that you do not love me . . . not as much as you do Leo, Bernard. . . . I don't think you know how much I love you either.

Francis. Why don't you tell me then like a man, instead of grumbling behind my back? Why let your heart suffer and grow hard and listen to the advice of the Devil whose breath scorches the fruit on the trees?

Elias. I am so ashamed, Father. Even at your feet I am not safe from the vilest temptations.

He weeps. FRANCIS *kneels before him.*

Francis. What about me? Do you think I am never tempted? If we were not to be tempted, we would have to be without desire. Our hearts would have to stop beating. . . . Be faithful to prayer. Temptation overcome is a gift to us from the Lord. You overcome temptations, of course?

Elias. No, no, I scatter them, I dodge them, and wear them out through prayer or fasting. I don't overcome them. They leave their mark on my heart—sorrow.

Francis. Sorrow! Oh, my child, what a wicked word! Leave sorrow to the Devil, who is always looking for new victims. Leave anxiety and disappointment to him. But you, the firstfruits of the harvest, be full of cheer, joy in the Lord. Be happy, gay, and affable toward everyone and you will inspire men with love of God. . . . [A *voice is heard singing offstage.*] Listen to that fine voice. I know it—it is Giles. Blessed be my brother that goes out without being asked, begs with humility and returns with joy. [FRANCIS *goes toward* GILES *who enters carrying a heavy bag and a goatskin bottle. Tall and powerful, he kneels before* FRANCIS, *who leans over and kisses his cheek. When* GILES *gets up,* FRANCIS *takes his bag.*] Give me your pouch. I want to carry it a little.

He carries the bag a few steps, then sets it down and pours the contents on the ground. GILES *holds up the goatskin.*

Giles. Cool water! cool water! Who wants cool water?

The monks, including RUFINO *and others—twelve in all— run up from all sides, and the goatskin passes from hand to hand.*

Francis. Come, brothers, come, and thank this poor man for the bountiful gifts the Lord has granted us.

Chorus. Lord, we humbly thank Thee. . . .

The friars say grace, and each, as he gets his share of GILES's provisions, bows to the BEGGAR, who also bows and beats his chest.

Beggar. I am not worthy. . . .

Francis. Sit down, poor people. Satisfy your hunger. But don't forget that redemption is coming to the world and its progress depends on each of us. Let us not sadden the Holy Spirit. [*All sit except FRANCIS, who remains standing among them. All begin to eat in silence except JOHN, who, with a piece of bread in his hand, looks intently at FRANCIS.*] Why don't you eat your bread, John? What are you waiting for?

John. I'm waiting to see if you are hungry.

Francis. I am not very hungry.

Beggar. I've had enough myself. Take some of mine, Father.

Francis. I will, my son. . . . And let us not forget our sister, the dust, that I love because she is pure. [*Sprinkling a little dust on his bread.*]

Giles. The truth is we are never as hungry as we think we are.

Masseo. Never as sleepy either.

Giles. It's just a matter of loving the Lord more than eating or sleeping.

Leo. A good theme to meditate upon is like a solid anchor to steady us.

The monks fall silent and are uplifted in ecstasy. Suddenly a voice is heard, singing a psalm.

Francis. Last night the Devil was noisy. He was bursting with activity, the fool. I was thinking of the voice of the Lord. You know what Saint John says: "he calleth his own sheep by name. . . ." By name!

Rufino. And the Apostle continued: "When he hath put forth all his own sheep, he goeth before them; and the sheep follow him, for they know his voice."

Angelo. The Voice of the Lord. . . .

Rufino. Let us listen to the Voice of the Lord.

Leo. And listen only to it.

Giles. Let us listen, listen, brothers. . . .

A silence, interrupted only by a soft, gurgling sound from
MASSEO, *expressing his beatific mood.*

Rufino. There was a time when just plain men could
hear their name called by the Voice of the Lord at any
hour of the day.

John. He called them like this: Peter . . . James . . .
John. . . .

Giles. And the one who was called turned round and
saw only a few steps away the face and smile of Jesus of
Nazareth.

Leo. His face . . . and smile. . . . We try to follow
them too. . . .

Masseo. We are not doctors of theology.

John. True!

Masseo. We don't ask for precise explanations. We
don't need them.

Leo. We always say and do the same thing.

Giles. Because we don't know anything else.

Francis. We are God's troubadours. . . . God spoke
a word to us one day and we have never been able to
forget it. And since that day we have not advanced in
learning, eloquence, dignity, or rank. Rather the contrary. We have gained nothing in the world, have we,
poor little Brothers Minor? But the mark of God has
deepened in us. It has bored, eaten, burned, further and
further into our flesh like the places which we wash and
care for, eaten away in the flesh of our leprous brothers.
It is said that if our senses were keen enough we could
hear the wheat grow and the grapes ripen and share in
the inner secret of life, instead of being separated from
it—observing, admiring, and only sometimes understanding it from the outside. So because God wants all the
thought and good will of which we are capable to turn
inward, we are allowed to cut ourselves off from the world,
shun its noise and turbulence, and sometimes hang sus-
pended between heaven and earth to listen to God grow

inside us, like a continuous prayer alive and powerful, which little by little fulfills in us God's promise to mankind, little by little makes us resemble God, replacing all we had ever loved before or longed for. Prayer restores to us man's innocence and strength and privilege before the first sin, first disobedience, and first violence. Let us pray, my dear little brothers

for all those who cannot see the miracles of nature mingled with those of divine love

for all who have not learned to read the word of God in the dove and the earthworm

for the unhappy kings whose fate it is to be consumed with ambition

for all men who in search of themselves go farther and farther from God

for all those whom Satan convinces in private little talks that they are masters of human knowledge and will rise higher the more they give freedom, latitude, and ferocity to their own will, the more they heap up riches and insist upon their own explanation of the world . . . which is not true, not true, not true! . . .

The friars remain silent. FRANCIS *looks at them, smiles, and calls them by name.*

Isn't it so? Bernard . . . Giles . . . Leo . . . Angelo . . . Juniper . . . Elias . . . John . . . Masseo . . . Rufino . . . simple children. . . .

A pause.

Bernard. We also have heard ourselves called each by his name. . . . See, brothers, we also are twelve gathered round Francis. . . .

Francis. Bernard, Bernard, what are you saying? A demon put those words in your mouth! [*Throwing himself face down on the ground.*] Oh, Bernard! In the name of obedience, I command you to tread upon me! I command you to put your foot upon my head and grind me into the dust. You must say: "Face down to the ground, wretched man! Where did you get your pride? Down to the ground! down to the ground!"

The friars turn their heads away and shroud them in their cowls. The Beggar *hides his face in his hands.* Bernard *gets up and goes to* Francis, *who is still stretched on the ground. He places his foot on the saint's head, then bursts into sobs and beats his chest with his fists.*

Bernard. Down to the ground! Down to the ground!
Chorus. Alleluia!
Bernard. Down to the ground!
Chorus. Alleluia, alleluia!

Bernard *hides among the monks, who also beat their chests. A pause.* Francis *gets up.*

Francis. Now go. Proclaim peace to men and preach penance for the remission of sins. Be patient in affliction, constant in prayer, courageous in good works, modest in speech, serious in conduct, and grateful for benefits received. In return, you will inherit the Eternal Kingdom. And when you see entering there with you all the souls to whom on this earth you have transmitted life eternal your hearts will rejoice!

Chorus. Alleluia, Alleluia! *Emitte Spiritum tuum et creabuntur, et renovabis faciem terrae.* Alleluia!

The friars file past Francis *in pairs and embrace him. You feel that* Francis *would like to say something special, personal, to each of his brothers as they pass. But he simply clasps each to his heart with transcendent emotion, repeating a single word softly but with increasing intensity.*

Francis. Charity. . . . Charity. . . . [*After the sixth monk has passed,* Francis *halts the rest.*] Charity . . . yes . . . first, last, and always. . . . Ah, little brothers, charity alone. . . . There is no other word, no other way. . . . Yes, I know you agree you want it. . . . I am not sure you know just how much. . . . Don't be too quick to answer. Don't nod your heads too soon. . . . One thing I beg of you: try to keep perfectly still and silent, and into the heart of the silence let fall of its own weight the word of Jesus—charity, charity. . . . Be men, the most human of men, and at the same time the most saintly. . . . Ah, let charity enter

your body, your blood. . . . Let it become the belief and
habit of your entire substance. . . . I think that is what
I wanted to tell you . . . to let not only your spirit and
heart be charitable, but your feet also of their own accord
and by themselves. Ah, little brothers, give yourselves to
me, give yourselves to God, give yourselves to mankind.
. . . [*As he speaks,* FRANCIS *embraces the six other
monks. The twelve, increasingly silent, formidable, and determined to be missionaries, start to exit.* FRANCIS *stops
them once more.*] Ah, little brothers, my children, my poor
friends, God's work needs all you have . . . all of you,
even your blood. As the Holy Scripture says: you have
not yet fought with your blood. You are called from the
far corners of the earth to bear witness. God expects no
less of us than He did of His first chosen few. He calls
us as He did them and sends us into the world like
them—into a world that has done far worse than not
to know—a world that has forgotten. It is not only sunk
in a bog of ignorance, it is crusted over with pride. It
thinks it has gone beyond the valley of darkness, but
never has it been plunged into so much gloom. You are
chosen, my poor little ones, to knock at the door of the
world—a door higher, more dismal and unfeeling, than
the desert rock. . . . Go out anyway in your poverty,
your weakness. Go and take your blood. Go, my beloved,
as pilgrims and strangers. Never despair. Go with your
blood . . . even unto death. . . .

A roll of drums is heard. The BROTHERS *file out.* FRANCIS
goes to the BEGGAR, *takes him by the shoulder and leads
him off.*

SCENE III

THE PLACE: *A village occupied by the enemy—the Sara-
cen soldiery of* EMPEROR FREDERICK II—*in the countryside near* ASSISI.

THE TIME: *Palm Sunday, April 18, 1212.*

A roll of drums is heard.

CHORUS LEADER [*Reading*]. "Prophecy of the fall of Baby-
lon as revealed to Isaiah, son of Amoz. . . . Set ye up
a banner upon the bare mountain, lift up the voice unto
them, wave the hand, that they may go into the gates
of the nobles. I have commanded my consecrated ones,
yea, I have called my mighty men for mine anger, even
my proudly exulting ones. [*Flourish of trumpets.*] The
noise of a multitude in the mountains, as of a great
people! The noise of a tumult of the kingdoms of the
nations gathered together! The Lord of Hosts is mustering
the host for the battle. They come from a far country,
from the uttermost part of heaven, even the Lord, and
the weapons of His indignation, to destroy the whole
land. [*Flourish of trumpets.*] Howl ye; for the day of the
Lord is at hand; as destruction from the Almighty shall
it come. Therefore shall all hands be feeble and every
heart of man shall melt. And they shall be afraid; pangs
and sorrows shall take hold of them; they shall be in pain
as a woman in travail; they shall look in amazement one
at another; their faces shall be faces of flame."

Sound of trumpets and drums. A CHORUS *member rushes
out of orchestra and onto stage.*

  Chorus Member I. Cursed be Emperor Frederick's Saracens who swarm over the whole land, burning and destroying strongholds, castles and cities, cutting down trees
and trampling vineyards and gardens.
  Chorus Member II [*Running on stage*]. Men, women,
children, they turn into prisoners, deportees, and corpses.
Curses on them!
  Chorus Member III [*Also running on stage*]. Quiet,
fool! You want them to burn our houses down? Take our
sons away into slavery?
  Chorus Member II. You always want to surrender.
  Chorus Member III. And you curse them behind their
backs.
  Chorus. Silence!

A silence. Three more CHORUS *members come on stage.*

  Chorus Member I. Who will tell us what we can do?
  Chorus Member VI. We must sleep on the ground and
swallow our rage while we wait for liberation.

Chorus Member IV. They will fight over our bodies and put as many soldiers in our houses as horses in our fields.

Chorus Member V. They may be hungrier still.

Chorus. That will be worse!

A silence.

Chorus Member I. We're completely defenseless.

Chorus Member II. Our Duke is too old.

Chorus Member V. And we are too cowardly.

Chorus Member IV. Speak for yourself.

Chorus Member V. I am speaking for myself. I'm forty years old. I'm unable to make a move or even think. But aren't you the same? The only difference is I admit it.

Chorus Member VI. What's the use?

Chorus Member V. It makes me feel a little better to say it.

A pause.

Chorus Member III. But I say there is only one sensible and useful thing to do.

Half-Chorus I. What is that?

Chorus Member III. Try to find a way to get along with them.

Half-Chorus II. Get along with them?

Chorus Member III. As well as possible, that is, since they are the masters.

Chorus. How can you say such a thing?

Chorus Member II. Didn't you know big Paul is on their side? He always has been for them.

Chorus Member III. You mean me?

Chorus Member II. We know you, old boy. You're rich. You don't mind greasing their palms so they will leave your cattle and chickens alone.

Chorus Member IV. It's always the same story. The rich suffer less than the poor.

Chorus Member V. You think we're blind? Why haven't your house and garden been touched?

Half-Chorus I. Tell us, why?

Half-Chorus II. You disgusting profiteer!

A pause.

Chorus Member III. Anyway, I wouldn't send my daughter to flirt with the commander in order to get favors from him.

Chorus Member II. What about your wife? Does she refuse to drink with them at night in your wine cellar?

Chorus Member III. You're jealous because your wife has a big, baggy stomach and breasts that look like empty bladders.

Chorus Member II. How would you like me to punch you in the jaw?

Chorus Member IV. Must we fight among ourselves?

Chorus. That's enough. Stop it!

Enter BROTHER GILES.

Giles. Peace be with you.

Chorus Member I. Ha, ha, that's very funny.

Chorus Member II. Ha, ha! Peace! It's about time!

Chorus. Ha, ha! Ha, ha, ha!

Chorus Member IV. If it's stones you're asking for, Brother Beggar, you came to the right place! Here are some!

Chorus Member V. What did you come here for, lazy good-for-nothing?

Giles. To help you a little, if I can.

Chorus Member III. To do what?

Chorus Member I. There's no work, no jobs.

Chorus Member IV. And we don't want any useless mouths to feed.

Giles. I understand completely, poor people. But if my mouth is useless, it is not very greedy. Maybe you have firewood to be gathered, water to be drawn, tools to be repaired, olives to be harvested—how should I know?— maybe sick people to be cared for, dead to be buried.

Chorus Member III. Dead and dying, yes. We cart them off every day.

Chorus Member II. As for the crops, if they wait for us to harvest them, they'll rot where they stand.

Giles. What did you say?

Chorus Member I. We're tired of working without pay.

Giles. Those fine grapes about to ripen, those trees loaded with fruit—you're not going to bring in the harvest?

Chorus. For whom?

Giles. What you've sowed, planted, grafted, pruned, my friends, you plan to abandon it?

Chorus Member IV. What can we gather it with?

Chorus Member II. They've taken our horses, carts, and tools.

Half-Chorus I. Everything!

Half-Chorus II. Everything!

Giles. What about feet to walk on, hands to pick, backs to carry, have they taken them from you? And the grace of God, have they taken it? You don't need anything else.

Chorus Member VI. Right! If you mean to die of hunger.

Giles. Eater of chaff, have you always eaten grain?

Chorus Member V. Chaff or grain, we used to eat. Look—our trousers are so big they almost fall off our waists.

Giles. So it's your stomach you're feeling sorry for? A big stomach has never given anyone strength or courage. Do you need your stomach to run, dig, love your neighbor? You should be glad to see your tyrant ruler overthrown. The Lord sends these rough soldiers over your bodies—just as you push a roller over your fields—to crush the clods.

Chorus Member II. Is it also the Lord who puts two armed soldiers behind every worker to take the fruit of his labor?

Giles. You consider the harvest a just reward for your labor. But how many of you have felt yourselves indebted to God? Now is the time to repent.

Chorus Member IV. He means, friends, our present suffering is a reward.

Giles. It should make you think and work. It enables you to make a fresh start. What have you done up to now?

Chorus Member V. Haven't we done plenty of hard work?

Giles. Yes, but nothing for your soul! Nothing for your soul! You have never done anything for your soul. You never think of it. You don't even know whether you still have one. The time of the soul has come.

Enter MARTIN.

Martin. The time of the soul, you say? Here, look at my soul through the hole in my backside. I'll give you my soul to make sausage with!

Chorus. Martin, Martin. . . .

Martin. What do you mean, Martin? What do you want with Martin? There's no more Martin. You can pinch me until I bleed, put a torch in my face, drive a nail into my eye—I won't feel a thing. I just jump and yell.

Chorus. Martin. . . . Please, Martin. . . .

Martin. I'm all alone in the world—no parents, no wife or children. . . . I live in a big house full of dark corners. The bed my mother died in has a big quilt that mice nest in. . . . The time of the soul indeed! The Saracens took my last potato! [*He howls like an animal. Enter* FRANCIS *with* BERNARD, ELIAS, *and* BEGGAR. MARTIN *begins to dance*]. Martin is the one who runs around naked at night in your kitchens. . . . It's Martin that eats your bread . . . and makes sport with your wives. . . .

Francis. Demon!

He comes down from platform and walks straight toward MARTIN, *who runs from him.*

Martin. No. Oh, no, don't touch me!

Francis. Demon, I command you in the name of the Almighty to leave this man. And you, poor brother, stop lying. It is not true that evil has disfigured you forever. Compel your spirit to look backwards and recover the purity of your baptism. Together we will build on it your deliverance. [*Seizing* MARTIN.] Ah! I have you!

Martin. You're hurting me!

Francis. Defend yourself. Grapple with me. Strike the most insignificant servant of God. Let your anger make the demon inside you loosen his grip. I won't let you go until you are free.

Martin. I don't want you to free me, damn you! Please.
. . . No!

*Surrounded by the crowd which is afraid to intervene and
which has been joined by* PRIEST, PHILOSOPHER, POOR
JOAN, BERNADONE, *and* PICA, FRANCIS *wrestles silently
with the man possessed of a devil.* FRANCIS *is thrown
to the ground. His face bleeds.*

Chorus. Oh! . . .

FRANCIS *pulls himself to his knees.* MARTIN *stands still
and looks at him.* FRANCIS *drags himself to* MARTIN *on
his knees, takes his hands calmly, and leans against him
to pull himself up.*

Francis [Speaking very gently]. Look into my eyes. Put
your hands in my hands. We'll crush the vile thing together.

Martin. Ah! You're making my bones crack, my insides
bleed, and my eyes water!

Francis. Be brave. Put all your strength into it. Get
rid of that filthy, slimy thing.

Martin. Oh-h-h! You're torturing me! tearing me to
bits! . . . Aaah!

He rolls on the ground, shrieking. FRANCIS *leans over and
pats him.*

Francis. Poor little fellow. . . . There, there, it's all
over. Be at peace now. Come and sit beside me. Come and
rest. Sleep.

He leads MARTIN *to platform and settles him down on
left. He looks at him for a long time and* MARTIN *falls
asleep. The crowd murmurs and stirs.*

Chorus. Ah . . . ah . . . ah . . . Francis . . . Francis. . . .

Poor Joan. Saint, saint, Saint Francis. . . . Ah. . . .

Beggar. It's a miracle . . . a miracle. . . .

He bursts into tears. FRANCIS *lifts his head, looks at the
sky, rubs his face, then looks at the crowd.*

Francis. What was I going to tell you? I don't remember. Forgive me, brothers. I don't remember. I will simply bless you and you will go back to your work. You must go with them, Bernard, Giles, Elias, and help them. . . .

All kneel obediently. They form three different groups, each of which is joined by one of the three friars. FRANCIS *makes the sign of the cross over them and they get up silently.*

Bernard. The hay must be gathered in before it rains.

The first group nods silently in agreement.

Giles. The grape vines must be tied.

The second group nods.

Elias. The lettuce must be watered.

The third group nods in assent. The three groups start off in different directions. FRANCIS *halts them.*

Francis. Oh, yes. I wanted to tell you. . . . Listen. . . . But you see him. [*Pointing to* MARTIN *at his feet.* MARTIN *stirs and groans.*] Pity him, I beg of you. Pity yourselves. [MARTIN *yells.*] Be peaceful, my poor Martin. You see, our sins make us rotten, repulsive, wretched. As Our Lord says in His Gospel: from the heart of man come evil thoughts, adultery, fornication, murder, theft, wickedness, fraud, evil looks, blasphemy, pride, and madness. This is hell, the rule of Satan, the black fire—alas, alas, my Brothers, eternal torment!

Beggar. It's true, it's true. Believe him. It's true.

Bernard. The soul must be tended. . . .

Chorus. Yes.

Elias. Pride must be cut off. . . .

Chorus. Yes, yes.

Francis. Also be pure, my children. This I ask of you. Do me the favor of not using profanity. It would be a very good start, a nice token of courtesy toward the Good Lord. Don't soil your lips or your heart by even the slightest coarseness. . . . I often walk on your roads and see you working in your fields, vineyards, and gardens. I see your horse giving of his best, your children and serv-

ants working with a will. . . . But suddenly you make
me bow my head in shame. My heart is torn by a frightful oath you swear at your horse or one of your children
or servants. You do this without anger, I know, without
even noticing it. But why? Has it never occurred to you
that the intelligent animals that live with you understand
you, that you hurt them by insulting them, that you in-
jure the souls of your little children and arouse secret
indignation in your servants? Respect—do you know what
this word means? To have respect for yourself, for all
creatures, and all things? Promise me, my children, to
have respect. . . .

Chorus. Yes, we will, we promise. . . . We'll try, we
want to try. . . . Francis, Francis, we'll follow you. . . .

Francis. Good, good. . . .

Chorus. But pray for us, you who are a saint. . . .
Pray for our salvation. . . .

Francis. And you—pray for me. Throw yourself into
prayer. Make it a part of yourself, in all humility. Pray
with confidence, enthusiasm, an ardor that cannot fail
to win heaven. Never be discouraged. And when you are
in distress, don't blame one another. You are not happy,
my poor little people, I know. It is frightful to have your
land trampled upon by men who were not born here and
your wheat harvested by hands that did not sow it. But
I promise you these misfortunes will pass in time. . . .

Chorus. "Thy paths drop fatness upon the oases of the
wilderness; and the little hills rejoice on every side. The
pastures are clothed with flocks; the valleys are covered
over with grain. They shout for joy, they also sing."

All faces are turned toward the CHORUS *as it recites this
Psalm, and* FRANCIS *is moved like the others.*

Francis. If only you believe me and pity yourselves! I
tell you, I tell you, things are not as bad as they seem.
Benefit from your lack of everything. Give and it shall
be given unto you. Forgive and you will be forgiven. I,
Brother Francis, your little servant, beg and entreat you
in the name of the love that is God Himself and our only
refuge, I beseech you with tears and the desire to kiss
your feet, I beseech you to receive with humility and

love—and love!—these words of Our Lord Jesus Christ,
who died for us, and to follow and practice them completely, completely! until your final hour, in all your
thoughts and deeds. . . . [A *piteous sob is heard.*] Who
is weeping?

Priest. Here, it's I! The village priest. The only help of
these poor people. . . .

Chorus. Hah! He has called down upon us the anger
of heaven. He has given us a bad example with his dis-
loyalty and fornication!

Priest. I am unworthy, unworthy, unworthy!

FRANCIS *comes down to him.*

Francis. Oh, poor little priest, how I pity you! Who
should be purer, more saintly, more honorable, than the
one who each day takes in his hands the body and blood
of Jesus to partake of them and give them to the faithful?
Poor brother, I weep for you. But I tell all those present
that nothing can diminish the supernatural power of your
hands which touch the Word of Life. You can lose your
own soul, alas! but you cannot fail to help save ours.
In honor of God, I honor his priest, even when he is
unworthy.

Kneels before the PRIEST *and kisses his hands.*

Priest. Mea culpa, mea culpa, mea maxima culpa. My
guilt is great.

Chorus. Mea culpa. . . .

Francis. There. . . . To each his own errors. We are
on our way; God calls us. Be as kind, O Lord, to me who
preach as to those that hear me. And Clare, Lord, the
little Clare that you promised me for tonight—is it not
so?—don't forget her, O Lord! [*Walking through the
crowd, speaking to one and another.*] As for you, start
by fighting covetousness. . . . You, evil gossip. . . . And
you, carnal desire. . . .

Philosopher. What about me, Master, what about me?

Francis. Simply bow your head very low.

Philosopher. See how deeply moved I am.

Francis. Dry your false tears.

Philosopher. I have studied your teachings for a long time.

Francis [*Turning on him abruptly*]. What have you given to the poor?

Philosopher. I will give.

Francis. Don't delay an instant. Give everything. The poor we have with us always. Do good works, good works!

Poor Joan. Saint . . . Saint . . . Saint Francis. . . .

Francis. Where are you?

Chorus. It's a woman. Here she is. . . .

POOR JOAN, *lost in the crowd, tries to escape.* FRANCIS
pursues her.

Poor Joan. No, no, no!

Francis. Where are you?

Chorus. We have her!

FRANCIS *reaches her. She falls on her knees.*

Francis. Who are you?

Poor Joan. I'm nothing. My name is Joan. I don't know the prayers. I need better eyes, quicker and less awkward hands, to do the little jobs I have to do. I have sinned very much. [*Kisses* FRANCIS' *feet.*]

Francis. So there was, O Lord, among your creatures a truly humble soul, a truly silent heart that compensated for the others. . . .

Taking her hand and leading her to the platform. As he passes by, the crowd presses forward to kiss his robe and hands. Night is falling. Torches are lighted among the
CHORUS.

Chorus. Brother, brother. . . . Is it true that you are our brother? Is it true that you love us?

A Single Voice. Glorious little poor man of Christ!

Chorus Leader. God. . . .

Chorus. God will take the poor man from his dunghill and seat him among the mighty and give him a throne of glory!

The BEGGAR *goes to* BERNADONE *and* PICA *who stand
alone, to left, near the audience.*

Beggar. You look very tired, poor people.
Bernadone. We have come a long way.
Beggar. To see the saint?
Pica. Yes, to see the saint.
Beggar. It's wonderful, isn't it?
Pica. Yes, truly wonderful.
Beggar. He sweeps everything before him.
Bernadone. Everything.
Beggar. Don't you want to go a little closer?
Pica. No, thanks. We're fine here. We have nothing to ask of him. Thanks. We're fine.

FRANCIS *climbs back to platform. He seats* POOR JOAN *to right, then turning to left toward* MARTIN, *who wakes up, he gives him his hand.* MARTIN *gets up.*

Martin. I dreamed I was lying on a very high, narrow, slippery bridge over a rushing stream full of snakes and dragons. I didn't dare move or stand up. An angel who had led me there over many bad roads said to me: "Follow me and place your feet where you see me place mine and you will be able to cross over. . . ."
Francis. You will cross over. Never fear.

He kisses MARTIN, *who turns toward the* CHORUS.

Martin. We'll all cross over, won't we, friends?

Going down. People kiss him and start a sort of dance.

Chorus. We'll cross over! We'll cross over!
Francis. Listen! We form a single body now and a single soul. We are like a forest when summer comes and clothes it in all shades of foliage, from the deep green of souls that have lived in the Lord for a long time to the tender light green shoots of spirits only recently touched by God's love. You even find still clinging here and there a touch of autumn rust and there is winter bareness which we will try to remove with our prayers and good works. The breeze that rustles through our branches, bends them toward one another and entwines them, is the breath of God, who is glad and urges us not to be divided any longer but to join and mingle our prayers and good works in a single love. Do you feel how good it is to breathe in

unity? And if you will, my brothers and friends, we will put to good use this wonderful moment when our entreaties must have an irresistible power with the Almighty. We will pray all together for our little Sister Clare, that we may take from the world such a noble being and enrich with her the Divine Master. We pray that she may have the strength and will to give up the world, its empty pleasures and transitory riches, as I gave them up myself, as we all give them up, and that she may join us here at the appointed hour—this very hour of Palm Sunday night. . . . In the name of the Father, the Son, and the Holy Ghost, Amen. Lord, give to our Clare, daughter of Favarone di Bernardino and the devout Ortolana, the courage and strength of Thy saints. . . .

Chorus. The courage and strength of Thy saints. . . .

Francis. Lord, let her rise at this very moment, holding in her hand the blessed palm leaf that our Lord Bishop gave her this morning, and let her cross forever the threshold of the room of her childhood. Lord, we pray Thee . . .

Choir. We pray Thee . . .

Francis. That she may go down the great stairway without trembling. That she may cross the courtyard without being held back by the familiar look of the home of her girlhood. O Lord!

Chorus. Lord, Lord . . .

Francis. Send Your angels to guide her steps in the night. Sustain her. Revive her spirits. Lift her up if she falls!

Chorus. Send Your angels!

Francis. Let our little sister Clare see in the darkness the light of our torches. . . . [*To the* Chorus.] Raise your torches . . .

Chorus. Sustain her!

Francis. And let her exchange her splendid raiment for the robe of poverty. [*To the* Chorus.] Prepare the holy gown . . .

Chorus. Revive her spirits!

Francis. And let her offer her long hair to the scissors! [*To the* Chorus.] Give me the scissors. . . .

Chorus. Lift her up if she falls!

Francis. For ever and ever, for the salvation of souls and the glory of the Father, the Son, and the Holy Ghost, world without end. . . .

Chorus. Amen.

During a prolonged and increasingly intense pause, all heads turn, outstretched, to the right. Suddenly all straighten their heads together.

The Entire Crowd. She is here! . . . She is here!

CLARE *enters, elaborately dressed, holding in her hand a blessed palm branch. She runs to* FRANCIS *and kneels. Torches surround her. The* CHORUS *rises. Two of its members climb to platform, holding aloft the robe of poverty and the scissors. A third removes* CLARE's *headdress. Her hair tumbles about her shoulders. Angels carrying flowers and censers move among the crowd. All strike up a hymn of triumph.* BERNADONE *and* PICA *fall on their knees.*

SCENE IV

THE PLACE: *The* PORTIUNCULA, *a Benedictine abbey on a mountainside near* ASSISI. *It was given to* SAINT FRANCIS *and became the headquarters of his* BROTHERS MINOR.

THE TIME: *Christmas Eve, 1220.*

GILES *and* RUFINO *sit in silence.* RUFINO *utters a deep sigh.*

Giles. Why do you sigh, Rufino?

Rufino. Because Francis won't be here tonight to celebrate the birth of the Child of Bethlehem with us.

Giles. I was thinking the same thing. [*A pause.*] Do you remember what he said about Christmas Day? He said that if he knew the Emperor he would ask him to order all his people to put out grain for the birds on that day and anyone who had cattle to give them a double ration of the best feed for love of Jesus who was born in a manger.

Rufino. I remember. And he said: "I would especially like the rich throughout the world to invite the poor to their table on that day."

Giles. Yes, and I remember just how he said it and his look when he said the name of the Lord Jesus.

Rufino. Yes. And I still see trotting behind him the lamb that all the Holy Innocents seemed to be following. The little animal went with him everywhere, even to church. Its gentle bleating accompanied our chants. Do you remember?

Giles. Yes. [*A pause.*] Where is he now?

Rufino. Among the infidels.

Giles. Maybe his blood has been shed.

Rufino. Maybe his eyes are closed.

Giles. What will become of us without him?

Rufino. What will become of the world?

Giles. Never since the time of Jesus has the world known such charity.

LEO *runs on stage.*

Leo. Francis is not dead!

Giles and Rufino [*Rising together*]. Oh!

Leo. He has reached Venice. He has spoken at Bologna. We will see him soon. Maybe before dark.

Rufino. God be praised!

Leo. Peter Catani, Caesar of Speyer, and Elias are coming ahead of him. They were with him at Acre when our brother Stephen joined them. They are following me. Bologna gave Francis a triumphal welcome.

Rufino. Everything will be put to rights again.

Giles. And not too soon either.

Leo. Many of the doctors in Bologna asked to become monks, they say.

Giles [*With a grimace*]. More learned men!

Enter PETER CATANI, CAESAR, *and* ELIAS.

Peter Catani. It's a great consolation, Brothers, to see you here.

All embrace.

Rufino. How is our beloved father?

Peter Catani. Francis is exhausted from the hardships of his long stay in the Orient, the difficult journey, and the sad news brought by Brother Stephen.

Elias. Yes, I am worried about his health.

Peter Catani. During the sea voyage home we often heard him utter great sighs and cry out in displeasure.

Caesar. His heart is so pure that he seldom shows indignation.

Giles. Indignation, did you say?

Elias. Human emotions don't seem to affect his weary body any more.

Caesar. Indignation would do him good. I tried several times to communicate mine to him. He turned me aside. Or rather I turned aside myself on seeing the expression on his tormented face. Although he has never shrunk from any human ugliness when a cure was needed, I fear he will never get over the ingratitude of his brothers.

Peter Catani. Yet his spirit has never been more alive or courageous.

Elias. It is not his courage I am uncertain of, but his will.

Giles. When love weakens or is withheld from him, Francis feels lost.

Leo. Here is Monsignor Ugolino.

Enter CARDINAL UGOLINO. *The three travelers kneel to receive his blessing.*

Ugolino. I salute you, my brothers, and give thanks to God for your safe return. [*The three get up.*] They tell me you have come ahead of Francis.

Peter Catani. Only a little, Monsignor.

Ugolino. We very much need him here.

Elias. Your Lordship will find him changed.

Ugolino. Yes, his disappointments . . .

Elias. His illness . . .

Ugolino. Poor Francis! Always in a hurry, never sparing himself. . . . Yet I am sure he finds great consolation in the tremendous success of his Order in Christian lands.

Elias. That, of course, is the main thing.

Ugolino. The main thing, of course, Brother Elias. At least for the time being. In Tuscany, Umbria, Emilia, and the Marches of Ancona—everywhere he has preached—the abundance of the harvest goes far beyond our hopes. Before thinking of journeys overseas we should store the harvest. . . . I mean, yes, organize these riches on a firm basis . . . with an eye to the future . . . that is, for the greater good of Christianity and the Holy Catholic Church. I hope Francis will see it that way.

Elias. He certainly will see it if your Lordship, with your high authority, takes the trouble to give him the necessary explanations.

Ugolino. That is just what we intend to do. Francis knows how much I love, admire, and respect him.

Giles. First we must clear up certain misunderstandings, and then rebuild the prestige a long absence has undermined.

Ugolino. That goes without saying. . . . You certainly have not forgotten, brothers: it was at the express and repeated demand of Francis that the Holy Father appointed me protector of your Order. I haven't the slightest doubt I'll find you amenable to the reasonable measures required. . . . Mind you, these measures will be discussed openly in a Chapter meeting, with the aid of the Holy Spirit. I don't want to weary you at this time. And it would not be right to start the debate without our beloved Francis. Go, my brothers, take a little rest. May God keep you.

The friars bow and go out. UGOLINO *calls* ELIAS *back.*

Ugolino. Brother Elias!

Elias. Monsignor?

Ugolino. I have heard much about you, my son. I wanted to tell you so. . . . That is all.

Elias. Monsignor. . . .

Bowing and pretending to go but not doing so. UGOLINO *sits down wearily.*

Ugolino. Indeed, everyone agrees as to your prudence, the extent and worth of your knowledge, the purity of your way of life. I have made inquiries here and there and

know something about your career. You were one of the
first to follow the holy man. You are devoted to him. He
has entrusted you with the most delicate tasks and mis-
sions.

Elias [*Draws near the* CARDINAL]. I have always served
him. I have no other ambition but to serve him until his
death and beyond—Francis and what he stands for.

Ugolino. I know, I know.

A *pause.*

Elias. Ever since his conversion I have shared his life
and his ideas, enthusiasms, and illusions. So I am well
able to understand his work, how he has done it, and
what he can still do.

Ugolino. I know. . . . Believe me, no one is more aware
of this than I. I have observed his efforts—less closely than
you, but with no less devotion—and rejoiced in his success. . . . Hence my present anxieties. . . . I fear that
too little life is left to him . . . or that his strength may
decline.

Elias. Yes.

Ugolino. For he hasn't finished his fight.

Elias. Alas! . . . This anxiety is shared by all who love
him.

Ugolino. I am old. Not much of life is left to me. I
confess it would comfort me to find a man still young, at
the height of his intelligence and strength—a man having
full understanding of Francis and his work who could
support him when I am no longer useful. [*Rising.*]

Elias. Yes, Monsignor.

Ugolino. Good. We will talk of this again later.
[*Stretching out his hand.* ELIAS *kneels and kisses the*
CARDINAL's *ring.* UGOLINO *takes him familiarly by the
arm and they walk slowly together toward the right.*]
You see, Elias, Francis is a saint. Everyone knows it.
Between ourselves, he is one of the greatest saints the
Church has ever had. Through him the world has been
reborn to God. What this little man has done with his
charity, with his charity alone, neither you nor I could
have done, could we? Not even with better brains than
his. Not everyone can be a saint. And the Church is not

made of saints alone. It has even had many excellent
servants who were not saints. From time to time it needs
extraordinary men and deeds. But alas! life is such that
the time always comes, Elias, when a leader is needed to
carry on the work a saint has begun. You understand?

Elias. Yes, Monsignor.

UGOLINO *goes out to right.* LEO *enters from left, followed
by* GILES *and* RUFINO.

Leo. Francis is coming.

Giles. I saw him a short way off. He needs a staff now.
He walks slowly and is a little stooped, but his step is
firm.

Rufino. Bernard has gone to meet him.

Giles. We must tell the Cardinal.

Elias. I will go to him. [*Exits to right.*]

Giles. Listen to me, brothers. Let us not give way to
the increasing number of gossips, malcontents, and
worriers. Let's rally firmly round our Francis.

Rufino. We'll help him rebuild his position.

Giles. If only he has the strength!

Leo. Here he is.

The three friars kneel. FRANCIS *enters from left. He supports himself with a staff held in his right hand and leans
on* STEPHEN's *arm with his left.* BERNARD *is on his right.*

Francis. Satan is at work among us, my Bernard. At
Siena, Perugia, Lucca, and even at San Damiano, our
Poor Ladies are being subjected to pressures which would
already have misled them were it not for the firm stand of
our Clare. I know that missionaries just back from Ger-
many and Hungary have gone around spreading a spirit
of discouragement. As for the ministers, men like Matthew of Narni and Gregory of Naples that I trusted, during my absence they have constantly introduced rules of
their own which threaten to destroy all my work. This is
real sedition. The work of Satan, I tell you—Satan!

Bernard. But now you are back.

Francis. Back, my Bernard, yes. But very weary. And I
tell you in confidence, very disappointed. Among the
enemies of our faith I exposed myself to danger, rather

hopefully. God judged me unworthy of martyrdom. He did not want my blood. [*Discovering at his feet* GILES, RUFINO *and* LEO, *he motions them to get up and embraces them.*] Giles, Rufino, Leo, excuse my bad eyes. The flies of the Orient infected them. The flies are the only living creatures for which I have not been able to find a little friendship in my heart. They have taken their revenge, you see. . . .

Leo. Is it you, Father?

Francis. Changed, am I not? But only on the outside. I am still your little brother Francis. But tired, very tired. Very happy, too, to see your good faces again, my sons, and on this Christmas Eve.

Bernard. Go and rest.

Francis. Rest? I have to run from one end of the world to the other. Oh, I made a great mistake in going. Everything crumbles as soon as I take my hand away. While I bring the Scriptures to the unbelievers, those that I called believers distort my preachings and make of them something only faintly resembling what they really are. What can I do? I am only one poor man. Let me sit down a moment. . . . Is our Cardinal here?

Leo. Elias went to get him.

Francis. I must speak to him at once. . . . At Bologna, where I just stopped, do you know what they have set up? A college, my friends! A sort of institute! I spoke to them. I said: are you mad? What have you turned yourselves into? Imitation Benedictines? You're going to study religion? Why? To talk about it? Go see whether the Paladins talked about their great deeds. They knew that God put them on earth to do tremendous exploits. They did them. Do as they did. For God gave you a very clear and precise mission—to live the Scriptures and convert the world by your acts. If you cut yourselves off from mankind, you betray your calling. . . . So I had the house closed— closed and emptied—from top to bottom, including the sick people. The leader, Peter Stacia, refused to confess his error. So I denounced him. [*Enter* ELIAS *on the right.*] May I see the Cardinal?

Elias. He will be here soon. . . . But now your brothers want to greet you.

Enter several monks, among them MATTHEW OF NARNI, GREGORY OF NAPLES, JOHN, FATHER PHILIP, PETER STACIA, *etc. They appear slightly embarrassed as they move toward* FRANCIS. *Several of them kneel.* FRANCIS, *sitting, does not move, looks at them, then begins to speak in a sad, monotonous voice.*

Francis. So you are here, my brothers. I greet you. I would like to greet you more joyously. What shall I say? . . . My brothers, my brothers, the Lord called me to walk in the paths of humility and simplicity and called along with me all those who want to follow me and do as I do. . . . The Lord told me He wanted me to be a simple man and His intention was to lead us along paths other than those of knowledge and learning. . . . There, my brothers, I have nothing else to tell you. The only thing I know well—and that is enough for me—is that I will not give up my royal dignity, my patrimony, my profession and that of my brothers, which is to beg from door to door.

As FRANCIS *speaks, some raise their heads. Others get up.* PETER *comes forward a little.*

Peter Stacia. I would like to be allowed to make a few remarks.

Francis. Peter Stacia, I have already denounced you.

PETER STACIA *goes back among the friars. He hesitates a moment, then exits to right with two other monks.* ELIAS *leans toward* FRANCIS.

Elias. They are waiting for your blessing.

Francis. My blessing? Alas! I see among them some who are wearing double and triple robes and I expect soon to see them put on cloth of purple lined with fur. . . . That is why to my sorrow I cannot bless you.

A Monk. Don't be so hard on us, Francis!

Francis. How can I bless your desire to be better clothed and lodged? Yes . . . it is harmless, you say, to seek shelter in a house. But I ask you, when will you start carrying weapons to defend these earthly goods? After living in houses you will want to live in palaces and have exquisite food on your table and horses in your stables.

I warn you again that there is only one way to be free, pure, and strong before God—only one, do you hear?— and that is to live in wretched huts made of branches and mud, as I commanded you.

Little groups of persons come in, among them the CHORUS. FRANCIS *is supported by a group of five:* LEO, BERNARD, RUFINO, GILES, *and* STEPHEN, *who answer in unison in the following passage.*

Chorus. Without any possessions?

The Five. None at all.

Francis. Except the robe and its cord.

Chorus. Without any books?

The Five. None at all.

Chorus. Not even a breviary?

The Five. Ashes.

Francis. Ashes—they are your breviary. Tribulations will come. The books will be thrown out the window. Only ashes, the ashes of Ninive, will save your lives.

Chorus. How shall we enter into the knowledge of God?

The Five. On your knees.

Francis. Through prayer.

Chorus. What inspiration shall we have for our preaching?

The Five. Prayer.

Chorus. Through study some of us have already acquired knowledge.

The Five. Pride.

Chorus. Must we forget it?

The Five. Yes.

Francis. There are so many who like to acquire knowledge that happy is he who makes himself barren for love of the Lord our God. [*A pause.*] God Himself has taught me these things. I have seen Him and He has spoken to me.

A Voice. How about the Pope?

Francis. Great Saint Peter, whom I saw in Rome just as I see you now, took the trouble to appear to me to confirm me in my vocation.

A Voice. Yet in the name of Jesus Christ the Pope decides and commands.

Elias. We are not here to discuss Francis' orthodoxy. We are here to discuss calmly whether the Rule he laid down for us when we were only three or four, or a dozen or even a hundred, is still applicable without any change now that we are a multitude.

Francis. Elias, you are leaving me. . . . I was waiting and yet dreading to hear your voice. You are leaving me, Elias. I felt a long time ago that someday you—one of my first-born—would allow yourself to be led astray. [*Embracing him.*] God gave you too much intelligence. I will pray for you. . . .

Elias. Father, without disrespect or disobedience, may I ask whether strict observance of an almost savage poverty and ignorance will not in the long run mean for some a risk of wallowing in laziness, and for mankind to whom you propose this as a model, a threat of stagnation?

Francis. Don't you see that the world is rotten with sensuality, injustice and lies? That is the real stagnation. Don't you see that the world must surrender to the Holy Spirit, that it must burn? How can you speak of laziness and stagnation when each of us must first win his place near Christ and then keep it? Have you never known the wonderful renewal of recognition and joy which contemplation of the Holy Trinity brings? Have you never fought to become saintlike? Don't you know this effort calls for an iron will, more strength and discipline than if we try to satisfy all the needs of the body and go beyond them by seeking sensual pleasures? I know of only one road to progress for mankind—the road to redemption and holiness. To cleanse the world of evil, starting with ourselves—isn't this harder and more courageous than to try to enrich ourselves and enjoy worldly pleasures—which often means resorting to violence? We have seen these things cause the decline and fall of great empires and their leaders. . . . So we must make a fresh start. The day will come when men won't know what to do with all the marvels they will achieve at heavy cost of pain and grief, and with waste of their genius. And they will rend their hearts with their own hands. That day is not yet. But I foresee it and you are preparing it spiritually. If you loosen your grip on poverty today, you will lead unhappy mankind to this immense despair.

Elias. That is possible, Francis. Of course, if we must go to extremes, we will never be able to compete with you. . . . Some of us are not rebellious in our hearts but nevertheless are dissatisfied. If you make a Rule, it is for all to follow, not yourself alone.

Francis [Getting up]. Here is what the Lord told me: "Nothing in the Rule of the Order is yours. It is all Mine. And I want it to be observed to the letter—to the letter. Without comment, without comment, without comment. I know how much human weakness can bear and to what extent I will come to its aid. Those who refuse to follow the Rule, let them leave the Order!" Do you understand? Do you understand? Must I repeat it? [*Sitting down.*] That is what the Lord our God told me. Pardon me. . . .

Hiding his face in his hands. The monks withdraw in little groups as they had entered. Elias *is the last to leave.* Leo, Giles, Rufino, Bernard, *and* Stephen *do not move. Night falls. After a moment* Francis *lifts his head. He continues as if all his listeners were still with him.*

I see on the public squares of the cities, in the pulpits of the churches, at the courts of the mighty, sons of Francis preaching and arguing magnificently. . . . I see on the barren shores and arid mountains wretched little brothers, poor and saintly, humble and naked, weeping for their sins and the sins of the world, and hiding. . . . I see both groups meet some day at the gates of Paradise to be presented by the angels to Our Lord Jesus Christ. The Saviour, addressing the troop of humble ones, will say: "Come and see, my beloved brothers, how many and what souls have been saved by your prayers and your tears. While the others preached and spread their wisdom, I achieved the world's salvation through your prayers and your tears. Receive therefore the reward of your good works, which is life everlasting." And the poor workers, carrying their garlands of flowers, will enter God's kingdom, singing and leaping with joy.

He rises and feels his way toward the brothers who have departed. THE FIVE *follow him.*

Which of you, which of you, brothers, will take my hand and be the first of these chosen dancers, these happy singers that the angels will crown with flowers and embrace at heaven's gate? Come, my brothers. Don't let the time of pardon pass. Brothers, do you hear me? Brothers, where are you? [*The Five join him and surround him.* FRANCIS *looks at them and looks around.*] Bernard, Giles, yes. . . . Leo, is it you, my lamb? Will they wrong Jesus once again? Will they condemn Him? My God, my God. . . . [FRANCIS *sobs.*]

Chorus [*Kneeling and chanting softly*]. Christ is born today. O come let us adore Him. *Venite adoremus. Venite exultemus domino, jubilemus Deo Salutari nostro: preoccupemus faciem ejus in confessione, et in psalmis jubilemus ei.*

FRANCIS *kneels.* THE FIVE *stand round him.*

Bernard. This is the day of His birth.

Francis. Jesus was born to be crucified.

Chorus. Betrayed, sold, captured.
       Abandoned, denied, bound.
       Mocked, beaten, scourged.
       Tried, condemned.
       Stripped.
       Crucified.
       Slain.

Leo. How beautiful He is, the Newborn Babe, with His fresh cheeks.

Francis. O my God and my All! Grant to me to be born to your suffering. Reveal to me the secret of your Passion.

Giles. Gently He moves His hands and feet.

Chorus. Nails crude, dirty, and square. . . .

Francis. Shall You pierce His hands and feet?

Rufino. O most beautiful of the children of men.

Francis. Shall You become the most pitiable of men?

Stephen. Newborn Babe, Conqueror of death.

Francis. Shall You suffer as a helpless man? No torture is spared Him, not even thirst. Not even to feel forsaken by His Father. He sees deep into the souls of His torturers. He sees the punishment that awaits them. He takes it and suffers it.

Chorus. The cowardice of the judges, the howling of the crowd, the anger of the executioners, the rage of the malefactor, Judas's despair.

Francis. He pities them.

Chorus. The reed, the crown of thorns, the scarlet cloth, the hammers, the nails, the sponge.

Francis. He pities them.

The Five. Christ is born today. Come let us adore Him.

Francis. Yes, Lord. Yes, Lord, here am I. My soul shares the Passion of Christ. My soul suffers. Ah! Don't take away its torment. Let it slip into torment. Let it leap into torment. Let me take from the Lord Christ the part of His torment that He will grant to me.

Chorus. Venite adoremus, et procidamus ante Deum; ploremus coram Domino qui fecit nos; quia ipse est Dominus Deus noster; nos autem populus ejus, et oves pascuae ejus.

The Five. Christ is born today. Come, let us adore Him.

The six friars bow their heads to the ground. Enter Cardinal Ugolino. *He climbs slowly to platform.*

Ugolino. Come, Francis. Everyone is in the church, ready to sing Matins.

Francis [*Getting up*]. Yes, Monsignor. Come, brothers.

The Five *rise.*

Ugolino. We will spend the night in prayer. I will officiate myself and you will be my deacon. You will read the Gospel and pronounce the Word of God.

Francis. Yes, Monsignor.

Ugolino. Then tomorrow we shall meet to take up, all together, in the most brotherly spirit, three or four points on which you must reach agreement with your brothers as soon as possible.

Francis. Monsignor, I have given my brothers all I could, in love. I told them just now, with complete frankness, what I had to tell them. I do not intend to use the slightest compulsion or impose their conduct on them by force. . . .

Ugolino. I will be here to help you, Francis, to guide them . . . and if necessary, to defend you. . . .

Francis. It has been done, Monsignor. God Himself has just defended me completely.

Ugolino. I don't know what you are trying to say, Francis.

Francis. Tomorrow I will resign my functions and powers and turn them over to Peter Catani, if you consent. And he, again with your consent, may give his authority over me to any one of my comrades, even if it be the humblest novice, and I will obey him as I would God.

Ugolino. Beware, dear Francis, of a decision inspired perhaps by your weariness.

Francis. I don't know whether it is weariness, but I feel inside me a great emptiness and a strange call. . . . Pray, if you will, that I may at least become for my brothers a model of obedience and an example . . . yes, an example, not surely of the Christlike, but of what an ordinary man, among the errors, ills, and debauchery of the world, can become if he determines to follow the Lord and imitate Him in all simplicity and steadfastness. . . . No, no, Francis, rid yourself of pride. . . . There shall be no torture for you, no martyrdom. . . . It is from my own self that my humiliation must come, if God will help me begin my penance all over again and pursue it to the end. . . .

FRANCIS *goes off to right, followed by* THE FIVE. UGOLINO *stands still a moment, then goes off after them, slowly.*

SCENE V

THE PLACE: MOUNT ALVERNA, *in the* APENNINES *northeast of* ASSISI—*a place of great natural beauty which was also a gift to* SAINT FRANCIS.

THE TIME: *Before dawn on the Feast of the Holy Cross, September 12, 1224.*

BROTHERS ANGELO *and* ILLUMINATO *meet.*

ILLUMINATO. Glory to God.

   Angelo. Glory to God.

   Illuminato. Brother Angelo?

   Angelo. Yes, I'm Angelo.

   Illuminato. And I'm Illuminato.

They embrace.

You are looking for him too?

   Angelo. He has probably found some new, more remote refuge.

   Illuminato. He escapes us.

   Angelo. Like a bird.

   Illuminato. Let us wait for the dawn.

A silence. Enter SILVESTER.

   Angelo. Here is Brother Silvester.

   Silvester. Glory to God. . . . You are not worried about Francis?

   Angelo. Saint Michael is watching over him.

   Illuminato. He doesn't even need his eyes any more.

   Silvester. It is as if there is almost nothing between him and the Eternal Kingdom and he hears the choirs of angels.

Enter LEO.

   Leo. Did you hear that terrible noise?

   Illuminato. When?

   Leo. In the middle of the night. I think the Devil is doing battle openly. I ran to the cave. It was empty. I called for a long time. There was no answer. So I began to look for our Francis among the trees in the light of the moon.

   Angelo [*Going off*]. You didn't find him?

   Leo [*Also exiting*]. No.

   Silvester [*As he too goes offstage*]. Often Jesus, Mary,

the angels, and the saints who visit him take him some
distance away.

Illuminato [*Going off also*]. Then some day they will
take him from us forever.

*As the four friars disappear, a sustained note drawn with
a bow on a stringed instrument by an invisible angelic
musician is heard. Then two* ANGELS *pass by silently.*
FRANCIS *appears. Grievously stricken by illness and priva-
tions, he is only the shadow of his former self. He can
scarcely see and his gown is made of tattered, ill-matched
patches.*

Francis. The falcon wakes me before dawn. The angels
call and I follow. The rabbit goes with me through the
thickets. The music and the voices of the angels are so
beautiful that often my eyes that see no more seem to
revive again in the light of Paradise. I do not know
whether I walk or float, whether it is the wind or the Hand
of God that moves me, whether I tread on moss in the
path or on the tops of the oak trees. Lord, you have
brought me into this wilderness and I run to and fro,
calling your name. Why do you sometimes allow me to
see you but never suffer me to come to you? Lord, you see
that I am mad! Will you not cure this madness of love?
You, O Lord, can love boundlessly! But can the lowliest
creature do so without being destroyed?

The CHORUS *and* CHORUS LEADER *rise slowly and lean
slightly toward* FRANCIS.

Chorus Leader. Courage. . . .

FRANCIS, *guided by his hearing, walks toward the* CHORUS,
kneels, and leans out toward the orchestra.

Francis. Oh, Saint Michael, sir, you do me honor and
pleasure when you come to me. Will you please ask a
favor for me of Our Lord Jesus?—that before I die I may
feel in my soul and body, as keenly as possible, the pain
my sweet Lord had to suffer in His very cruel Passion.
. . . And one more thing, please. Tell Him I now have
but one desire—to break this final bond so weak and yet

so strong—this web of life which keeps me still from touching Him—this body—this body. . . .

Enter from the rear SATAN, *a tall, glittering angel with black wings.* FRANCIS *groans and falls face down on the ground. He has not seen* SATAN *but has felt his presence.*

Chorus. Courage, courage, little poor man. Even a little more courage.

FRANCIS *braces himself like a wrestler. The* CHORUS *and* CHORUS LEADER *go back to their seats in the orchestra.*

Francis. I know you are here. And I know who you are. . . . You are the most beautiful of the angels. But I know you are a serpent . . . much larger and stronger than I. But the Son of God promised his apostles they would crush the serpent. . . . You are infinitely more intelligent. But I am faithful. . . . I hope you will have no power over me. You encourage what is most frivolous in man—his curiosity. I believe I have no more of it. What is basest in him—self-indulgence. I hope I have no more of it. Your great achievement is to have made our animal needs so compelling, so potent, that they seem a distorted reflection of the godlike—evil counterfeiter that you are! But as for me, I have sewn myself into a sack and rolled my head in the dust. That is why you will neither trouble my freedom to distinguish between good and evil nor trap my redeemed spirit in your paradoxes and absurdities.

Satan. But what about your humility?

Francis. God did not command me to be humble in front of the Devil.

Satan. So you are not afraid of vainglory?

Francis. Not if I glory in the Lord.

Satan. My little Bernadone, I confess you upset me. Why are you so bitter? I don't want to quarrel with you. Why provoke me? I am interested in your work. I admire your miracles, your saintly perfection. I may want to be converted. Does this surprise you? Why? And why not answer a few questions? [*A pause.*] You are comfortable now in this solitude of Alverna with your flowers and birds. But are you quite sure you are following your calling? Looking at things from the outside, quite objectively, it seems to me you didn't put up much of a fight against your brothers—those who opposed you. Why? Was it laziness? Discouragement?—And why have you suddenly lost interest in martyrdom after seeking it on the Barbary Coast with a courage that we all admired? Tell me, why? And above all—oh, above all!—why did you decide to set adrift generation after generation which from now on will drink iniquity like water? Tell me, why did you do it, Francis?

Francis. Lewd and curious spirit! You try to throw your coils around me and trap me with your deceitful questions. There is no "why" for me. I have obeyed from the beginning and I still obey.

Satan. I wonder whether you don't need me to give this perfect obedience its true name—fear?

Francis. I always fear to disappoint the Lord my God. And soon I must appear before Him.

Satan. Will you be completely safe?

Francis. The Lord owes me nothing. He can, if He chooses, leave me in exile among the poor men who did not want Him. But I had set out to find Him and restore Him to poor mankind.

Satan. On one of the arms of the cross, Francis, a demon crouched to try to trap the spirit of Jesus. Did you know that?

Francis. So they say. Demons cannot conceive of anything completely pure. That is the infirmity that proves how stupid they are.

Satan. Will the angels and Mary watch over you on your deathbed, Francis?

Francis. God has promised certain things to me.

Satan. Will the spirits of your disciples also be defended, Francis? Are you not afraid many of them will be weak and may even be condemned to hell-fire?

Francis. You and those like you on earth and in hell are always ready to rejoice over the scraps that fall from the table of salvation. Keep trying, Satan! I know you have an inexhaustible supply of persistent, clever, brilliant, and false arguments. But the pride that makes you scintillate and that you inspire in others only gives birth to failures. You will never create anything. You stir people up, intoxicate, and drug them. You don't give any nourishment to their souls. The world doesn't need the glorious illusions you distribute so lavishly. It needs the humble creatures who, although they may have little talent, take life as it should be taken, give of themselves fully day by day, and work without stint quietly to repair what you destroy with such a clatter.

Satan. What you have done, Francis, shall nevertheless be undone.

Francis. All too true! . . . But you shall not disturb my meditation.

Satan. Saintly ignorance shall be made mock of.

Francis. All too likely, since you never rest for a moment.

Satan. Saintly poverty shall be forsaken.

Francis. It well may be. But we have received the lessons and the example of a God. We have a model. I know you will never destroy completely the human being shaped by a God who has suffered in human form. However stupid, proud, and arrogant the freethinkers and tyrannical minds may be, there will always be someone, even if it's only a little girl—you look frightened already! —who will ponder in his heart of hearts the teachings of the humble Master who walked before His disciples in Galilee. As long as there is a soul——

Satan [*Interrupting him*]. I warn you, Francis, there will be no more soul. We will wear out the human soul. We will plunge the world into lust and brutality. We will make history with the iniquity of flesh and blood. Flesh and blood, flesh and blood! After twenty centuries of Christianity, enormous armies, refusing to be baptized, shall write upon their flags the motto: Flesh and Blood.

Francis. Then the persecutions shall bring forth armies of saints.

Satan. When the Devil appears the saints arise. Francis Bernadone, my friend! Soon you will go to sit on the glittering throne I occupied on high. The richest throne in Heaven. They have kept it for you. Enjoy it! I am and will none the less always be the Prince of this world.

Francis [*Laughing quietly*]. Ha, ha . . . ha, ha, ha!

Prince of this world! You make me laugh, poor outcast. Pride, despair . . . negation, sterility. . . . Poor Satan, how envious you must be of the host of good angels! Tell me, Prince of this world, what about the crescent moon and the little silver star? Is it you that place them on night's curtain? And what about the little flower at your feet, whose Father is God? He brought it out of the void and it mirrors Him. He loves it because He created it. But you cannot love it. You don't even know it. You know nothing but yourself. This cyclamen . . . lean down, Prince of this world. Show me that you can pluck it—the flower of Alverna—without scorching it with your fingers, the fingers of the damned! [SATAN *furiously whacks* FRANCIS *a great blow over the head. The saint slumps to the ground with a cry.*] Ah! . . . I truly pity you, Satan. . . . But you, dear Saint Michael, give me your hand. . . . [*Taking in both his hands the hand of* SAINT MICHAEL *which emerges from the orchestra pit and leaning his cheek upon it. From the* CHORUS *comes a musical phrase which makes* SATAN *shudder, back off, and disappear.*] Even if I had to fight off the seven spirits more evil than the spirit of Satan, I believe I would conquer them by the pity which the Lord placed in my heart and which I cannot cast aside. . . . It helps me come a little closer to God, and, having come closer, to see a little better the unfathomable sorrow which is the center of His Mystery. I don't understand it but I see it. The more I see it, the more I love it. The more I love it, the more I long to be drawn to it and changed into it. . . .

Chorus Leader. Francis. . . .

Francis. O Saint Michael, sir! At last I near the goal. . . I hope I am free!

Chorus Leader [*Climbing to platform and standing behind* FRANCIS]. Francis, I have been commanded to tell you to prepare very humbly to endure in all patience that which is pleasing to God.

Francis. I am prepared, my lord, to endure whatever pleases God.

The CHORUS LEADER *grasps* FRANCIS *by the hand, pulls him to his feet, then leads him off while the sky gradually lights up.*

Chorus. "I saw also the Lord sitting upon a throne, high and lifted up, and His train filled the temple. Above it stood the seraphim: each one had six wings; with twain he covered his face, and with twain he covered his feet, and with twain he did fly. And one cried unto another and said: Holy, holy, holy, is the Lord God of Hosts: the whole earth is full of His glory."

Six CHORUS *members, dressed as shepherds, emerge from orchestra and stand in two parallel lines on stairs.*

Old Shepherd. The light came and sought us in our sheepfolds.

Shepherd I. To wake us and draw us outside.

Shepherd II. It made us ashamed of our laziness.

Young Shepherd I. The dogs sniffed at the doors.

Shepherd III. The little bells tinkled as the sheep stirred.

Old Shepherd. But it seemed that the light wasn't the light of the sun that rises and sets.

Young Shepherd I. Do you think there can still be miracles in our time?

Old Shepherd. You think you are cleverer than our ancestors. They were poor people like us. They were hungry. Heaven sent them a sign. They went straight to the House of Bread with their dogs and flocks.

Young Shepherd II. Are you still hungry, Grandfather?

Old Shepherd. Grandfather is always hungry for love and hope and for the old paradise. But he is like everyone else: lazy, full of doubt, and selfish.

Shepherd II. What is hard for me is not to quarrel with my neighbors. People who live near each other always have little things to blame on one another.

Young Shepherd II. I love the bottle. I admit: I love the bottle.

Shepherd I. I am ungrateful by nature. Not that I like ingratitude. It makes me sad and discontented. But I'm just that way: I'm ungrateful.

Shepherd III. We are not really bad. We are weak, we are small, we make a fuss about nothing. If we could only do penance once and for all and not sin again. That shouldn't be impossible and we would be so much happier.

Old Shepherd. Everything always has to be started over and over again. . . . "Peace on earth to men of good will." Peace? Don't you believe it! Neither on earth nor in our hearts. No matter what you say, people just don't want it. Every day we manage to pass it by. Then from time to time someone—a man or a woman—steps out of the crowd and says: "So that's the way it is, is it? Well, I'll show you how to follow in the footsteps of Our Lord Jesus Christ."

ILLUMINATO, ANGELO, SILVESTER, *and* LEO *enter.*

Illuminato. Shepherds, have you seen him?
Shepherd II. Who?
Leo. Our father Francis.
Shepherd III. We don't know him.
Young Shepherd II. Is he here?
Angelo. If God has not taken him from us.

The CHORUS *rises and strikes up a stirring Alleluia.* FRANCIS *appears. He staggers along on his wounded feet and hides his hands in his sleeves.* SAINT MICHAEL *follows at a little distance.*

Francis. Pray, my beloved. The Lord is here. Open your hearts. Forget me.
Illuminato. Careful! You will fall, Francis!
Francis. No, do not touch me. No, do not ask me any questions. . . . Happy the servant who keeps in his heart the secrets that God entrusts to him. [*Singing softly.*] "Thou art holy, Lord God, Thou art God above all gods. . . ." Illuminato, Angelo, Silvester, Leo. You are here, I am sure . . . and you that I can hardly see . . . and all men on earth. Ah! How I would like to share my happiness with you! But I am going away. Live in peace, my beloved. I am going away. My body is leaving you but I leave you all my heart. I will go with our brother Leo. . . . Come, little lamb of God. . . . No, do not touch me. . . . We will go to the Portiuncula. And I shall never return. . . . Farewell, farewell, farewell to you all and to all things here! Farewell, holy mountain; farewell, Alverna; farewell, mountain of the angels! Farewell, my dear brother falcon who awakened me with your

cry. Farewell, charming birds who greeted me. Farewell, great stone under which I prayed so often. Never, never will I see you again. [*He takes several steps and sings.*] "Thou art strong, Thou art great, Thou art the Most High. . . ." [*Stopping again.*] Farewell, divine mountain, holy mountain, abundant mountain where God was pleased to dwell! Farewell, Mount Alverna. May God the Father, God the Son, and God the Holy Ghost bless thee! But I shall never see thee again! [*He goes away, singing, with* LEO.] "Thou art good, all goodness, the Supreme Good, the living and true God. . . ."

ILLUMINATO, ANGELO, *and* SILVESTER *follow* FRANCIS *at a distance. The* CHORUS LEADER *goes forward toward the audience.*

Chorus Leader. He will not be able to walk far. But do not worry. He will find a peasant who will lend him his donkey with much kindness and piety. There he is on the donkey, followed by brother Leo. . . . It is a triumphal march, up hill and down dale, always riding the donkey, always aided by some companion, from town to town, from church to parsonage, from convent to hermitage . . . San Eleuterio, Alberino, Fonte Colombo . . . his spirit uplifted and transported in God. . . . For weeks and months the saint journeys, a pure image of Christ, aiding the people with countless miracles great and small. There is no house in Umbria too humble or remote for Francis to visit it, no family so poor that worship of him does not ennoble and sanctify it. As death draws near and his body weakens, his spirit becomes ever greater and more ardent. Here is Francis at the end of his last journey. Bernard and Leo take him back to the Portiuncula to die. . . . [*Appearing to listen to a distant sound.*] It is Francis. . . . He is singing. . . .

SCENE VI

The Place: *The* Portiuncula.

The Time: *October 4, 1226.*

Francis, *supported by* Leo *and* Bernard, *comes in singing in a very weak voice the* Canticle of the Sun.

Francis [*Singing*]. O most high, almighty, good Lord God, to Thee belong praise, glory, honor and all blessing!
Praised by my Lord God with all his creatures, and especially our brother the sun, who brings us the day and who brings us the light; fair is he and shines with a very great splendor: O Lord, he signifies to us Thee!

He is out of breath and leans on Leo's *chest.* Bernard *takes his feet and* Leo *his shoulders and they stretch him on the bed.* Leo *stifles a sob and sits at some distance on the right.* Bernard *stays at the foot of the bed, then goes to* Francis *and leans over him.*

Bernard. Are you in pain?
Francis. Not at all. I know that my errors and sins are forgiven. There is no more distance. No separation. The Lord Himself is caring for me. I am waiting for Him. He is coming. It is finished.
Bernard. I envy you.

A pause.

Francis. Give me your hand, Bernard. . . . I can't see anything at all. . . . Your hand is warm. . . . Flame, fire, light, it's beautiful. Listen to me. . . .
Bernard. Yes, Francis.
Francis. If I have ever caused the slightest shadow to come over your spirit, forgive me.
Bernard. Nothing but light has ever come to me from you.

A pause.

Francis. My first-born. . . . My youth!

Bernard. My master!

Francis. It was so simple. We were simple people, humble toward all.

Bernard. Yes, Francis.

Francis. Why couldn't it be as simple today? My Rule and Testament are simple and plain. One only need look at them the same way—plainly and simply—and put them into practice until the end. . . . You see, I am at the very end of my life but I am still looking toward the beginning. That is what I've done always. It is what I urge you to do—look toward the beginning always.

Bernard. Yes.

Francis. Only you still must suffer much.

Bernard. That doesn't matter, Francis.

Francis. Suffer with patience, gratitude, and joy. God has told me that you will dwell in the Eternal Kingdom. We will meet again.

Bernard. Then all is well.

Francis. All is perfect. All is more and more luminous and clear.

They fall silent.

Bernard, do you hear me?

Bernard. Yes.

Francis. Giacoma. . . . Do you remember Lady Giacoma di Settesoli? I jokingly called her Brother Giacoma, remember? She was always so good to me. If she heard of my death and had not been here, she would be very sad.

Bernard. Yes.

Francis. So tell her that if she wants to see me alive, she must come at once.

Bernard. Yes.

Francis. Write to her. Tell her to bring a shroud to wrap my body in and wax for my tomb. Also please ask her to bring me some of those little cakes that she used to give me when I was sick in Rome.

Bernard. Yes, Francis.

Francis. Thank you, my child.

ELIAS *enters.*

Bernard [*Aside to* FRANCIS]. Elias is here.

Francis. Welcome, welcome, Father. . . . Father, please forgive me for having asked my brothers to sing for me several times and even singing with them myself. I know you don't consider that suitable at a time like this and you are uneasy lest it seem scandalous to some people. But you see, by the grace of the Holy Spirit, I feel so deeply united with my Lord God that I can't help rejoicing in Him and singing His praises with joy.

Elias. It would be splendid if all of us could end our earthly lives in this way.

Francis. My time is drawing near, Elias. The Most High has already multiplied and will multiply still further the number of my brothers and children in your hands. Promise me that you will never give up the Portiuncula, which is truly the home of Christ and His Holy Mother and the Gate of Heaven. It was here that Jesus enlightened the spirit of his little poor men. I ask that absolutely nothing unnecessary be said or done here ever. I want this little enclosure to remain completely pure and holy.

Elias. I will see to it. [*A silence.* ELIAS *looks intently at* BERNARD, *who takes the hint and exits.*] Francis, you will soon be with the Lord.

Francis. I wish you could share the joy it gives me.

Elias. Don't forget your brother Elias.

Francis. And you—don't forget your brother Francis.

Elias. Your name will be honored. Your relics will be glorified. . . .

Francis. My name is nothing. I would like it to be blotted out and my remains to be buried in some secret place.

Elias. But pray, Francis, for poor Elias as you know him—irritable, barren, tormented. Pray that he may carry to the end his almost unbearable burden: the eternal salvation of a multitude.

Francis. Love! There is no other law! I will pray that

in your heart, more and more, everything may be simpli-
fied by love. Believe me, you will be a good servant of
God, if you do not cease loving the brother who gravely
sins. And if, prevented by some human fear, the sinner
doesn't dare come to you, go to him and ask him gently
whether he wants your pardon.

Elias. I know how thankless my nature is. I will never
have your saintliness. I wish I were not so envious of you.

Francis. That in itself is very good. God's love will
find a way to go through the narrow passage. . . . Pray,
watch, warn, work, feed, love, wait, fear.

Enter GILES.

Giles. The Lady of Settesoli, with her two sons, has
just arrived from Rome.

Francis. She is answering my call before it came to her.
Bring the Lady of Settesoli and her two sons to me. And
you, Elias, call in all the brothers. [ELIAS *and* GILES *withdraw.* LEO *sobs.*] What is this I hear? Is it you, Brother
Lamb?

Leo. Yes.

Francis. I thought so. Come here. [LEO *comes to him.*]
Are you crying? How inconsistent men are! I mean spiritual men. They spend their lives here below wishing for
the sight of God—for themselves and those they love.
You love me, Leo. You see me reach the end of my
journey and you cry!

Leo. No, no, I'm not crying.

Francis. You must not cry. Leave tears to the poor
men of the flesh.

Leo. I won't cry any more. I am not sad. It's rather
that I feel uplifted.

Francis. Well then, cry, my little child. I don't see why
I should keep you from crying, if it does you good. [LEO
throws himself on Francis and sobs. FRANCIS *strokes his
head and weeps too.*] My child, these are the last tears we
will shed together. They are sweet. I wanted to ask you
something, Leo. Are you listening?

Leo. Yes, sweet Father.

Francis. When I am gone, I would like you to watch

over Clare, help and support her. I would like her to be
able to find me in you.

Leo. Oh, Father!

Francis. You don't want to?

Leo. I would like to with all my heart. But how could
I replace you with her?

Francis. I entrust her to you because you are completely
pure. . . . [*A pause.*] Clare, my little soldier! Brave . . .
that's what she was. Almost foolhardy. She was even sorry
she wasn't a boy. With what fire she embraced poverty!
All her actions breathed this ardor. How eagerly she
threw herself at my feet and asked me to give her to God.
How she ran to join us on the night of Palm Sunday.
. . With her thin figure, her pure face, and beautiful
gray eyes, her chin thrust forward a little, her hair short
after I trimmed it, this virgin looked like a young crusader.

Leo. Before leaving this world, dear Francis, wouldn't
you like to see your young crusader again?

Francis. No. Oh, no!

Leo. I thought you would find consolation in her.

Francis. Jesus Christ had much less consolation than
we. . . . You see, Leo, my friendship for Clare was the
purest, most perfect, Christ-like thing in my life. I don't
want to bring to it—especially at the last moment—anything suggesting human affections. I am both father and
mother to her. A father or mother, with God's help, can
be somewhat aloof without being cold. I know that no
hardship troubles her and no penitence is too much for
her. I love her spirit so much! I want this self-denial to
be credited to her in Heaven. No. I will not see her again
on earth. [*Enter* BROTHERS BERNARD, GILES, SILVESTER,
ILLUMINATO, RUFINO, MASSEO, ANGELO, JOHN, *etc.*] Ah!
Dear brothers, blessed brothers, you see, I take with me
only one regret—not to have spent all the love that God
provided to me, as to a king's son, for the duration of
my journey. All that remained for me to love on earth
I leave to you, little brothers . . . all I don't know and
no one knows in the depths of the seas and deep inside
matter but which Thou knowest, O Lord! Therefore I

ask pardon of all that I have not known, of all the humble hidden things, of all our humble, shy virtues . . . and also of my humble brother donkey, my body, that I have perhaps mistreated often and yet it has borne me faithfully, somehow, all the way to the edge of eternity.

Illuminato. Alas, good Father, your children are going to lose you and be deprived of the true light that guided them.

Francis. Shhh. . . . When death comes, be sure to strip me and place me naked on the earth. [*Enter* ELIAS *with* LADY GIACOMA *and her two sons,* JOHN *and* GRATIANO. GIACOMA *bows her head to the ground at* FRANCIS' *feet.*] Here you are, Brother Giacoma. . . . You have come a long way. Did you have a good journey?

Giacoma. Father, I have brought you some of the sweet almond cakes that seemed to do you good some time ago in Rome.

Francis. You must have guessed how I yearned for them. It's my last bit of greediness. I will take a little, so that God will not have inspired in you this great act of charity for nothing. . . . I am most pleased. . . . And you, my fine young men, what are you carrying?

John. The shroud.

Gratiano. The wax and incense.

Francis. Thank you. Now God is calling me. I forgive all my brothers. I bless them all I can and even more than I can . . . And all who are not here—take them my blessing—and all those who in the future will come to join you—bless them in my name. . . .

Chorus [*Singing very softly*].
Praised be my Lord for our sister the moon, and for the
    stars, the which He has set clear and lovely in heaven.
Praised be my Lord for our brother the wind, and for
    air and clouds, calms and all weather by which Thou
    upholdest life in all creatures.

Francis. I have heard crystal waters flow from the spring, the new leaves rustle and seen the seasons come and go. Thou hast let me take part in this chorus of praise, O Lord! I have done my utmost and now I go. . . .

Bernard. Is your joy perfect now?

Francis. Yes, yes, yes, soon. . . .

All the FRIARS *and* CHORUS [*Singing*].

Praised be my Lord for our sister water, who is very
serviceable unto us and humble and precious and clean.

Praised be my Lord for our brother fire, through whom
Thou givest us light in the darkness; and he is bright
and pleasant and very mighty and strong.

Praised be my Lord for our mother the earth, the which
doth sustain us and keep us, and bringeth forth divers
fruits and flowers of many colors and grass.

Praise ye and bless the Lord, and give thanks unto Him
and serve Him with great humility.

A pause. FRANCIS' *hand moves several times indicating
he wants to speak.*

Francis [*Singing*].

Praised be my Lord for our sister the death of the body
From which no living man escapeth;
Unhappy only those who die in mortal sin,
But full of joy those who have done Thy very holy will!

A pause. Then he calls in a loud voice:

Leo! [LEO *comes to him.*] When winter comes, little
brother Leo, be sure that my sisters the bees are not forgotten and see that they have a little honey in their hives.

*Chorus of Friars. Voce mea ad Dominum clamavi: voce
mea ad Dominum deprecatus sum; effundo in sospectu
ejus orationem meam et tribulationem meam ante ipsum
pronuntio. In deficiendo ex me spiritum meum, et tu
cognovisti semitas meas.*

Chorus [*From a distance*]. *In via hac, qua ambulabam,
absconderunt laqueum mihi. Considerabam ad dexteram,
et videbam: et non erat qui cognosceret me. Periit fuga
a me, et non est qui requirat animam meam. Clamavi ad
te, Domine, dixi: Tu es spes mea, portio mea in terra
viventium.*

*A silence. Then a lark song of ethereal joy rises and is
soon lost at a great height in the air. Then those nearest
to* FRANCIS *lean over his body, then straighten up ab-
uptly. A general sobbing bursts out but is quickly stifled.
All the brothers fall on their knees and* GIACOMA *lifts*

her head. BERNARD *and* LEO *hasten to loosen* FRANCIS'
gown. They lift him and start to place him on the ground.
But for a few moments his body remains on the edge of
the bed, his head sagging on his shoulder, his legs dan-
gling, his arms outstretched, and one sees his feet, his
hands, his side, bearing the marks of the Holy Stigmata.

Giacoma. In the perfect image of Christ's Passion—
five bleeding wounds from which mankind will come to
slake its thirst. Crimson jewels cut in the flesh of Francis
by the Hand of the Lord.

During the reading which follows, they lay FRANCIS' *body*
on the ground, finish stripping off his gown, cover him
with the shroud, and kneel round him—all in an other-
worldly silence.

Chorus Leader. "And we, the Brothers Minor, your
useless servants, we pray and humbly beseech all those
who wish to serve God in the Holy Catholic Church,
all those who live in the churchly state, all priests, deacons, assistant deacons, acolytes, exorcisers, readers, door-
keepers, and all clerics, all monks and all nuns, and all
children, little boys and little girls, and all the poor and
needy, and kings and princes, and workmen, peasants,
servants, and masters, and all virgins, all who are conti-
nent and all who live in the state of matrimony, all lay
persons, men and women, young and old, the well and the
sick, great and small, of all nations and speaking all
tongues, in short, all men now living or who yet shall
live—we humbly entreat them to persevere in the true
faith and conversion, for there is no other way to be
saved. And let all of us, with all our heart, all our soul,
and all our bodily and spiritual strength, with all our reason and all our faculties, all our love, all our intimate
being, let us love the Lord our God, who gave us all—all
our body and all our soul and all our life and who continues to give them to us, who has created and redeemed
us and who out of pure compassion today still wants to
save us and who has pardoned and pardons daily the
miserable, lazy, impudent, ungrateful and wicked scoun-
drels that we are! Amen."
Chorus [Singing]. Amen. . . .

SELECTED READINGS IN ENGLISH

Beauvoir, Simone de, *The Second Sex*, Bantam, 1961 (on Montherlant and Claudel).

Bentley, Eric, *In Search of Theatre*, Knopf, 1953 (on Copeau).

Chiari, Joseph, *The Poetic Drama of Paul Claudel*, Kenedy, 1954.

Claudel, Paul, Two Dramas: *Break of Noon* [*Partage de Midi*] and *The Tidings Brought to Mary* [*L'Annonce faite à Marie*], translations and introductions by Wallace Fowlie, Regnery, 1960.

Fowlie, Wallace, *Paul Claudel*, Bowes & Bowes (London), 1957. *Dionysus in Paris: A Guide to Contemporary French Theater*, Meridian, 1960.
An Introduction to Contemporary French Literature, Meridian, 1957.

Ghéon, Henri, *The Art of the Theatre*, translated by Adele M. Fiske, Hill and Wang, 1961 (on Copeau).

Grossvogel, David I., *The Self-Conscious Stage in Modern French Drama*, Columbia University Press, 1958 (on Claudel).

Guicharneau, Jacques, *The Modern French Drama*, Yale University Press, 1961 (on Claudel, Montherlant, Mauriac).

Hobson, Harold, *The French Theatre of Today*, Harrap (London), 1953 (on Montherlant and Claudel).

Montherlant, Henry de, *The Master of Santiago and Four Other Plays*, translated with an introduction by Jonathan Griffin, Knopf, 1951: contains *Queen After Death* [*La Reine Morte*], *Malatesta*, *No Man's Son* [*Fils de Personne*], *Tomorrow the Dawn* [*Demain il fera jour*], *The Master of Santiago*.

Pucciani, Oreste, *The French Theater Since 1930*, Ginn, 1954 (on Montherlant).

Steiner, George, *The Death of Tragedy*, Knopf, 1961 (on Claudel).